FLYING ON THE EDGE

Bush Flying in
Newfoundland/Labrador
People and Politicians
Seals, Ice and Rocks

A Collection of True Incidents and Bizarre Stories of Aircraft
and People Encountered While Trying to Develop
a Small Airline Business in Newfoundland and Labrador

1960 -2000

From the Recollections and Log Books of
Gene Manion

mury w. Knowles

GENE MANION

DRC PUBLISHING

3 Parliament Street
St. John's, Newfoundland and Labrador
A1A 2Y6
Telephone: (709) 726-0960
E-mail: info@drcpublishingnl.com

Library and Archives Canada Cataloguing in Publication

Manion, Gene
Flying on the edge / Gene Manion.

ISBN 978-1-926689-05-0

1. Manion, Gene. 2. Bush flying--Newfoundland and Labrador.
3. Airlines--Newfoundland and Labrador.
4. Bush pilots--Newfoundland and Labrador--Biography.
5. Newfoundland and Labrador--Biography. I. Title.

TL540.M278A3 2009   629.13092   C2009-903627-4

Aircraft on cover: foreground: Grumman Widgeon
middle: Noorduyn Norseman
behind: Beechcraft -18
helicopter on back cover: Hughes 500 C
Cover painting by: Don Connolly
Layout by: Becky Pendergast

Published 2009
Printed in Canada

We acknowledge the financial assistance of the Government of Newfoundland and Labrador, Department of Tourism, Culture and Recreation

Dedication

I dedicate this book to the devoted airmen and the unwavering entrepreneurs who have tested the edge, endured the adventure, and enjoyed most every minute.

"This first hand account brings together the world of the aviator with that of the entrepreneur in a graphic way. To turn the love of flying into a self-sustaining business is something that has been attempted by many but accomplished by few. In these pages the conception, financing and creativity shown to nurture a start up enterprise into a substantial business is woven into the exhilaration of flying! Common sense, hard work and fun, accompanied by the necessary luck, all show through and make for a great read!"

Bob Beamish, Found Aircraft Corporation, Mississauga, ON

* * * * *

Acknowledgements

Thanks to the pilots, engineers, and labourers whose stories are told in this book. And thanks to their wives and other wonderful people who welcomed me into their homes and willingly shared their stories about aviation in Newfoundland. I thank Ben Davenport and Willy Wilson who pushed me to do this. I appreciate the guidance and encouragement that Christine Hamelin and Steve Wormington provided.

Thanks to the Honourable John Crosbie, Lieutenant Governor of Newfoundland and Labrador, for his kind advice and for writing the foreword.

Special acknowledgement goes to Brenda Keyes for the photo of her parents, Flossie and Frank LeDrew, and for her family's tolerance during the difficult times. Also, I am very appreciative of the assistance provided by Jean and Peter Stacey of DRC Publishing.

Cover Artist: Don Connolly of Sydenham, Ontario.

Foreword

I am pleased to extol high merit to Gene Manion's book *"Flying on the Edge."* This book provides a vivid description of the Newfoundland people, politicians and sealing industry during he period from 1960-2000. It is the best account I have ever read of bush flying in this province or anywhere, and the best descriptions of coastal and inland Newfoundland and of our rivers and wildlife.

I was lucky enough, during my career, to have gained considerable experience travelling in bush planes and helicopters. My family connection with EPA and the demands while serving as MHA and as Member of Parliament provided me with extensive travel opportunities throughout Newfoundland and Labrador. Much of my flying took me to wilderness fishing rivers, hunting excursions, and to the coastal outports. I knew many of the remarkable pilots, who were flying with EPA from the mid 1950s – Royal Cooper, Marsh Jones, Austin Garrett, and others.

Manion's book is an excellent account of the dedication and perseverance of his team of pilots and staff who would not give up, of how they dealt with inadequate funding and countless difficult situations. These are dramatic exploits that never made the news, although they are still remembered around the kitchen tables and bush camps by those who were aware.

"Flying on the Edge" is an appropriate title because to fly on "the edge of the envelope" is to know your capabilities and to fly the aircraft to its maximum design limitations. It is very important to know when you reach the edge. The author often pushed the envelope, frequently on the brink of financial disaster and often risked personal tragedy in his determined pursuit of success.

The book reveals that Manion is a man full of drive and resolve, used to and capable of tremendously hard work, and a true risk taker in his piloting career. It was Bernard Baruch who wrote that "A ship in harbour is safe but it is not what ships are built for."

In other words, ships are built to be used, not to be kept safely in harbour and this certainly was Manion's philosophy. With the fierce competition he faced in 1961, Manion knew his ship wouldn't come in unless he sent it out. The author was born in the Thousand Island are of Ontario, learned to fly in the RCAF, and spent seven years in the military as a pilot instructor and flying the CF-100 Interceptor aircraft. He left the air force in 1959 to pursue a career in bush flying.

When Gene Manion first came to Newfoundland in 1960 he flew for Wellon's Flying Service for a few months until they were taken over by EPA. He, with some friends, started a bush flying business called Newfoundland Air Transport Ltd. He had very little capital but lots of purpose. His drive equaled that of a businessman named Huntingdon who said, "Anything that is not nailed down is mine, anything I can pry loose is not nailed down." In the early years, his company had many problems with financial shortages, intense competition from large established companies (EPA), and the difficult weather that Newfoundland presented.

Our island is a triangle of rugged land, separating the North Atlantic from the Gulf of St. Lawrence, with all the communities situated along our extensive coast. With the high hills and vast amount of ocean nearby, the weather is always a concern and common enemy of bush pilots. The province has 196 rainy days each year, parts of the south coast with 200 days of fog, some areas with over 450 centimeters of snowfall and the ground snow covered for 183 days each year. Forty kilometer winds are considered normal.

Under Manion's direction, his company progressed from a borrowed Piper Cub to Cessna, Norseman, Beaver, Otters, Beechcraft and eventually acquired a Dehavilland Heron four-engine craft and other commuter type wheel planes. Later, he diversified the business by offering Hughes turboprop helicopters to his customers.

His company catered to the wilderness tourist camps, serviced the exploration camps and ferried mining personnel and their freight. The book describes many flying adventures involving medivac flights and rescue operations. NAT was called upon to evacuate people from communities that were threatened by forest fires and to fly doctors to remote settlements.

The book often describes and pays tribute to the unique character and boundless hospitality of the outport people who were unfailingly helpful and generous, despite the fact that they did not have much in the way of wealth or comforts, whenever the pilots or aircraft needed assistance.

One of the most interesting parts of this book is its description of the company engaging in the gulf seal hunt in 1963. They employed sealers, took them to the offshore ice, and flew the pelts and carcasses to a base on the Magdelan Islands. It was risky landing the ski planes on the drifting ice sheets some fifty miles from shore, but the operation greatly helped the company's teetering financial situation.

The author flew many interesting people including the famous fly-fisherman Lee Wulff, who Manion once rescued when Lee's float plane flipped over during a landing in high winds. His passengers included Albert Martin when manager of Bowater Paper Company, Chester Dawe, the Irving Brothers, Margaret Lake on the south coast at Ramea and Helge and Anne Ingstad, the Norwegian visionaries who later discovered the Viking site at Lanse-aux-Meadows.

The company also had many unusual flights and encounters when flying to Sable Island and to the French Islands of St. Pierre and Miquelon. In 1978, Manion assisted the RCAF with a search and rescue mission on the northern peninsula looking for some lost snowmobilers from Daniel's Harbour. The author had some remarkable encounters with Premier Smallwood during an election campaign and also flew him to Boston after his defeat – when he had to get away from the turmoil in Newfoundland.

During his flying career, Manion logged over 13,000 hours on 25 different types of aircraft and helicopters without an accident. There is no doubt that this accomplishment involved considerable skill, and as he says, "A large infusion of luck at crucial times!"

I unreservedly recommend this book to anyone who has

interest in our people and how they lived in the outport communities. It is a superb account of the seal fishery, mining development, hunting big game, and fly-fishing for salmon and arctic char. *"Flying on the Edge"* is an outstanding example of how success can be achieved by individuals who are prepared to engage in hard, risky work with drive and strength of mind.

This is one of the best accounts I have read of the way life was in Newfoundland and Labrador and of the travails of bush flying in that era. Gene Manion has told his story superbly, and it is one well worth telling.

Honourable John Crosbie
PC, OC, ONL, QC

Preface

Flying on the Edge is an account of my most vivid experiences, and those of others, while flying in Newfoundland and Labrador. It is about aviation during the frontier era long past. My objective was to describe some of the exciting incidents that took place while I was developing a small business, and to share with you my love of Newfoundland – its vibrant characters, its wildlife, and its outport culture, and the way things were.

My detailed logbooks and diaries were used in recalling these events. To fill the gaps, I had many discussions with others who were involved. Some dialogue was recreated from memory and I used the real names of people and places, except in a few instances where I could not trace or recollect the names. This story would not have evolved had it not been for the dreams, skills, trust, and devotion of many friends, staff and associates. Their names are listed in the Endnotes.

Two excellent books describe the early days of aviation development in Newfoundland and Labrador: *The Little Engine That Could*, written in 1998 by Marsh Jones, the legendary vice-president of Eastern Provincial Airways,provides a vivid historical account of that airline from 1949 to 1965: *Tales from a Pilot's Logbook* is Royal Cooper's colourful 1999 account of his personal aviation experiences as an RAF fighter pilot and of his many dramatic flights during his career with Eastern Provincial Airways.

The late Bill Bennett, of Gander Aviation Limited, also deserves mention for his legendary contribution to bush travel in the province. The late Len Rich is the author of *Bill Bennett: A Biography*

I hope this book will add another notch to the rich testimony of those great aviators.

Introduction

Fifty-six years ago, my passion for flying began as I watched the RCAF Harvard trainers practicing low flying sorties in Ontario over our Wolfe Island dairy farm. Little did I realize that this obsession would lead me to the exciting shores of Newfoundland many years later.

My career suddenly changed in 1959 when the Avro Arrow (CF-105) program was cancelled. The training and instrument flying experience that I gained in the air force would prove very beneficial in the years ahead. Fate took me to Newfoundland in 1960, where I tried to establish a small bush plane service. It was quite a struggle.

The chapters that follow are about that struggle. This book is not meant to tell the story of "Newfoundland and Labrador Air Transport Limited" nor is it meant as the personal memoir of Gene Manion. Rather, it is an account of the dedication and perseverance of a team of pilots and their staff who would not give up, and of how they dealt with inadequate funding and countless difficult situations. This story would not be complete if I failed to describe some of the interesting people I encountered, including the politicians, who played an unusual role in everyday life. These events did happen, and I apologize if any important details have been forgotten or if names have been omitted.

Some attempt has been made to bring to life the primitive beauty of this great province and to sketch the compelling humanism of the colourful Newfoundlanders. I was not able to recreate all the joyful, soul-stirring moments that occurred during those harrowing years, but I try to present the gusty reality of how it was, how we behaved, and how most of us survived and enjoyed it. I recount these yarns in "down home" terms, since not many writers are pilots and not many pilots are writers.

Climb in the cockpit, snug up your straps, and share this thrilling journey with me – expect some turbulence! To enhance your trip and assist you in visualizing the events, a working knowledge of the general topography and the severe Newfoundland weather will prove beneficial.

The province of Newfoundland and Labrador is divided into two geographical parts: Labrador and the island of Newfoundland. The province has a small population (508,990 in 2009) spread over a huge land mass (405,720 square kilometers, just less than that of California).

The island is a triangle of rugged land in Eastern Canada that separates the North Atlantic from the Gulf of St. Lawrence, and has 9600 kilometers of coast line. Having evolved with the fishing industry, all of the towns and small communities are situated along the extensive shore area – except for Gander, Grand Falls and Deer Lake. Until the 1960s, the sparse road system extended only from Port aux Basques to St. Anthony (along the western coast), and across the central area from Corner Brook to the St. John's region.

During the 1950s and 1960s, bush planes were used extensively for travelling throughout Newfoundland and Labrador – by all segments of society. The western and northern parts of the island are a mountainous extension of the Appalachian Chain, with massive fjords indenting the coast. The central and eastern areas are relatively flat. The entire land mass is strewn with lakes and rivers and the rest is saturated with a green profusion of boreal forest. Bush planes have a landing site at every community – either on a lake or salt water bay. Unlike most other provinces, there is a noticeable lack of ground lights at night, since the total population less than one person per square kilometer.

The common enemy of all Newfoundland bush pilots was the threatening weather, which could rapidly change. Fog, low cloud, and high winds often plagued our paths. Rigorous winds are common, occasionally toppling large trucks off the highway when reaching 150 kilometers per hour. Their ferocity is a threat to small, low-flying craft. Not only is the air turbulence and the rough water a flying concern, it can cause havoc to parked aircraft if they are not properly secured. One wintry morning, after a windy night, I looked out at the open field by the LeDrew airstrip and couldn't believe my eyes. The field was dotted with large balls of snow the size of watermelons. Frank said they were "Newfoundland Snow Devils." It's a unique phenomenon, requiring an extreme gusty breeze and soft, damp snow. As the willy-wa * tears at the snow, small balls are rolled along with each gust, becoming larger on each roll. Growing in size, they provide more surface for the air to catch. Rolling along, they leave a long trench as their footprint. During my fifty years of weather watching, I have only witnessed the snow devils on two occasions in Newfoundland, and once during a severe Chinook along the foothills of Alberta.

Often the snow conditions on the frozen ice present a hazard. Strong winds blow the snow into sharp, compacted drifts which freeze as hard as cement. Landing on those ridges can break a ski axle, crack struts, or tear off the tail skids.

Please note that in aviation circles, we used feet not meters, for expressing altitude. For speed, our terminology was knots or miles per hour. Since most Canadians have gone metric, I use kilometers (herein) to express distances.

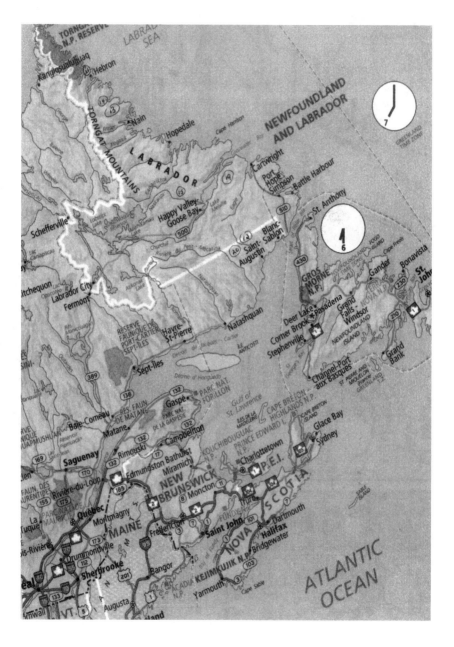

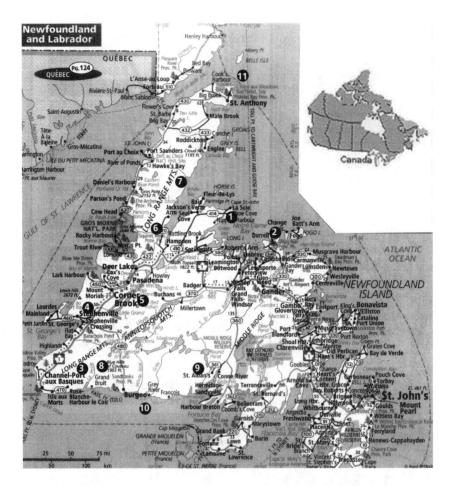

1	Tilt Cove	7 Harbour Deep
2	Twillingate	8 Rocky Ridge Pond
3	Crash Pond	9 Baie D'Espoir
4	Gallants Pond	10 Ramea
5	Saddler Lake	11 Quirpon
6	Main River Lodge	

1	St. Paul River	6	Charlottetown
2	North River	7	Tesuiyak Lake
3	Liberator site	8	Saglek
4	Groswater Bay	9	Susan River
5	Voisey Bay		

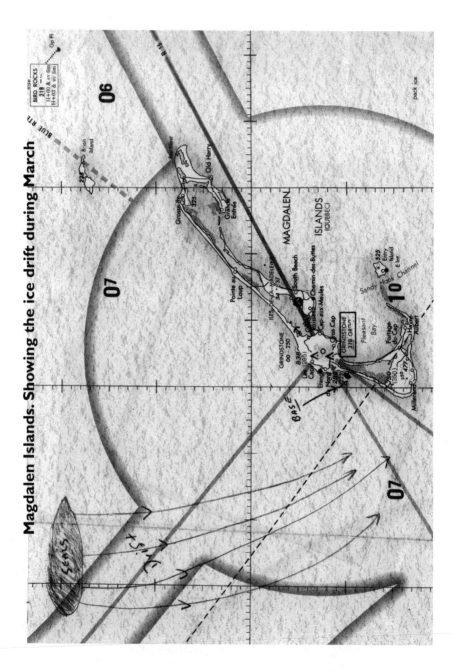

Magdalen Islands. Showing the ice drift during March

Table of Contents

COMMERCIAL FLYING

Chapter 1 Getting off the Ground

"Borrowed" Piper Cub CF-JAM on small pond at Tilt Cove

It was while lurking behind a tree early one freezing winter's morning in 1961, taking a bead with a 30.06 on the doorsill of my former partner, with my crew scrambling to steal back the plane he had stolen from us, that I began to seriously question whether becoming a bush pilot in Newfoundland had been, after all, a good idea.

In 1959, I had been ready for a change. I had just finished a seven year stint with the RCAF as a fighter pilot with a CF-100 squadron stationed in Canada and Europe. Looking back that night, after less than two years as a bush pilot and would be businessman in Newfoundland, leaning against that tree with a rifle in my hands, life in the Air Force suddenly seemed pretty tame.

I had been very happy with my lifestyle in the Air Force and had been planning on making it a permanent career. But that suddenly changed. The CF-100 was being replaced by an advanced Canadian-conceived jet interceptor, the Avro Arrow, which was being built in Toronto.

In 1952 the Canadian Government contracted with A.V. Roe of Toronto to develop a replacement aircraft for the CF-100 interceptor. It would be supersonic, capable of high altitude flight, and have sophisticated weaponry and advanced fire power. This unsurpassed machine would make Canada the leader in supersonic flight technology. Six aircraft were built, with two completing successful flight testing. The Arrow was fifteen years ahead of similar productions by any other country. Legendary test pilot Jan Zurakowski had described its performance to us as nothing short of awesome, showing 1,400 mph at 55,000 feet and still climbing and accelerating! We could only fantasize about where it would go with the larger Iroquois engines, which were soon to be installed. The seasoned CF-100 pilots thought they would be in line to fly this machine as soon as it went operational. The cancellation of the project in 1959 was a shock. The disappointment was so great that many of us resigned in frustration.

While waiting for an economic turnaround with the major airlines, I found work doing some bush flying in Baie Comeau and the St. Lawrence River area until something better came along. The first two job offers came on the same day. One was with a large U.S. carrier opening up a transport service in a remote jungle area of South America; the other opening was with Wellon's Flying Service in Corner Brook, Newfoundland. I had a close friend, Jim Roe, who was flying on contract with Eastern Provincial Airways (EPA) in Greenland. Jim encouraged me to take the job with Wellons. He knew how much I loved the outdoors and was sure Newfoundland would appeal to me in many ways. I took his advice and joined Wellon's Flying Service.

In 1960, Newfoundland was still in catch-up mode with the other nine Canadian provinces. Many coastal communities were still very isolated because of the lack of road access, and were still dependent upon boat and air service. Except for the vicinity of St. John's, the provincial capital, the Trans Canada Highway was a muddy trail during the spring thaw and little more than a rough, dusty path during the summer. Most hotels and restaurants offered basic amenities and no more. The tourism industry was in its infancy. Jobs were scarce, although the seasonal fishing industry was still prospering. Some mining companies were becoming active with exploration programs. Skiplanes and dogsleds provided the winter mail service to many outport communities.

Most of the economic activity throughout the province was in the hands of a few wealthy families in St. John's. The wholesale distribution of goods and all industrial and fishing activity was controlled by these fiefdoms. The same elite groups had considerable political influence with Joey Smallwood's Liberal government. Newfoundland's powerful Crosbie family was among the most influential of that group, with their sprawling empire encompassing some seventeen different enterprises. They controlled all air service on 'The Island" and in Labrador – except for the small fledgling operation of Wellon's Flying Service. The financial power and political weight of the Crosbies created a high barrier for any would be aviation entrepreneurs. Ches Crosbie, the family scion, was often ruthless in protecting the family's empire.

The Crosbie family owned: Newfoundland Engineering & Construction Ltd., insurance, international shipping, machinery distributing, building supplies, real estate development, sugar refinery, drug retail & wholesale, margarine plant, hotels, taxi companies, fish processing plants, a whaling enterprise, a brewing company, soft drink manufacturing, stevedoring, steamship services, sealing, offshore terminals and Eastern Provincial Airlines (EPA). As well, they owned many lease-back buildings, including hospitals, schools, banks, hotels and nursing homes.

To successfully compete against this powerful monopoly would inevitably require ingenuity, perseverance and perhaps an unfounded optimism. A willingness to resort to unorthodox measures wouldn't hurt either.

Wellons operated two Cessna 180 aircraft from a base in Pasadena, near Corner Brook, on the west coast of Newfoundland. They had been successful in making some basic inroads with two of the large mining companies at Tilt Cove and Baie Verte. The upstart company was the first air service in the province to compete with the large, well established bush plane operations of EPA.

In the fall of 1960, Wellons was financially troubled and on the verge of bankruptcy. By this time, I had been flying their bush planes for eight months, and had established good relations with the officials of the two mining companies at Tilt Cove and Baie Verte.

The Tilt Cove Maritime Mine was a large, self-contained copper mine situated near La Scie on Newfoundland's northeast coast. The mine was owned by the M.J. Boylen group of Toronto. The site was inaccessible by road until 1964. Over six hundred personnel lived in the isolated rockbound community. Transportation requirements were met by a charter boat that brought supplies across 55 kilometers of unfriendly ocean from Springdale when possible. Although the mine provided family housing, a medical clinic, a grocery store, a bank and an entertainment center, there was still a pressing need for a year round charter air service, especially during the winter season when the coastal boats were moored.

The Baie Verte mine, 60 kilometers north of Tilt Cove, was enjoying the early stages of a mining boom. Advocate Mines Ltd., owned by the Johns Manville Corporation, had discovered a rich asbestos ore body and was committed to the construction of a $230 million production facility. Road transport to the mine was difficult and they had budgeted for considerable expenditure on air services over the next few years.

Both of these mining companies had used the services of EPA and Wellon's Flying Service for their air charter work. When they discovered that EPA had purchased Wellon's two aircraft in January of 1961, they were somewhat perturbed and that created an opportunity. Bob Baker, the manager of Advocate Mines, preferred the personalized service he had enjoyed with Wellons. "Manion, if you can't get something going quickly, we will buy our own aircraft – but we would rather concentrate on mining than becoming involved with an aircraft," he said. Holland Smith, the manager of Tilt Cove, had a soft spot for the struggling underdog

Johns Manville's Advocate Mine at Baie Verte (1963)

and also believed that some competition for EPA would result in better air service to his mine. At the time EPA had four DC-3s, three C-46s, three Cansos, four Otters, seven Beavers, one Royal Gull, three Cessna 185s, two Cessna 180s and three helicopters (a formidable fleet with no competition). Baker called me and suggested that I somehow acquire an aircraft to immediately resume their interrupted mail and express service between Corner Brook and Baie Verte on a regular basis. He also told me to retain the keys to their forwarding facility in Corner Brook, which had formerly been in the hands of Wellon's Flying Service. He said he didn't want to be forced to use the services of EPA. The manager at Tilt Cove also encouraged me to provide their mining complex with an aircraft as soon as possible, for much the same reason.

Eastern Provincial had a long list of lucrative contracts. Under a federal postal contract, they provided winter mail delivery to various isolated areas of Newfoundland and to the entire Labrador coast. The Greenland government retained EPA to provide their coastal transport. They provided all provincial government departments with air carrier service, including Medivac flights and forest fire suppression. They had a supply contract with the U.S. Air Force to service their remote radar stations. As well, they were heavily engaged with tourism and exploration service agreements. The two mining companies had good reason to suppose that their needs would not always be a priority with EPA.

To start a commercial bush plane service, there were formidable barriers to overcome: the procurement of a suitable aircraft, insurance coverage, the basic mandatory infrastructure for a base of operations, ground equipment, a suitable winter airstrip near Corner Brook, the hiring of maintenance personnel, compliance with Air Transport Board licensing requirements, acquiring a Ministry of Transport operating license, establishing radio communications, and above all, obtaining operating capital. It seemed overwhelming. Obviously, there was a rare opportunity knocking at my door, but decisive action had to be taken immediately or the door would be quickly slammed shut by the powerful Crosbie interests.

I found two willing partners and we wasted no time incorporating a company called "Newfoundland Air Transport Ltd. (NAT)." Rick Richard, an aircraft engineer from Moncton, and Frank LeDrew, a retired business manager, came in as my partners. Rick held a commercial pilot's licence. He had no experience on floats or skis, and was known more for his uncanny ability to repair the machines. Frank owned land in Pasadena that would serve as a winter airstrip and he had a managerial background and a passion for airplanes. Pasadena, near Corner Brook, offered a sheltered lake area for floatplanes and was a suitable location to establish our base on the west coast. A tentative aircraft lease was obtained on a Cessna 180 from Stan Deluce in Shipshaw, Ontario. A temporary operating certificate arrangement was made with a friend, Arnold Bradley, who owned Northern, Quebec Air Service Ltd. in Chicoutimi, Quebec, 1,200 kilometers away. This arrangement was legally questionable, as it stretched the interpretation of the Air Transport Board basing regulations. Our radio station and office was set up in Frank's home. The airstrip behind the LeDrew residence was lengthened to 1,700 feet and the snow was cleared. The mining companies were told that NAT would have a skiplane in service near Corner Brook within a week to look after their needs.

Things were moving right along, but after pooling our

combined cash resources we only had a total of $2,000 to invest in the operation. It would cost that much to travel to Northern Ontario and ferry the aircraft back to Corner Brook. The minimum deposit required for the aircraft lease and insurance was $5,000. It was obvious that this operation couldn't get underway without a loan. All of the banks in Corner Brook refused to discuss any loan arrangements without substantial collateral. They emphatically told us that our business plan was doomed to fail. "The aircraft industry is too risky," they said."The services already being provided by EPA are adequate. You have no experience in corporate management and you have no assets or working capital." It was hard to argue against their reasoning. None of our friends were in a position to loan us money for such a wild scheme. Our prospects, then, were pretty dismal, but we were so naive that we thought it was achievable.

I firmly believe in the philosophy that if you make a solid commitment to a goal, no matter how difficult, you'll be obliged to find a way to make it happen. So we went ahead anyway. It was decided that Rick would proceed immediately to Shipshaw with his credit card and prepare to ferry the leased skiplane back to Newfoundland. Somehow we would come up with the $5000 and forward it to White River Air Service within a few days.

Occasionally, I had socialized with the bank manager at the Tilt Cove mine. After a long telephone conversation, it seemed there was some small hope of obtaining a loan from that little branch, though it would take more persuasion. However, Tilt Cove was totally inaccessible, except by aircraft, and it was 180 kilometers away from Pasadena. There simply were no funds to charter an EPA skiplane and no other aircraft were available.

We mulled the problem over. "I have one suggestion," Frank said. "But it's pretty farfetched." He wasn't kidding.

A Doctor Erb owned an old Piper Cub, CF-JAM, and when he'd moved to Toronto three years earlier, he'd left it parked on Frank's farm.

"There's a set of skis for it in my shed, but I don't know if it'll fly," Frank said."It hasn't flown since he left here and there's been no maintenance."

We worked all afternoon and most of the night scraping snow from the fabric surfaces, fuelling, changing the oil, installing the skis, checking the engine and the flight controls and, finally, hand-starting the small 65 horsepower engine. Early the next morning, the little yellow bird taxied out onto the strip and climbed into the sky. After my satisfactory test flight, Frank, with some reluctance, climbed in the back seat and we set an easterly course for the Bank of Nova Scotia in Tilt Cove.

I had never flown such a small plane as a Piper Cub before, but soon enough Frank and I were settled in for the long, slow flight. The weather en route was high overcast with good visibility and a nippy minus12C. Our thoughts were focused on somehow acquiring the loan, rather than on the lack of instruments or heat in the tiny cockpit. A small oil streak stained the windshield, the compass seemed off by about twelve degrees, and the only flight instrumentation was a needle ball, an oil pressure gauge, an altimeter and an airspeed indicator. The fuel gauge was a little crooked wire bobbing from the cowling as its cork float bounced in the light turbulence.

The needle/ball is a rudimentary instrument. The needle shows if the aircraft is changing direction and the ball shows slipping due to asymmetrical flight. All modern aircraft have an artificial horizon, which is much more precise and easy to read.

Tilt Cove is situated in a rocky concave depression by the coast on Cape St. John. Granite hills 700 feet high rim the perimeter of the bowl where the buildings perch on the edge of a small pond. The mine is on the south end of the enclosure where there is a jagged opening to an ocean wharf on Notre Dame Bay. Windsor Pond, by the townhouses, was never used as a landing area owing to its small size and the lack of a reasonable approach. An elongated lake called Long Pond was situated on top of the hills, which served as the aircraft staging area. A steep, two kilometer road had been carved on the hillside to provide access from the mine. A J-5 Bombardier vehicle provided transportation from the mine to the landing site. However, the mine was not expecting any aircraft that afternoon. Only the bank manager knew we were coming. Without radio contact, we had no way to notify the mine office that we needed a lift had we landed on the upper lake. After considerable circling and a practice approach, I set the craft down on the small pond by the houses. Our arrival caused quite a stir among the residents as it was the first time an aircraft had ever landed on the little pond between the rocky cliffs.

Bank negotiations took up most of the afternoon since their head office had not agreed to grant the loan, but my youthful enthusiasm and determination seemed to be getting through to the branch manager. After using as many compelling arguments as we could conjure, some helpful interjections by the mine manager, Holland Smith, and enjoying a few encouraging offerings of New Year's cheer, a demand loan for $6,000 was finally granted.

With the bank draft carefully tucked in my vest pocket, an elated Frank and I took flight from Tilt Cove. The sun had set, the temperature had dropped, and the overcast sky was threatening. Progress was slow against the westerly headwind, with our ground speed down to about 50 miles per hour. By the time we reached Birchy Lake, it was dark and light snow was reducing visibility, so we went down to 400 feet to maintain some visual contact with the ground. The sky ahead promised worse weather to come. Soon there was no visual reference whatsoever. The lights had gone out in this roadless, uninhabited area. We began to slide in and out of low stratus cloud with wispy snow further obscuring our vision on that moonless night.To further complicate the situation, there were no instrument or cockpit lights in the Piper. Luckily I did have a flashlight, and fastened it to the seatbelt strap to provide some illumination on the rudimentary panel.

I weighed the situation. With ground reference rapidly deteriorating, to continue the flight in darkness and at this low altitude was foolhardy with high terrain all around. On the other hand, landing on a lake would not be prudent either, since we were not equipped to spend a night in the bush in those frigid temperatures. We had no sleeping bags or survival equipment. We didn't have a radio and hadn't filed a flight plan. My main concern was about making sudden and fatal contact with the high ground surrounding us. Despite being low on fuel, I elected to climb into the cloud layer to a safer altitude and make for Deer Lake. Thinking it was time to ease the tension, I told Frank not to worry: "These little planes are quite safe if you crash, they will just barely kill you!"

Instrument flying was risky, since the craft wasn't equipped with an artificial horizon or directional gyro. Intense concentration was required in using only a needle/ball and airspeed indicator to keep the plane in a stable, upright state. While I kept a careful eye on the needle, the Cub climbed slowly to 3,000 feet. The higher altitude brought on extreme cold and numbed my fingers. Careful attention had to be brought to bear on maintaining a compass course toward Deer Lake otherwise the dark, invisible hills would take their vengeance. I made time estimates for reaching the lowlands of the Humber Valley, where I anticipated making a slow, blind descent. It was a long, nerve racking forty minutes of basic instrument flying.

Finally, a faint glow of lights blinked below. We presumed they were radiating through the falling snow from the small village of Howley. After a slight navigational correction to the northwest, we descended cautiously through the thick darkness. It was a tremendous relief to finally spot the twinkling rays of dim light beaming at us from the larger town of Deer Lake straight ahead!

Deer Lake was at the east end of a large lake of the same name which extended 32 kilometers through the Humber Valley to Corner Brook. This valley was free of obstructions so a safe altitude reduction was now practical as we made for home. Soon we were gliding low over the lake using the south shore as a reference. At last, in a blinding snow squall, CF-JAM landed on the frozen surface behind Frank's house in Pasadena. Floss LeDrew greeted us and we all enjoyed hot toddies in front of the glowing fireplace.

We had won our first of many battles. The next morning a wire transfer was made to White River Air Service and Rick was soon on his way to Newfoundland with NAT's first aircraft a Cessna 180, CF-LWT.

Feb. 16, 1961

The first of three aircraft to be operated by the newly-formed Newfoundland Air Transport Ltd. arrived at Pasadena Tuesday shortly after noon.

The aircraft, a Cessna 180, was flown from Ontario by one of the founders of the company, R.W. Richard, who will be chief engineer for the company. The company was formed by Frank LeDrew, Mr. Richard and Gene Manion, all of whom formerly worked with Wellon's Flying Service, which is now incorporated with Eastern Provincial Airways.

Mr. LeDrew will manage the new company with Mr. Manion, the chief pilot. The company will operate between Pasadena, Tilt Cove and Baie Verte. It has radio communications between Pasadena, Tilt Cove and Baie Verte and also with mining towns on the east coast.

It wasn't long thereafter that I was summoned to court for breaching air regulations. I was charged with flying an aircraft without the owner's permission, unauthorized servicing of the aircraft prior to flight, and flying the aircraft without a current certificate of airworthiness. I pled guilty to the last two charges and was fined fifty dollars for each offense, or thirty days in jail. We scraped together enough to pay the fines. Jail time would hamper flying the charters we had already booked.

By late 1961, our company had three leased Cessna 180 aircraft in operation. They were all very busy but cash flow continued to be a major problem. While I was devoting most of my energies to flying and promoting traffic, my partners were fending off creditors and trying to scrounge money for fuel, parts, supplies, and the payroll. Then, the bank called in our demand loan without offering an explanation. We later found out that Ches Crosbie was a director of the bank and had no doubt influenced them in their decision to withdraw the loan. We also discovered that Ches Crosbie had threatened our suppliers so that they would cut off our credit.Our major part suppliers in Montreal refused further shipment without cash payment. And just to top it off, the aviation fuel distributors told us the only fuel we'd get would be cash on delivery. No credit!

We were making the absolutely necessary payments to some creditors each month, while living on starvation wages. It was hard to understand why we were not getting ahead financially. We were flying about 90 hours each month on all three aircraft; our gross income seemed substantial, but there was little left in the bank account to pay all the bills. We had no experience in running a business. We only knew how to fly, fuelled by plenty of confidence and enthusiasm.

After moving from Moncton with their three children, Rick and his wife, Jeanine, rented a small house in Pasadena. Frank had a home to maintain and he and Floss still had four children in school. Since I wasn't married, I boarded at the LeDrew home when I was staying overnight at the base. The company didn't have the funds to pay us a normal salary so we drew the absolute minimum for our basic necessities; the first year I received $737 in wages. The meager wages squeezed out of receipts made it especially difficult for the Richard and LeDrew families.

We consulted with Merle Belanger, an accountant. After considerable deliberation he informed us that our main problem was the aircraft leasing costs: White River Air Services was making the profit and we were doing all the work. If we were to survive, we had to find a way to purchase our own aircraft. The bank managers all sang the same song: "We'll loan your company money equal to the cash you have on hand." The trouble was there was no cash on hand. Winter was looming and that meant reduced demand for our services. We needed to find a lucrative winter contract if we were to hang on.

The large coastal freighter that supplied Tilt Cove's cargo and passenger service would soon be blocked by ice. After lengthy negotiations with Holland Smith, the mine manager at Tilt Cove, we were awarded a winter supply contract. The terms of the deal involved basing a large skiplane at the mine site to haul freight and passengers between Springdale and Long Pond, and using smaller aircraft for passenger trips to Gander and other communities. To begin the operation in early January, when the supply ship service was halted, a larger aircraft had to be procured and a sizeable cache of aviation fuel would be required at the mine site, or Springdale, within a month. Some kind of ingenious financial scheme had to be worked out in a hurry.

We tried to order 150 drums of aviation gas from both Shell and Imperial Oil in Lewisporte, to be delivered to the lake near Springdale. Both fuel companies refused the request, something about our poor credit rating! Without funding or credit, it would be impossible to acquire a large skiplane for the service. It seemed that we had hit a dead end and our dream was all but over. Rick and I decided to have a wrap-up dinner at the Lakeland Motel. The next day we would advise our customers that we were closing shop.

The motel in Pasadena was a regular hangout for EPA and NAT pilots and mechanics based in Pasadena. Bob and Edith Skinner always provided good service and a sympathetic ear. Mrs. Rogers listened to all the shop talk and kept our glasses filled. Sitting in a secluded section of the dining room, we dug into our big T-bone steaks and decided to wash our problems away with some fine wine, figuring we might as well go out in style. We thought we could probably obtain employment with EPA.

The dining room was deserted except for a large, boisterous, well dressed man who had been standing drinking by the bar since we arrived. Suddenly his weaving bulk sauntered unsteadily over to our table. Without warning or ceremony, he slammed his beer glass full of dark rum onto our table. We looked up at the Hitler-like stranger in utter disbelief, dodging the flying booze. Before we had a chance to retaliate or even ask what this was all about, he bellowed at us.

"Do you know who I am? My name is Ches Crosbie and I control all the flying services in this province. And you are the pair of goddamn reprobates who are trying to compete with my establishment. Let me tell you this loud and clear. I will continue to control all the commercial flying in this province. Not only will I use all my resources to put you out of business, but I'm going to make sure that you are personally driven to Hell – right out of this fair province of mine!"

With that, the obnoxious hulk lumbered away as quickly as he had come, leaving us wide-eyed and speechless. As his words sunk in, I was boiling over in rage and had an almost overwhelming urge to kill or maim. "That son of a bitch has just changed our future," I told Rick, my voice quaking with rancour. "Now we have to find a way to make that bastard eat his words!"

Ches Crosbie - founder of EPA

I ordered another bottle of Chablis to fuel the discussion. Without speaking, we both knew things had suddenly changed. We were now filled with more passion and determination to succeed than we had ever had before. We could taste it. "Damn that Crosbie Dynasty!"

The next morning I called my friend Rolly Weir in Little Bay Islands. Rolly was the owner and captain of the Tilt Cove supply boat. I asked him how closely he could estimate when the ice would prevent further voyages from Springdale to the copper mine. Rolly said that when the slob ice thickened in the seawater, he could normally provide three day's notice before his last trip. Emphasizing the urgency of the situation, I asked Rolly to be sure to call us three days prior to his suspension of service. We would have some important cargo for shipment on his last trip. The following week we received his call.

After some fancy negotiating, we convinced the Imperial Oil depot in Lewisporte to deliver150 drums of aviation gas to the vessel in Springdale for shipment to Tilt Cove on the last trip, which would be on Friday. I assured them that we had the cash for payment, but in view of the current ice conditions I said we doubted the voyage would even take place.

"Ship it C.O.D. and we will be on the dock to pay in full if and when it's unloaded at Tilt Cove," I assured them. Reluctantly, they agreed.

On January 16, we made sure that we were not to be found in Tilt Cove when the shipment arrived at the unloading wharf. The manager of Imperial Oil was livid when he discovered that Rolly had offloaded their drums without payment. When he finally tracked us down, we patiently explained to him that some completely unforeseen financing delays had arisen and we were very sorry to have caused any inconvenience. In no uncertain terms, he ordered us to leave the fuel on the dock. "Don't use any of it," he barked. They would have it returned on the first boat in the spring. But we knew our fuel problem was now solved and we would pay them for it during the winter as we used it.

Meanwhile, I had made arrangements to lease-purchase a Norseman skiplane from my elderly friend Ray McLeod in Montreal. Bob Noordyn, an aviation engineer from the Fokker plant in Holland, had come to Canada in 1934 to design a rugged bush machine for the unique needs of our harsh north country. The Norseman was built of steel tubing rather than wood framing, and was covered with fabric. The landing gear had to be strong to withstand the punishment of rough ice and heavy waves. It was fitted with a 550 horsepower radial engine. In early January, Eric Watson arrived in Pasadena with our fourth aircraft. It was previously owned by Austin Airways with registration CF-GMM.

We were now ready to begin the winter season. Many times in the subsequent years, silently but sincerely, we would give thanks to Ches Crosbie for providing us with that last bit of motivation that inspired us to forge ahead.

But that being said, it was beginning to seem that one problem solved was usually a sign that another crisis was just down the road. Our partnership fell apart during the early winter of 1962.

A serious dispute erupted between Frank LeDrew and Rick. Rick suspected that Frank, who was handling the administration, had siphoned a small sum of funds from company coffers for his personal use. With a bit of evidence, Rick's suspicion grew and he suggested that there was not room in the business for both Frank and him. I had enjoyed a close friendship with the LeDrew family and couldn't believe that Frank would hurt me. I found that I could not properly concentrate on my flying with such heated accusations and discussions going on. Reluctantly, I finally sided with Rick and we relieved Frank of his share in the business. Actually, Frank's share at that time would have been one third of many large debts since the planes were all leased and we owed a number of suppliers.

Without Frank, we had to find another winter airstrip. An arrangement was made with a farmer, Hugh Atkinson, to use his pasture adjoining Frank's property in Pasadena. At the new field on Green Acres Farm, we erected a small maintenance hangar and installed a mobile trailer to serve as an office.

Frank was furious. He remained adamant that he'd been mistreated and threatened to sue us. His hostility became very clear when Rick and I went to his house to remove our base radio, which we had installed there. While Rick was picking up the radio, I climbed up an apple tree to remove the antenna. When I heard the icy clank of his rifle bolt slamming shut, I looked down to see that he had his .300 Magnum pointed at my head!

"I'll give you three minutes to get down from that tree and to get the hell off my property!" he ordered.

After having enjoyed a long and cordial relationship with Frank and his family, I couldn't believe what I was hearing. He can't be serious, I thought. But then he clicked off the safety and I saw that his features were weirdly menacing, especially his bizarre stare.

"Take it easy, Frank, we're leaving," I said. Slowly, I dropped the wire antennae and descended to the ground. The muzzle of his rifle followed me to the car!

Rick didn't speak until we were driving out of the gate: "Holy shit! I think he would actually have pulled the trigger. Did you see his weird eyes and how crazy he looked?"

To recoup his losses and avenge what he considered an injustice, Frank devised a plan with Clayton Hutchings, an EPA pilot, to reclaim one of our floatplanes as payment for his past contributions to the company. Deer Lake, where our seaplane base was located, was not yet frozen. Clayton crept onto the base early one morning, started the engine on a Cessna 180, took off from the lake and landed the craft on the small, snowcovered airstrip behind

Frank's house. This machine was urgently needed to conduct skiplane charters to keep our company afloat. An immediate solution had to be found and the only answer was somehow to reclaim that plane from Frank.

To take off from Frank's short runway on floats would be tricky. Even gaining access to the plane would require trespassing. No doubt the fuel had been drained and the battery removed. The airstrip would need to be cleared of snow and packed. And to make it even more interesting, we knew Frank could be dangerous and would be sure to react with force if he caught us trespassing. But a plan soon materialized.

"Operation Recovery" began before daylight. We borrowed a John Deere 440 bulldozer from a neighbour. Rick was the driver. I cut the wire fence between the Atkinson property and Frank's strip to allow access for the dozer. While Rick was plowing and grading the field, Eric Watson and Eddy Oake refueled the aircraft, installed a new battery and warmed the engine at idle. The men working on the airfield had only agreed to the mission provided they were adequately protected from the gunfire that was likely to burst from Frank's back door. Frank had been known to use his .300 Magnum to fire over his orchard trees when he spotted kids stealing apples. We were also aware that when Frank lost his temper, he would often take action without much rational reckoning to diminish his resolve. In fact, I recalled, he had recently threatened me with his loaded rifle over the stupid antenna.

And so it was that I found myself hiding behind a tree before dawn taking a bead on the doorway of the LeDrew house fifty yards away. And while I asked myself, shivering in the predawn gloom, how it had all come to this, I was prepared, if necessary, to dissuade Frank from retaliatory fire by shooting at the door casing with a scoped 30-06, should he emerge with a gun. I knew this was the only way we could safely recover the aircraft, but I had a queasy feeling about firing at the house in which Frank's family had treated me so well. I prayed that I wouldn't need to pull the trigger.

Fortunately, as we later learned, although Frank had indeed tried to use his rifle to thwart our reclamation project, members of his family physically restrained him and prevented him from opening fire.

Eric's takeoff from the field was chancy, but proved uneventful. He landed the craft on our new winter strip, where we soon had the floats replaced with wheel-skis. We were back in business.

From then on, we posted a night guard in our office to keep a careful watch on our equipment. Frank made a second attempt to confiscate our aircraft, but Rick, armed with an axe, quickly dissuaded his scoundrels as they were in the process of towing it across the field.

Len Hawco, Frank's lawyer, later won a judgment against me for $120 with respect to unpaid board and lodgings. This entire ordeal gave me much personal torment since I had great admiration for the LeDrew family. But there was more corporate trouble looming on the horizon!

Atkinson's field office and hangar (1962)

Flossie and Frank LeDrew

Maritime Mine at Tilt Cove

Note Windsor Pond where I landed Piper skiplane

Wellons Cessna landed short

Corner Brook Harbour -1962

Chapter 2 Coastal People

Battle Harbour, Labrador (1962)

It was during the winter of 1961 that I made my first charter flight to Labrador. Prior to this trip, I hadn't taken the time to appreciate the unique character and boundless hospitality of those hardy and enduring coastal people.

Flying north along the west coast of Newfoundland, I reached the tip of the Great Northern Peninsula. I was delivering a large electrical dynamotor that had been ordered from Corner Brook to repair a diesel generator.

The island of Newfoundland is separated from southern Labrador by 30 kilometers of restless ocean called the Strait of Belle Isle. It was a wintry day but with adequate visibility, allowing me a good look at the stark, rounded hills of southern Labrador as I set course across the water from the town of Flowers Cove. The strait is seldom covered with solid ice, owing to the rapid tides and currents and the large outflow of water from the Gulf of St. Lawrence.

Ten minutes over the steel-gray water brought me to the

desolate fishing village of Forteau on the Labrador coast. Turning to a more easterly course, I followed along the coast for another fifty kilometers before reaching the small settlement of Battle Harbour. It was a bleak coast, barren and rough. All the scattered fishing ports were located in secluded coves, but separated by miles of sea-swept shore with ice-encrusted islands. The small community looked naked with the absence of trees. It comprised dreary wooden shacks scattered along the shore, square clapboard houses, fishing stages and battered warehouses perched on the edge of the rocky bay. Most of the saltbox houses had two stories and low peaked roofs, and needed paint. They appeared to sprout from the rocks. The harbour was a narrow tickle (slender water area) rimmed with makeshift wharves suspended on staunch strouters projecting up through the snow. A large group of men straggled to the ice as I taxied the skiplane to park by the big steamer wharf. They eagerly greeted me with firm handshakes and gathered around to help with the offloading of the heavy freight.

It was mid-afternoon and knowing that darkness came early there I had planned to return as far as Flowers Cove, but the friendly villagers were relentless in coaxing me to remain with them for the night. Their heartfelt invitation finally convinced me that this would be a more interesting stopover. My new helpers eagerly brought an assortment of ropes and bollards to secure my craft to the ice.

"Yes, me son," they said. "You'd better snug er down good, fer they speaks of a heasterly blow. When she blows ere, she can be a wunnerful dirty night."

When I inquired about a boarding house,they just laughed: "You won't find any dem fancy sleepin' places ere, but ya gits a choice of twelve ouses to be at, and they's all better than dem city places."

Good-natured arguments broke out among the villagers about why it was best the stranger stay at their place and not another. Finally, a man who seemed to have won the debate beckoned me to follow him. After climbing over the icy stage and passing through the dock sheds, which reeked slightly of rotting fish, we went up the winding path and past an array of drying flakes and weathered hulls of overturned boats. I followed through stake-fenced yards and around various homes where chained husky dogs lunged and growled at the new intruder.

Labrador is a sparsely populated land, legendary for the harshness of its terrain and climate. Indians, Inuit, and finally Europeans, attracted by its wealth of teeming fish, all settled on this incredibly challenging territory over the years. The sturdy, resourceful fisherfolk took root on the rugged land, mingled, and multiplied. The isolated bays offered stout timber and boat shelter and thus evolved the "outports." Tragedies were common at sea, but the generations that survived produced a rare breed of courageous, keen-witted, and generous people. In 1961,the men built boats to catch fish while the women gutted, split and dried the cod fillets on the flakes. Seals were caught in the spring, their oil was rendered, the pelts used for clothing and the meat eaten. Nothing was wasted.

Caribou and rabbit were normal winter fare and their hides provided warm winter garments. The children, pressed into service at a tender age, could sail or row a dory by the age of eight. The girls assisted with sewing, cleaning fish, cooking and gathering wood, the boys did men's work by the age of twelve.

The salthbox house to which I was brought that night long ago, bound with whip-sawed planking, was simple, warm and cozy. Inside the porch, the kitchen area was spotlessly clean. Above the steaming kettle on the woodstove an array of mitts and homespun wool socks were drying in the heat. The wall next to the stove was neatly stacked with cleaved firewood. Thomas O'Brien introduced me to his wife and then ushered me into a small parlour where his elderly father greeted me from his squeaky rocker: "Tis good to see ya, me young man. Please sit and tell me of de news from de houtside. Sharon will fetch us some tea bye and bye."

Mr. O'Brien was a hardy looking man with thinning gray hair and a tidy white mustache. He wore a warm and gentle smile that lit up his weathered features. His large, gnarled hands rested on the table. They were twisted and scarred from a lifetime of rough work and hardship. Four sturdy homemade chairs surrounded the card table ornately covered with white, handstitched linen. The centerpiece was a cracked blue vase holding a colorful clutch of dried marsh flowers.

The kerosene lamp, with blackened chimney, threw long shadows on the hand-hewn wallboards. Hanging opposite me was a print portraying the Last Supper and on my right hung a larger framed portrait of Joey Smallwood, Newfoundland's first and only premier since the province joined the Canadian federation in 1949. Scratchy music echoed softly from a shelf box nestled between the flimsy plastic window curtains. Across from the entrance there was a door, slightly ajar, leading to another section of the home, from which we could hear the wound up chatter of children.

As Mr. O'Brien refilled his blackened corncob pipe, he became quite talkative: "Dis has been me ome fer years. Me old father built she, God bless his soul, and we keeps hadding on wit each generation. T'is not fancy, but keeps out the starms. Thomas and Sharon ave six young-uns, and when they gets growed, we'll shove hout another wing. Me old woman passed away some years ago wit the TB, but I angs on and tries to rally Tom wit de chores."

Sharon tapped timidly on the door before bringing in a steaming dish of caribou stew, a teapot, freshly made warm buns and two bowls of canned peaches.

"Please call to the kitchen if ya be needin anyting else," she said. "And ifen that radio bothers ya jist turn he off."

I asked my elderly host about life in this remote part of Labrador. Before speaking, he reached down and disconnected the battery wire that led up to the old radio set: "Jist listens to de ships at sea an the galling news bulletins hout'a St. John's, tis good I don't ear too well, but it lets us know as much as we care ta know," he said. "But ta hanswer yer question, tings are very good ere. We gits by quite fine, since there be plenty to heat, the country feeds us well. When we sells de fish we gits credit fer de winter flour and next spring's boat fuel, tabaccy, and ar hother needs tis hard ta keep squared up on the merchant's books. There ain't much call fer cash, but would like to see a heasier life fer de kids when dey grows. I's gittin' hold and me legs aren't so spritely but at eighty yars I shan't complain, since dey's the same pair He started me wit."

I asked his opinion of government services.

"Oh, they sends in a young teacher,but de learnings could be better," he said. 'Most of us knows ow to deal wit bad sickness and de medical boat comes by each summer. Joey Smallwood has been a Godsend. Before he, we was some frightfully poor and no one cared or knowed we was ere; there was no government dock fer de supply boats, and ye knows that de worse ting you can have is no wharf." He paused to take a pull on his pipe, warming to the subject.

"We ad no hold age money, poor heducation and little medical tention. Why dey says he's even puttin in a big ospital at St. Anthony fer we! De fish prices was worser afore confederation, and we ad no regular boat service in dose days."

By regular he meant about twice each summer. We finished the hot stew and began the dessert and tea.

"Yes me son, Joey be a blessin fer we," he continued. "As I said, before he, we was strugglin fer survival and lots of us didn't make it. Now when the sea permits, we even ave a parson who comes fer de Sunday service and gives de marriage and de funerals. Some more 'ouses are getting the electrics soon, and dey even says dat fisher people may get paid in money during the hoff season! We got it some good, I says, but t'is ar nature to complain."

Through the far door, three children of various sizes were stacked by the sill. They stared at me with wide, innocent eyes. I thought they were showing curiosity about the stranger in their home.

"No sar," the old man explained. "They's not lookin ta yee, they's spying yer peaches! They don't hever see de canned peaches ceptin' Christmas." After that, each spoonful produced a twinge of guilt as I swallowed the children's special treats. I didn't know whether to continue eating or set them aside.

"Joey seems to have some weak government ministers surrounding him," I commented.

"Yiss," the old man replied. "He's making hall the decisions, so peraps he don't suffer fer strong voices that might hinterfere. Some a dose politicians got less sense den a codfish. But we hopes he won't let his success be a bulge on is head. I've seen some good men go rather foolish dat way and we fears Joey may ang on too long."

We talked for some time longer and I was sorry to end a very pleasant evening, but it was time for rest. I thanked Mr. O'Brien for sharing his thoughts with me and Sharon showed me to my comfy bedroom.

"The houthouse is a stone's throw from de back door, but if'n ye minds the snarly dogs or de frost ye'll find a potty under yer bed. Now you ave a good sleep," she said.

That night, underneath the feather-stuffed quilt, the increasing cold of the room wasn't even noticeable. I slept soundly, waking only once to stretch and smell the sweet aroma of woodsmoke.

After a pleasant breakfast of partridgeberry jam and more of Sharon's delicious bread, I tried to pay for my lodging. Sharon and her husband were plainly insulted by my offer.

"You jest come ere whenever yer on de Labrador," Tom said. "We'd be onored to see ya hanytime."

Most of the population came to the harbour to say their goodbyes. Observing Tom's older boy peering at the aircraft, I quietly slipped a $20 bill into his torn coat pocket. The crowd was still waving as my skiplane lifted from the harbour ice.

On the long flight home, I reflected upon what I had seen and heard. There are hundreds of similar coastal settlements around the province's rockbound shores, I thought. The hardy inhabitants are fighting a daily battle with the elements to wrest a subsistence living from the windswept sea. Their survival demands unrelenting courage and toil. They are stranded, in complete isolation, for half the year by the ice. Wood gathering and social communication beyond their villages can only be carried out by grueling dog team trips. There are no roads, little education, scarce medical care, and the monotonous repetition of unending labour. They are without the ordinary entertainments and conveniences which modern man considers essential.But they are independent and content and show a delightful humour about their constant striving. Their remarkable generosity in the face of adversity was unsurpassed in my experience. I strongly believed they would share their last crust with a needy neighbour or a complete stranger.

For these hardy folk, I thought, the fishery is their tender and wealth and is measured on a different scale from what we know. Success is simply eking out a lean existence. Yes, I thought, most of us could learn a lot from these extraordinary people. To me this certainly was a "New Found Land." Before this trip, I had often second guessed my decision to come to this new and remote Canadian province, but now, after a night in the outport of Battle Harbour, I was convinced my choice had been the right one. It seemed that I had entered the heart and soul of Newfoundland and it fit the frontier like lifestyle that I was seeking.

Chapter 3 On the Brink

Rick Richard in front of hangar on Atkinson Farm

In the winter of 1962, though business was picking up, we encountered new problems at every turn. There was considerable freight to move to the various mine sites on the Baie Verte Peninsula. Our winter strip at the Atkinson's field was too short for the fully loaded Norseman. The Deer Lake Airport was the nearest suitable runway, but it was not yet in use by any other carrier and therefore it had no snow clearing crew, fuel or terminal buildings. We had to transport cargo by truck from Corner Brook and plow the access road to the airport. We fitted straight skis (without wheels) to the old Norseman, making it usable without removing snow from the runway.

Throughout the 1960s, Newfoundland suffered severe winter weather with huge volumes of snowfall. The snow on some lakes was so deep and loose that the aircraft would get bogged down when turning with heavy loads. The pilots spent many frustrating hours shoveling snow to free their craft, especially on the lake we used for Advocate Mines and on the pond that we used to service Rambler Mines.

The pilots regularly endured many freezing and tiresome chores before flight in the early morning and at the end of their day. It was routine procedure to run the skis up on spruce branches so they wouldn't be frozen into the snow the next morning. Tarpaulins were set over the engine cowlings to prevent snow from blowing into the various intakes. Before shutdown on the last flight, it was necessary to use oil dilution on the engines. This dilution technique injected fuel into the oil reservoir so the engine could easily rotate on the morning start; otherwise the low temperatures would congeal the oil and prevent the battery from turning the motor over. After the engines idled and warmed up, the injected fuel would evaporate, creating normal viscosity for lubrication. Even with this system it was usually necessary to apply heat for some thirty minutes using blowpots placed under the engine tarp. When extreme temperatures were expected, the aircraft batteries had to be removed and taken to our sleeping quarters for warmth. The fuel drums were shoveled out of the snow and rolled over to the parked planes. There was no electricity at these remote lakes, so all the refueling had to be done by hand pump and felt strainer. The wings and control surfaces were scraped free of snow and frost before takeoff. Nevertheless, the pilots loved flying so much that they accepted these frigid hardships day after day without complaint; it was just part of the job.

Consolidated Rambler Mine near Baie Verte

The Rambler Mine, a small start-up gold/ copper producer near Baie Verte, was also without road access for much of the winter and early spring. Its normal landing area was some distance from the mine site, so we routinely made airdrops with the mail and lighter parcels. We got to be quite proficient at these drops. On one occasion, I had a mailbag and two bags of cooked lobster that the manager had requested. After dropping the mail, it was announced over the radio that the bag had landed about 30 feet in front of the administration building. On the next pass, I was told that the package landed 12 feet southwest of the door. On the last run, by sheer luck and some correction, the lobsters bounced off the snowbank and flew through the open door of the mine manager's office. There was applause on the radio and compliments for my display of expertise. Perhaps I should have told them that it was just pure luck, but I decided that if they wanted to credit my remarkable skill for the last drop it would be unkind to disillusion them.

During the winter of 1962, the Lundrigan Construction Company was continuing to work on a new road link between Baie Verte and La Scie, a distance of about 60 kilometers. The area consisted of only a barren piece of rock and tundra interlaced with small lakes and bogs. Late in the afternoon, on my last flight of the day, I was returning to Tilt Cove in the Cessna after completing a trip from Gander to Baie Verte. An advancing trough of rough weather was beginning to deteriorate flight conditions, forcing me to skim the scrub treetops to maintain visual contact with the ground.

Suddenly, without any warning, the engine gave a few quick backfires and died! All instrumentation was normal, but there was no time for troubleshooting. Fortunately, the aircraft was light and could glide a short distance even from only 200 feet of altitude. There was a clearing in the trees to my left. The Cessna responded immediately as I desperately banked toward the opening in a rapid descent. The wind was behind me, but there was no choice but to attempt a landing straight ahead and downwind. The clearing widened to my left, just as the skis slapped the snow. The aircraft came to an unceremonious stop on the lake. Both the aircraft and I had escaped unscathed, but it appeared I would be stranded on Armchair Pond.

All our aircraft were equipped with single side-band radios, normally allowing communication with the mine sites and our base in Pasadena, but I couldn't get a response on the radio. In the air, we used a trailing antenna that would unwind a coil of wire in the slipstream behind the rudder. This allowed an optimum wavelength for each frequency used and provided more signal strength. But I was on the ground.

Donning my snowshoes, I unwound 38 feet of coiled wire and laid it out on the snow behind the aircraft. On my next attempt I got a response. I was relieved to hear the voice of Ernie Creighton, the company dispatcher at Tilt Cove, on the other end of the line. I asked him to contact our base in Pasadena and advise Rick that I was near Lundrigan's construction camp on Armchair Pond, that a new carburetor was urgently needed, and that I had an extremely important flight to make in the morning to pick up the vice-president of Johns Manville Corporation in Gander.

I walked down the lake about a kilometer through the storm. Although there was only a light breeze, the falling snow bit at my face as I slogged through the knee deep drifts. After half an hour trudging, I rounded a point and was relieved to spot the lights of the construction camp with its stovepipe spewing a welcoming stream of smoke. The fire in their kitchen warmed my chilled bones while they fed me. When the staff learned of my problem, they fired up their road grader and opened a path down the trail to the Baie Verte junction. It was about two in the morning when Rick pulled into the depot with the company truck. He had been battling snowdrifts on the road for five hours. Under protective canvas, at minus 15C, we worked together through the stormy night with a flashlight and blowpot. Before daybreak, the new carburetor was installed and we roared into the predawn sky for a test flight. I then dropped Rick off at the construction site and began the one hour flight to Gander. At 7:30 a.m. Mr. Karl Lindell boarded my aircraft at the Gander terminal. With a firm handshake, he apologized for getting me up for such an early departure.

"You look a bit weary this morning, Gene," he said, pleasantly. "I suppose you were up partying all night, were you?" I thought it best not to answer.

Faulty carburetors weren't our only problem in those days. Our combative relationship with EPA's head office in Gander hadn't improved with time, although most of their pilots and maintenance staff were friendly and cordial. Their large fleet of modern DeHavilland Beavers and Otters looked sharp, with freshly painted company colours and logo. The crews were smartly attired in company flight suits. Our planes and staff were motley by comparison. Although we placed a high priority on maintenance, the funds for fancy paint jobs were just not available. The Norseman that we operated was a tough workhorse, but did not compare with the performance of their Otters, nor could our Cessnas do the work of their Beavers. We concentrated on service rather than looks.

About this time, we discovered that Ches Crosbie was a director of the bank we had been dealing with, and behind the scenes, had been the source of many of our banking and financial problems. The unavailable credit with the oil companies, Laurentide Aviation and Leavens Brothers, could also be traced to EPA's powerful propaganda campaign against us. As well, someone had convinced government officials that our equipment, pilots, and service were substantially inferior to those of EPA. Government officials were told by someone that our operation was marginal and probably not very safe!

Many of our charter flights for the various mining companies involved shuttles in and out of Gander Airport since it was the main hub for Air Canada flights to the mainland. Advocate Mines owned a staff house in Gander that we looked after for them, and we used it for our crews when they had to overnight at the airport.

In the early years of NAT's operation, we didn't have our own docking facility at the lake in Gander. Since it was the main base for all EPA operations, they had large facilities on the lakeshore that we frequently used for docking and embarking our passengers. Although their seaplane base was listed as a transient facility, the management of EPA had instructed their dock staff to untie any of our floatplanes if we used their wharf. This major irritation continued until our lawyer put them on notice that they would be held responsible for any damages that resulted should our planes drift onto the rocks or shore.

EPA also refused to sell us fuel or parts. We both maintained fuel caches at various remote locations on the coast of Labrador. Owing to their large mail delivery service, the EPA storage sites were quite numerous, but they refused to sell us fuel at any price, even under the direst of circumstances. All of their station agents were instructed "Give no assistance to NAT personnel."

In the spring of 1962, Long Pond at Tilt Cove became unusable due to mild conditions that left two feet of slush on the ice. Our freight hauling from Springdale was still a necessity for the mine, since ice breakup wouldn't occur until mid-May. In order to continue our airlift, we located a large flat bog near the U.S. Air Force radar station. It was 10 kilometers from the mine by J-5 snow machine. Our fuel drums were moved to this new operating site where we now based our aircraft and discharged our freight.

On a particularly stormy April afternoon, four EPA Beavers and an Otter were caught in a blizzard on their return flight to Gander after delivering mail to St. Anthony and Labrador. The pilots were aware of our new bog runway on Cape St. John, and after many diversions in the snow squalls, they had no choice but to land on the big marsh. We arranged ground transportation for the five pilots and provided overnight accommodations for them at the mine. During the evening the pilots informed us that they were too low on fuel to return to Gander, but the planes were desperately needed back there in the morning. The manager of EPA, Jim Lewington, called me several times that night pleading for me to sell them some fuel for their stranded fleet. I knew, for the first time, that I held the trump cards in my hand that would determine the fate of their five aircraft. It was no doubt a spiteful feeling of triumph or revenge that I felt, but I decided to let them dangle for a while in their pleadings for fuel.

On the third call, I said, "Jim, for the last two years your company and its owners have used every damn tactic available to hurt our business. Now, I don't mind competition, but some of your antics have been ridiculous. Ches Crosbie swore that he would bankrupt us and he sure as hell has tried. Now you have a serious predicament and you expect me to cooperate! I may be stupid but I'm not a fool. If the situation was reversed, you know damn well that you wouldn't provide us with fuel."

"Gene, I can fix all that if you can see your way to fuel those aircraft," he begged. After lengthy negotiations, a satisfactory deal was finally reached whereby we would refuel their planes provided that they changed their policy towards us immediately and extend similar cooperation at all their remote sites. It was possibly the single most expensive fuel-up they had ever purchased, but Jim Lewington did keep his word and the tension between our two companies diminished considerably following this fortuitous incident. Meanwhile, other people were having problems.

Our early base at Pasadena -office and maintenance shed (1963)

In the early 1960s, many of the rural coastal communities on the island of Newfoundland were very isolated, especially during the winter. The coastal boat service was suspended from

December until May, blocked by ocean ice. Many of the fishing villages didn't have a road connection. On the Northern Peninsula, a coastal road joined the small towns in the summer months, but the ferry service across St. Paul's Inlet was curtailed at freeze-up, leaving the northern region without road access. Winter mail service was provided by skiplanes and dog sleds. The telephone system was archaic in these villages. Those lucky enough to have a phone used a party-line crank mechanism that was seldom workable because of the static.

We had hired some of the hardy fishermen from the Portland Creek area to construct and guide at our remote hunting camps, another business we were developing. Although they lacked much formal education, these men were extremely capable at carpentry and mechanical repairs and had an unbelievable work ethic under very trying conditions. The fishery provided a meager existence, so they were anxious to augment their income at any part-time job that cropped up. During the long spring ice breakup, they would venture through the ice flows in small open boats to collect a few seals for food and saleable pelts. As we got to know them, we "come from away" mainlanders became very attached to these resilient, hardworking people.

One evening, in mid-April of 1962, I received a scratchy phone call from Jessie Caines. After apologizing for bothering me with her worries, she asked for help.

"I'm some worried about me husband Tommy," she said. "He and six other friends left yesterday morning in two small lobster boats to *swatch seals in the hice leads along the Gulf Coast. They planned to return in the evening, but there's no sign of they yet, probably got theyselves nipped in the hice."

I asked her for more details.

"Well," she said, "they's in two 27-foot open wooden boats that the men made theyselves, and they's got the houtboard motors. The men weren't too stoutly dressed, but they did take some bread and they took lots a gas wit em. Though *scrammed, no doubt they'll get back come mornin."

She went on to describe the local conditions: "The heasterly wind has opened up the hice pack along the shore, which made the yearnin' by the men to go swatchin in the first place. But during the hafternoon, the wind went round to the west and she's been blowin' a gale with blindin snow hever since. I don't want to put trouble on you, but ifin you have a plane up this way, maybe you could scout the hice flows to see how they's doin.'"

I was very concerned although Tommy's wife hadn't seemed overly worried. Immediately, I contacted the Search and Rescue center in Halifax to advise them of the missing men. The next morning we sent a skiplane up the coast. But due to the continuing storm, the aircraft had to return to base when it reached the snow-obscured inlet near Bonne Bay, halfway to Portland Creek. Captain Tenet of the Coast Guard notified us that they had dispatched a large rescue plane from Halifax, but the mission was scrubbed due to lack of visibility over the gulf ice.

The spring storm continued for three more days. Finally, after we had repeatedly expressed our concern to the Coast Guard for the lives of the seven men, they agreed to divert their large icebreaker to the area for surveillance. The *Sir Humphrey Gilbert* (one of Canada's largest ice-breakers) had been attempting to open a shipping lane to Bowater's paper export wharf in Corner Brook when the captain received the new orders.

Most of the masters who commanded these huge ice ships were British and former naval captains.They tended to be quite aloof, in my experience, and conducted their operations in the pompous, somewhat high-handed manner that they felt befitted their exalted position. Normally, they clear a path and guide large cargo vessels through the ice and, local captains often complained, haughtily ordered the other captains about. Nonetheless, their radio commands were generally obeyed and the wisdom of their orders was rarely questioned by anyone.

Tommy and his men had become trapped about 40 kilometers off the coast when the wind jammed and closed the open water leads. They were forced then to haul their two open boats onto an ice pan, propping up one boat on its side to act as a windbreak. They contrived a stove-like device from scrap metal, used gas and seal oil for fuel, dined on seal meat and bread, and huddled together for warmth, awaiting a change in wind.

Wilfred Caines, the youngest member of the group, had fallen into the sea when they struggled to haul their boats onto the floating ice. Tommy stripped him of his wet garments and dressed him in pieces of clothing offered by the other men. They placed Wilfred in the bottom of the boat and covered him with sealskins. They tried to restore him with hot tea, but on the fifth day he was showing clear signs of hypothermia. The fire wasn't sufficient to dry their clothing or offer much comfort, but it did provide warm tea water and raised their spirits somewhat.

Aware of the danger of remaining immobile, Tommy wouldn't let the men sit on the ice and wait for help. He encouraged them to keep walking in circles while swinging their arms and clapping their hands. These coastal men. and especially Tommy, had a rare ability to cope with extreme hardship while retaining their sense of humour and optimistic outlook.

"It'll feel some good to cuddle me old woman when we gits ome tomorrow," Tommy would tell his friends, brushing snow now and then from Wilfred's face.

The disgruntled captain of the *Gilbert* had, no doubt reluctantly, obeyed the orders from Halifax and swung his big 7,000 ton vessel northward. There wasn't much prestige associated with the search for a small boat in the midst of a snowstorm. I was well acquainted with many of the officers serving on the icebreakers, and I can easily imagine the tenor of the outrage on the bridge.

"How dare they waste my precious time and skills by sending me on these ill-founded missions? The cost of diverting our vessel is utterly ridiculous," the captain would have muttered to himself. Perhaps even worse.

Early in the morning darkness, after steaming through the icy Gulf for ten hours, the captain was called from his stateroom and told by the first mate that an hour ago they had spotted a wispy fireball a few kilometers off the starboard bow, but they couldn't tell what it was, visibility being still very limited by the falling snow. Reaching the bridge, the captain ordered the 4,300 horsepower engines stopped and instructed the crew to stand off until first light. During the night the exhausted seal hunters had heard the faint rumbling of a diesel engine in the distance. They had prepared for such a happy eventuality and immediately torched a five gallon bucket of gasoline. One further attempt at signaling was made after the engine noise stopped. But, to the great disappointment of the men, there was no apparent result.

Coast Guard icebreaker in gulf ice

At daybreak, with their hopes rapidly sinking as the wind freshened, the stranded men suddenly saw the huge bow of the icebreaker looming through the driving snow. The great ship slowly moved alongside the ice pan that had provided a haven for the desperate men for six nights. The captain appeared on the port bridge with a megaphone in his hand. He was a stately looking gentleman, the sealers later said, dressed as he was in full uniform with the collar of his greatcoat turned up to shield himself from the howling wind. From far below on the ice it was difficult to be certain, but it looked as if he was sporting two rows of military medals on his left breast, but that might have been a trick of the early morning light.

"Cast the rope ladder over the side and prepare to board the party," he bellowed.

The long ladder clinked as it unfolded like a spider's web against the lofty hull of the ship. The captain must have been more than a little surprised when the tiny party on the ice remained motionless on the edge of their weatherbeaten boats. He would have expected any sane man to scramble aboard as fast as his legs would carry him after the ordeal he knew those men must have been through.

The megaphone resonated over the ice. "Are you able to climb up the ladder or do you require a stretcher to be lowered?" the captain shouted.

Tommy yelled back, "Most of us can climb yer damn ladder, but you gotta aul up ar boats first!"

The captain puffed up and blared back heatedly, "We didn't come all this way to retrieve your skiffs, we came to rescue men. Now come, my lads, leave your boats where they're at and scamper up the ladder, we don't have time to waste."

There was a short discussion among the men on the ice. Tommy then shot back at the captain: "If you aren't taking up our boats, skipper, then you might as well fuck off! Yer wastin ar time as well as yer own."

That may well have been the first time the skipper had ever been addressed in front of his crew in such a blunt and informal manner. But those small fishing boats were the most important asset the men had for eking out a living on that unforgiving coast and they sure weren't going to leave without them.

The captain found himself between a rock and a hard place. He couldn't turn his back on the stranded men. How would he explain that to his superiors? But the men had been quite clear in their message; they would not budge until their 'damned skiffs' were retrieved. There was complete silence for a few moments as the skipper sipped his tea and mulled over the situation. He knew these men from "The Rock" well enough to know they weren't bluffing. Finally, he came to terms with the inevitable and ordered the crew, in a somewhat less strident manner than before, to lower the derricks and lift the boats on board. Only then did Tommy and his beleaguered but unbowed men consent to climb up onto the deck and enjoy the comforts that awaited them.

Jessie, when advised of the rescue of her man, expressed her gratitude for our small part in the rescue: "I knowed they'd be OK," she said. "But if it weren't fer yous, they'd be waitin another few days fer the wind ta change."

Chapter 4 Crash Pond Salvage

CF –NXA after recovery from lake and refurbishing

Late in October we received a call from a Chicago insurance adjuster. "A client of ours just crashed a new float plane in southern Newfoundland," he said."I'm flying to your area tomorrow to examine the wreck, repair the damage, and ferry the machine back to Illinois."

He asked if we knew the location of the crash and if it would be possible to charter one of our aircraft to fly him to the site. We had heard about the accident. Three hunters had flown from Michigan to Newfoundland in their new Cessna to hunt moose. With the help of a local guide, they had set up camp on a small remote lake in the southwestern part of the province. On takeoff, under gusty wind conditions, the right wing tip had struck the water and flipped the craft upside down. The pontoons were floating the inverted aircraft, but the occupants were not seriously injured. They managed to escape from the sinking cabin and swam to shore. Their guide then walked 30 kilometers to the nearest coastal village for assistance. A Coast Guard helicopter was dispatched and rescued the stranded party and they returned safely to their homes in the United States.

The nameless lake was 150 kilometers south of our base in Pasadena. Some of the higher lakes in the region were already freezing and the terrain was snowcovered. We advised the insurance agent of the wintry conditions and of the difficulties he faced, but he was not deterred.

"I have considerable experience in salvaging aircraft all over the North Country and in very adverse weather," he assured us. "I'll bring suitable equipment and spare parts so the aircraft can be repaired and flown back to Chicago. If you can loan me an experienced engineer, it shouldn't be a big job."

Three days later we met Stan Clancy on his arrival at Stephenville Airport. He had two large crates and some heavy duffle bags. Stan was a self-assured young man who was gung-ho about the project. His enthusiasm was not in the least dampened by the worsening weather conditions, even though he was city-attired and without suitable warm bush clothing. I took him to our office for a briefing and we joined him for dinner later that evening.

Rick, my engineering partner, was recovering from stomach ulcer surgery and had just been released from the hospital. He joined us for the dinner meeting. Stan explained that he had brought considerable equipment: a new propeller, governor, magnetos, carburetor, VHF radio, a complete set of replacement instruments, and a tool box. He also had a new wet suit and snorkel gear. He asked how early we could start.

We pointed out that he would require warm clothing. The lake might be frozen and that would prevent a float landing. In case of bad weather we should take a tent, sleeping bags, food and a portable stove. Some tools, block and tackle and ropes would also be a good idea, we told him.

"In that case," he said, "tomorrow we'll just do a quick reconnaissance of the situation and return here with a list of what we'll need to upright and repair the machine."

The next day the three of us boarded a Cessna and departed for Crash Pond. One hour later I landed on the long, thin lake, where the inverted plane was clearly visible. It was at rest 100 feet from shore on a silty lakebed with the bottom of the floats sticking up through the water surface. Stan suddenly lost some of his confidence as he stood on the icy shore contemplating that frigid water. Shivering in the sub-zero wind, he timidly asked if one of us would care to don the wet suit and examine the wreck for him. It was amazing how quickly his enthusiasm had faltered.

While I wiggled into the suit, Rick took me aside and suggested that it might be in our best interests if the damage reports were somewhat exaggerated. By this time, we had both had enough of this young man's blatant impudence. It would cost him.

After the short swim, a feeling of warmth washed over my body as the layer of insulation did its job. The craft was in about 16 feet of water, partially suspended by the inverted floats. With my snorkel it was easy to dive around the machine for an inspection. Surprisingly, there was very little damage. Both prop blades were bent, one of the outer wing spars looked twisted, and the upper hinge on the pilot's door was broken. The plane was resting in soft mud with the vertical stabilizer a few feet from the bottom and that seemed to be the total extent of the damage. The new Edo floats were unscathed.

I entered the cockpit to examine the interior and discovered a large air pocket trapped by the inverted cabin seats. This allowed me to breathe without coming up to the surface. I was so caught up in what I was doing that I stayed in the cabin for a long time assessing the damage and examining the instrument panel. Little did I know that Rick and Stanley had begun to think I'd been snagged underneath the craft and was possibly drowning! Just as I popped to the surface, Stan was starting to get panicky and Rick was undressing to attempt a rescue.

On the flight home, I explained the seriousness of the damage I had discovered. Stan seemed overwhelmed by the situation. His haughtiness of the day before had dissipated and had been replaced with what to us was a more becoming meekness. During the discussion, it soon became evident that he was now ready to wash his hands of the recovery operation and return to the comfort of his cozy Chicago office. He had more than enough of what now appeared to be a futile venture in an extremely hostile wilderness.

"I think he's ready to deal," Rick whispered to me when we landed.

That evening, Stan treated us to a sumptuous steak dinner at the Lakeland Motel. We told him that if he preferred to go home, we would make him an attractive offer on purchasing the wreck "as is, where is." When we made the offer, I was sure I could see a twinge of relief settle on Stan's face. Earlier, in the washroom, Rick and I had conferred and concluded that the repairs would cost about $5,000, not counting our time and labour. The aircraft's value, after repairs and including the new parts, would be over $60,000. We promptly offered Stan $6,000 if he would include all the spare parts and equipment that he had brought. After a long phone conversation with his company, the arrangement was accepted. Now we had only one obstacle to overcome. We didn't have $6,000!

While Rick generously plied Stan with more drinks, I drove over to visit our good friend Hugh Atkinson at Green Acres Farm. Hugh was a very conservative, successful farmer and prominent businessman who had always shown a keen interest in the progress of our air service. After explaining the bargain at hand, Hugh reluctantly issued a cheque for the $6,000 in exchange for a one-third share in the ownership of our upside down plane.

Our good friend Hugh Atkinson (1963) Green Acres Farm, Pasadena

"If I didn't know you rogues, it would be sheer stupidity to buy part of a damaged plane that's still on the bottom of a remote lake," he exclaimed.

All that remained was to get the plane upright, repair it, and fly it home.

We purchased a complete new wing section for the Cessna.

After it arrived in November, Eric Watson made three trips flying Rick and me to what had become known as Crash Pond, with all our equipment and fuel. The smaller lakes were now solidly frozen, but the new wing would not fit in the Norseman and could not be fastened to a skiplane for exterior transport. In summer, it was routine to carry boats and large materials by strapping them to the floats of the craft for external transport. So it was with considerable apprehension that the big wing was securely lashed underneath the floats of a Cessna 180 by resting it on the two horizontal cross members that connected the floats. The wing root was placed just behind and underneath the propeller, with the tip extending well back beneath the fuselage. Surprisingly, the precarious load handled fairly well, although the extra drag reduced the speed by 30 miles per hour. Eric took off from our Pasadena Base on open water but had to land the floatplane on the ice at Crash Pond.

Eric returned to Pasadena, leaving Rick and me and all our gear on the north shore of Crash Pond. We set up camp under the trees and began organizing our equipment. At the end of the second day we had righted the aircraft with block and tackle and wedged it to shore by cutting a path with chainsaws. The floats were drained and our new plane was securely moored on the slippery beach next to our makeshift encampment. Rick was in poor physical condition after his operation and was heavily medicated. Nonetheless, he worked away methodically all day and used a generator night light. The engine oil was flushed a few times and the new propeller installed. The wing tanks were drained and replenished with clean fuel. The damaged wing was removed and replaced. Foul weather made the work particularly trying. The cold wind and the wet snow not only dampened our morale, but made it impossible to dry our clothing. Our workplace looked like a disaster area, with cowlings (engine coverings) scattered on the ground, black oil and grease pooled on the white snow, boxes of tools and parts spread about at random and empty fuel containers littering the shore ice. Our canvas sleeping abode was soggy with wet snow dropping from the spruce limbs. It became a menacing

45

enclosure. The makeshift outdoor kitchen held an array of canned goods, utensils and dishware, arranged in no apparent order on a shelf under a flapping tarpaulin, with strands of moss hanging over our cooking area. Everything was soggy as the scraggly spruce boughs steadily dripped moisture. Even our open-air privy was uncomfortable.

Finally, Rick suggested we try an engine start without replacing the magnetos or carburetor. One by one the pistons coughed and sputtered to life, and the prop started turning. In moments the Continental came to life with a roar, the exhaust spitting a mixture of flame and dense black smoke. Oil and dirty water spewed over Rick's entire body. When the engine finally gained a regular momentum, our spirits were lifted. Rick crouched beside the cowless engine, his greasy hands resting on his stained coveralls. Smiling through the grime, he reached over and removed a wrench that had been left on the oil cooler.

The ground running went fine; now an air test was required. The ice surface was sufficiently hard to make for good conditions for a float takeoff. The low cloud cover wrapped the surrounding hills and offered marginal room for a quick low level test flight. The short circuit around the lake went well, and all systems proved satisfactory for the flight home when the weather permitted.

Having already endured four nights in our sodden abode, we were very anxious to leave, but the weather closed in and stranded us for another three anxious days. Rick was now quite ill and we were gradually running low on food. We were wet and completely bored with just waiting. The time dragged. Had we brought some books or magazines, it would have helped to avoid monotony. I passed the day by cutting dry firewood for our little sheet metal stove. When Rick saw the huge stack of wood he wondered if I planned to spend the winter there! Our main concern was the possibility of a heavy snowfall which would prevent a floatplane takeoff from the lake. The daily calls on the portable radio didn't provide much encouragement regarding the prevailing weather, but it was the highlight of the day to speak to someone other than ourselves.

On the seventh morning, I peered through the tent flap. There was a low ceiling, but the sky seemed slightly brighter than it had been for days. It was time to go.

I rattled the tent to rouse my partner: "Hey Rick, better roll out. It's a beautiful day," I lied. "Let's get ta hell out of this hole."

We loaded the craft with most of our gear and quickly left behind what had become an appalling campsite, leaving only the damaged wing, empty fuel cans and the bent prop. In the minus 8C chill, we made our way homeward. Snow squalls were frequent, which necessitated diversions from a direct course. The cold breeze whipped at my left shoulder, since the door on my side of the cockpit had been removed for lack of new hinges. Most of the instruments had not been replaced and the old ones were frozen. I had a functioning altimeter, oil temperature and pressure gauge, and RPM indicator. The pitot tube was blocked with moisture, which made the airspeed pointer inoperative. Although we were very cold and damp, the flight went reasonably well for thirty minutes. But then, in maintaining a constant altitude we perceived a gradual reduction in speed. Was the engine losing power? It was difficult to diagnose the problem since the manifold pressure and speed dials were not functioning. The RPM was normal. Foolishly, we were anticipating major troubles, such as piston failure, contaminated fuel or a magneto malfunction,but in doing so we were overlooking the simplest explanation.

The carburetor had been accumulating ice in the cool, humid atmosphere. It was stupid of me, as an experienced commercial pilot, to fail to recognize the obvious. A student pilot would have been more quickly aware of such likelihood in this textbook icing atmosphere. I would not have accepted such a gross error from one of my students when I was a flight instructor with the RCAF. Suddenly, it dawned on me, and hastily I selected full carburetor heat, which killed the engine completely! Heavily loaded, we descended rapidly. Coming to my senses, I played with the mixture control to backfire the stumbling motor. This procedure proved successful in sufficiently discharging the ice buildup from the venturi to allow the engine to resume its normal performance. Fortunately, the lower lakes, including Deer Lake, were still free of ice. Soon, and much relieved, we arrived safely in Pasadena with our new possession.

The Grenfell Mission Hospital in St. Anthony employed Tom Greene as their pilot. We hired him to fly the salvaged Cessna to an over-haul depot in Bar Harbour, Maine. The engine crankshaft was checked and the craft was repainted and embossed with new Canadian markings. After completing proper importation, CF-NXA was flown back to Newfoundland. It was our first fully bought and paid for aircraft, destined to serve many areas of the province. Eventually we repaid Hugh Atkinson for his timely investment.

The old damaged wing and propeller that we had left on Crash Pond were still of value. We were anxious to retrieve them so they could be repaired during the winter. In early December, another Cessna 180, still fitted with floats, was used for the recovery. Rick advised against using this craft since its engine was close to expiry and was showing clear signs of needing an overhaul. He had grounded the craft for commercial use until time permitted an engine replacement. However, our other aircraft were heavily booked for customer charters, so I elected to use the plane anyway.

"Surely the engine will hold out for one more flight," I appealed.

"Maybe, but it sure won't be used for any passenger service," Rick said, adding the warning, "Remember, the compression on that one cylinder is well below normal."

Eric Watson decided to come with me, since I would need help in loading the wing on the floats. The one hour flight was uneventful, although the engine temperatures were watched closely for any signs of malfunction. As we landed on the ice at Crash Pond, the weather was threatening in the higher ground. Carefully we strapped the wing under the belly on the float cross tubes. After takeoff it was necessary to turn south in order to avoid the high terrain, and follow the small river valley toward the lowlands. But the weather was forcing us to attempt the long way home around the coast.

The aircraft's performance was reduced considerably by the

drag caused by our external load. It was not surprising that more power was required even with our lower airspeed. We were somewhat apprehensive about being forced to fly at such a low altitude with the ungainly load and a troublesome engine. Reaching the south coast, we turned west and followed the seashore toward Port aux Basques. The low visibility made it necessary to continue at 500 feet above the ocean. Routing ourselves around the southwestern tip of Newfoundland, our trip home would take over two hours. Eventually we crossed over the lighthouse at Channel Head and turned north to Stephenville. The weather didn't get any worse, but our oil temperature did. Power demands to the engine were reduced, but that only served to decrease our forward progress.

As we passed St. Fintan's, I called the USAF base in Stephenvillewith a position report and they advised that the weather was still fairly reasonable in their area. As we approached the base visibility improved, but the oil pressure was getting too low for comfort. Our seaplane base at Stephenville was closed for winter, but the lake was still free of ice.

"Eric, I think I'll put her down here and let things cool off," I said. "We've got a pretty sick engine." Cheerfully, he agreed, and we landed without incident.

There was a good highway from Stephenville to Pasadena, so we unloaded the wing and called the base to send a vehicle. Being rid of the ungainly external load and the weight of Eric, I decided that I would continue with the empty aircraft. In carrying the big load, considerable strain had been placed on the already shaky engine. Shortly after takeoff, there was a noticeable loss of normal power. A quick glance at the instrument panel showed the oil pressure down to the red line and a very high oil temperature. The flight to Pasadena would only take about thirty minutes; the craft was very light, with just 120 pounds of fuel and nothing on board. I radioed the base and advised of my intentions. Knowing that there was the possibility of an engine failure, I eased the plane up to the cloud base at 2,500 feet and pulled back the power to cool the laboring Continental.About ten minutes later, my apprehension increased. The engine began coughing. There was a short series of surges and burps before it stopped completely.

Fortunately, I had chosen a route that would pass over a few frozen lakes in case of such an eventuality. To hone our skills, it was fairly routine for us to conduct engine-out practice landings when returning from our charters without passengers. Emergency landings were not difficult if there was a lake within gliding distance. Ahead and slightly to my left was Gallants Pond. I judged it to be well within soaring range. My approach was quite high, so I held the nose up and applied left rudder in a descending sideslip. As the trees disappeared behind me, I kicked the right pedal to level the wings and guided the floatplane to a relatively smooth landing on the ice.

The narrow lake was about 1.5 kilometers long and surrounded by a mixed forest of birch and fir trees. The country road that skirted the east shore had been cleared of snow. I shared my predicament with Rick, who was standing by on the base radio. He said he would send the van down to pick me up on its way to Stephenville. During the one hour wait I tethered the aircraft to the ice in case of high winds.

We were anxious to ferry the plane from the isolated lake before receiving a heavy snowfall that would inhibit a takeoff on floats. A few days later, Rick and I drove to the site with two new cylinder assemblies and tools. An engine tent and heat pots were put in place. Rick completed a compression test and found one cylinder with a zero reading. Despite the freezing wind, lowering the chill factor to minus 20C, he soon lifted off the offending assembly and replaced it with a new one.

"Gene," he told me, "I replaced the really bad cylinder, but there's another one that is pretty weak. You should be okay for the short flight home. If it weren't so damn cold on my fingers, I'd replace the other one. What do you think?" Eager to get going, I agreed that the machine was airworthy enough to suit me.

After warming the engine, and with temperatures normal, I pushed the throttle forward. The little bird throbbed with the prop blowing great white billows of loose snow behind the tail section.

As Rick retreated to the shore with his toolbox, I shook the pontoons loose from their frozen encampment and taxied the craft to the southern end of the lake, turned into the light wind and applied takeoff power. With the floats rumbling over the ice, the Cessna rapidly gained speed and lifted from the surface. I kept the nose down to gain some extra lift before easing the controls back to clear the trees at the far end of the lake. The extra speed proved to be a blessing. At about 150 feet over the trees, I retracted the takeoff flaps. A loud bang echoed from the firewall and the engine rpm quickly decayed to zero!

Pilots are taught to crash land their aircraft straight ahead should the engine fail on takeoff. "Never try to turn back to the runway." But there was nowhere to land ahead or to either side, nothing but a tall, dense forest. Automatically and without giving it much thought, I pulled the nose above the horizon and banked steeply to the right in a *stall turn. An attempt to restart would have been useless. I yanked out the mixture control, turned off the magnetos and switched off the fuel selector.

My speed dropped rapidly in the chandelle, but the machine came around sharply in the 180 degree turn. Below, the thick forest revolved slowly, as it were turning and the aircraft stationary. I was now heading back toward the lake. There was little space between the dead treetops and me. The aircraft mushed downward at absolute minimum speed and yet fast enough to avoid a complete stall. Every aircraft has a critical speed at which there is barely enough airflow to provide the required lift to keep the plane flying. Should the speed go below that point, the aircraft will fall uncontrollably from the sky.

The shore of the lake was straight ahead, but numerous dead birch limbs were projecting skyward in my path. It seemed inevitable that the glide would end in the tall trees somewhat short of the lake, as my altitude was fast dwindling. Just as the pontoons started to strike the branches, I lowered partial flap. This bit of extra lift ballooned me through the top branches until somehow I was over the shoreline. As it happens, mature birch trees in Newfoundland are often infested with a "birch borer" insect, which kills the higher extremities of the trees, making the limbs very brittle, especially in cold weather. The floats made a noise like a machine gun as the little plane cut a swath through the frail branches. Pops and bangs echoed up through the aluminum pontoons as the dead limbs cracked and snapped. It sounded as though the belly of the plane was being ripped apart. Finally, I cleared the trees, watched the rocky shore pass beneath, and bounced to a stop on the ice. I silently thanked God for the birch insect that had weakened those branches!

It seemed unbelievable that this one trip could cause so much grief after all my years of incident free flying. With rubbery legs, I walked around the craft to examine the damage. Amazingly, there wasn't a scratch on the fuselage and only slight dimples on the bottom of the floats. Rick had been on the road listening to the departure. After hearing the engine bark and quit, he heard the horrific battering as the floats ploughed through the trees.

"I was sure you had crashed in the woods," he shouted as he ran up and shook my hand excitedly. "Am I glad to see you in one piece! On our next move we'll change the entire engine, as the manufacturer recommends. That may just extend your life, as well as the aircraft's." This time, he got no argument from me.

Chapter 5 The Work Was Never Routine

Tilt Cove freight haul from Springdale to Long Pond

Our flying was never boring. Each charter brought unexpected surprises, chance encounters, and challenges to overcome.

The regional office for administering air carrier operations was located in Moncton, New Brunswick. Ernie Savard was the Regional Superintendent. Ernie was a practical man with a no-nonsense approach to his job: he ensured safety in the industry while making allowances for the tremendous difficulties encountered by the smaller carriers. He was always helpful as long as, in his estimation, the service was operating safely. Many of his inspectors were not as understanding, however, and enforced the regulations by the book.

The ministry inspectors would frequently and unexpectedly visit our base to examine maintenance and flight records. During the inspection, they would check the validity of the pilot's license, examine the aircraft, and get a general overview of the operation. Following their inspections, a discrepancy report would be received listing required corrections that were to be effected. They would invariably find some faults.

During the early winter, our skiplanes were very busy when the weather was good. There was usually a backlog of freight to be moved to the mine sites, and often we had requests to airlift items that were critical for mining production. The senior mining staff did considerable travelling to and from their head offices in Montreal and Toronto. Our passenger charters were carefully scheduled to coincide with Air Canada arrivals and departures at the Stephenville and Gander airports.

One day in the winter of 1962 we had loaded a large electrical motor on board my Cessna at the Pasadena air strip. It was a special priority item for the Baie Verte asbestos refinery. We had a considerable amount of flying booked for the day, so we were not thrilled to see a black sedan driving onto the field and parking at the ramp just as I readied the Cessna for departure. A rather short, portly man with a florid complexion emerged from the car.

I recognized William Folit immediately. He was now a regulations inspector with the Ministry of Transport (MOT) out of Moncton. But ten years earlier, he had been an RCAF pilot stationed at the same training base in Alberta where I was during my instructing day. We had never been good friends. In my opinion, William had always shirked his duties, coming up with excuses about why he shouldn't be flying. He preferred to do ground school instructing or oversee the Link Trainer Simulater, but he would always scrounge sufficient hours each quarter to receive his flight pay bonus. His assigned students were then passed off to others for extra flight training. We'd had words with each other on several occasions during those earlier years.

As he carefully looked over my craft, he signaled for me to shut down the engine. Already I was late for departure and his surly insistence sorely tested my growing impatience. I locked the throttle at minimum idle and hastily disembarked from the cockpit. Shaking his hand, I couldn't resist a snide remark: "I see you finally landed a cushy job with MOT. What can I do for you?"

Folit shot back: "I see you're as unpleasant as ever in your new endeavour." I had a sinking feeling, as I realized that I should have greeted him with a little more respect if I hoped to get cooperation from his department.

He did nothing to disguise his anger: "I told you to shut down that engine. I want to see your log book and license. That left ski axle has a non-compliant weld. Your aircraft needs a paint job and I'm sure there are plenty of other serious discrepancies!"

My blood pressure just kept rising: "Sir," I said. "For someone who couldn't even fly a link trainer, you seem to have become an instant expert in ski plane operations. I have an urgent flight to make and you are interfering with my work. If you want to see mechanical records, go and speak with Rick Richard. If you want to examine my log book, grab tightly to that tail ski and hang on. We'll both be in Baie Verte in about one hour!" Before he had an opportunity to respond, I was in the aircraft applying full power for takeoff.

As I flew away, I was annoyed with myself for having provoked this altercation when a little diplomacy might have saved me a lot of trouble. I knew that I had an unfortunate habit of expressing myself too quickly and that I held stupid officialdom in utter contempt. However, these agents are directed to conduct their inspections without interrupting normal flying activities unless there is an obvious and critical safety factor involved. I convinced myself that we had both been wrong in our dealings. At the next opportunity, I had a long, frank discussion with his superior, Ernie Savard, which included an apology. Ernie agreed that in the future, it would be in everyone's best interest to avoid sending Mr. Folit on departmental visits to our base.

Mechanics were needed but difficult to find. We knew that some industrious men from the coast were quite adept at mechanical work, so Rick trained a few of them as apprentices. After a few seasons, with careful supervision and instruction, they became very proficient. Owing to their lack of education, their written exam scores for the MOT qualification were not high enough. Ernie Savard was instrumental in arranging oral exams for these fine men and some went on to become licensed aircraft engineers. Ernie was one of the few top level civil servants who achieved the goals of the department by using common sense rather than dogmatic adherence to the bureaucratic bible. He was greatly respected by the bush carriers.

Before the supply ship service stopped in December, the grocery warehouse at Tilt Cove was fully stocked for the long winter. The cookhouse fed all the personnel who did not have family housing. Our crew ate their meals in the same busy mess hall. Normally the food was adequate. However, as the winter season progressed, we noticed that the taste of the morning eggs and bacon had taken a turn for the worse and it was difficult to obtain a palatable breakfast.

Securing the planes for overnight

On their long weekends off duty, the cookhouse staff would often charter our planes to fly them home for some time out. Their families were scattered around Notre Dame Bay in the various coastal villages. During one such flight to Change Islands, I mentioned the problem to George Billings, one of the senior chefs: "It's getting hard to get a tasty breakfast lately. What's going on with the cooking?"

He smiled and asked what I normally ordered in the morning. "I have tried fried eggs, boiled eggs and scrambled eggs, but since none of those were edible, I've switched to pancakes," I said.

George chuckled: "Our eggs are over three months old and will soon be unfit to serve. We try to sort them out by age and put the worst ones in the pancake batter!" He seemed to take some delight in describing how every morning the staff carefully shaved a layer of mold from the bacon before frying it. After this revelation, we settled for toast and jam at breakfast, although the butter seemed a little off as well. As the season progressed there were more complaints, so the demand for our fresh food airlift increased.

Warr's Wholesale Store in Springdale provided the supplies. To load the cargo, our ski planes would land on the salt ice harbour and taxi to their wharf behind the storage warehouse. Lanky Jake Decker handled the delivery with his old horse and sleigh. He was dedicated to his job and would obligingly assist with the loading of supplies into the aircraft. The pilot estimated the weight of the cartons as they were piled on board. Jake would chide us for not taking more boxes: "Them miner boys at the Cove are gonna starve unless you fellas loads up them planes with more stuff. Why, dem big gulls can carry more than that!"

But Jake did give us something to think about. We were getting backlogged with freight as the demand increased and the early spring storms often grounded us for two or three days. A heavy rain had melted most of the snow that covered the icy surface. When the temperature dropped our landing areas became smooth sheets of hard ice. We decided to remove the skis and operate on straight wheels. The reduced weight and drag of the ski assembly allowed much better performance and increased our payload. We then suggested to the mine manager that more goods could be moved if they would pay us by the weight instead of by the trip. This new system, although not entirely legal according to Air Transport Regulations, proved beneficial to both parties.

The Norseman aircraft was extremely rugged. It had a fifty foot wingspan and a radial engine developing 550hp. The undercarriage was very strong and its large cabin provided good cargo space. Using a low amount of fuel, the prescribed payload was about one ton. The load limits normally specified by the manufacturer for single engine aircraft are fairly conservative, providing a good margin of safety. Both Eric and I were very familiar with the aircraft, the terrain, the weather, and the minimum safe fuel requirements. There was no climb required after taking off from the sea ice in Springdale and we could fly the twenty minute flights to Tilt Cove over the frozen ocean at low altitude. The cold temperatures gave extra power and lift performance. Without the cumbersome skis and with the ideal conditions that now prevailed, we gradually pushed beyond the load limits.

On a good weather day, we were hauling over 3,000 pounds (1,364 kilograms) in the Norseman and doubling the normal load of the Cessna 180. There were no passengers carried during these overweight flights. Jake was happier now that his sleigh loads moved more quickly and the mine officials were pleased with the increase in supplies they were receiving. It was a win-win situation for everyone.

Later in the spring, the salt water ice gradually deteriorated with sporadic rain and the increased heat from the sun. After two days of being grounded by fog and warm rain, we called Warr's warehouse to obtain an ice report from Springdale.

Our horseman, Lanky Jake, answered the radio: "The sky looks some good to me and I can see hall the way hout the bay. The hice should be ok. Is you flyboys comin hover?"

"We should have both aircraft over there in an hour, so you better get your old sleigh loaded," I replied.

We flew the Norseman and the Cessna over in close formation and circled the area before landing. Eric's calm voice crackled in my headphones: "That ice has all turned black and looks like black, open holes off the point!"

"It doesn't look good," I acknowledged. "But surely old Jake would have told us if it was unsafe."

With more than a little trepidation, we landed and taxied fast to the loading wharf. The engines were shut down, but the horse and sleigh were nowhere to be seen. As we walked up to the warehouse to inquire about our freight, we met Jake sauntering down the dock with his hands in his pockets and the ear flaps on his cap drooping over his ears.

"What the hell is wrong with you today? Where are the loads?" Eric shouted at the forlorn-looking figure.

Jake pulled his floppy cap down over his eyes. "Well, I checked the hice after talking wit you hon the radio and decided that she were'nt safe to risk me 'orse and sleigh!" he said, a bit sheepishly.

We were astounded. "Why you old son of a bitch, you!" I shouted. "Do you think that decrepit old nag of yours is more valuable than these planes?"

We wasted no time getting off that rotten bay ice and moved the freight deliveries to Davies Pond, which was a large lake five miles north of the town. The thick ice on the fresh water lakes remained safe for another four weeks. We were learning to be somewhat less trusting of the local baymen for our weather and ice reports.

Joseph Alexander was a tall, Irish thrill-seeker; he was also a doctor employed by the Maritime Mine at Tilt Cove. He and his lovely wife, Maureen, were provided with a comfortable home and clinic at the mine site. He received many calls from the scattered villages in the region to provide medical services. When not busy with the mining fraternity, he would arrange to be flown to the outports to perform his medical magic. For us pilots, these outings were always interesting diversions.

On a cold, stormy morning, after cancelling our daily bookings due to adverse conditions, Dr. Joe came to visit me at the staff house.

"Gene, I've a request to go over to Round Harbour. There's a very sick lady who needs my care. Would you be able to fly me over?" he asked.

That tiny community was only 10 kilometers away by plane. There were high rocky hills between Tilt Cove and the other side of the peninsula. I knew the fishing village was situated on a small bay at the base of those hills. Most likely, the ice was sufficient for landing in the small harbour, but that coast was completely exposed to the open Atlantic.

"Well, Joe," I said. "It's doubtful if we've got enough ceiling and visibility to even fly that short distance. Look out the window.

You can't even see across Windsor Pond. If we did get there, I'm not sure there'd be room to land in that tiny cove. I've never landed there and with that rough terrain, I don't imagine there is any other suitable place to put down."

Joe placed a call on my phone. When he hung up, he announced with a confident grin: "I talked with old Mr. Connors and he says there's a level field behind the village where the EPA planes land their mail. He said he'd pay for the flight even if you have to abort."

"I suppose it won't hurt to have a look," I said, not entirely convinced. Time after time I had been led astray by trusting local advice.

Eddie Oake met us with the tracked Bombardier and delivered us up the hill to our aircraft. The weather was really unfit for flying, but with light fuel and just one passenger as load I knew the Cessna would handle very well at reduced speed. We managed to weave around the steeper hills in the blinding snow at very low altitude. With a partial flap setting, the nose was tipped down to provide better visibility and the extra lift gave improved response on the controls. Moderate wind sheer bounced the light craft in the turbulence as we skimmed down the steep cliffs to examine the harbour. When I glanced over at the always enthusiastic doctor, I could see he was enjoying the wild ride.

"We should do this more often," he said. "It sure beats tending pregnant women in the clinic!"

The small fishing village was nestled around the shore of an oval indentation in the rock face that was exposed to the open north Atlantic. Clusters of boxy houses huddled under the cliff. The homes were basic square structures constructed of locally hewn lapstrack planks, some with the bark still attached. The black tarpaper roofs showed their ragged beating from the constant sea breeze. Curls of gray wood smoke swirled from the makeshift chimneys and steel stove pipes. Each of these humble homes had small outhouses in back. The shore was lined with upturned dories, fish flakes, log wharves and storage shacks. These self sufficient coastal folk are very proficient at being their own carpenters.

The strong northeast wind was whipping the North Atlantic into a rage. I shook my head as I looked down and saw the surging sea battering the unyielding ice edge at the mouth of the inlet. The huge white rollers threw columns of spray up the cliff on both sides of the harbour. The ice on the cove was a mass of jagged pans that had frozen together to form tortured sculptures.

"There is no way we can land there," I muttered. "But I'll have a look at the field behind the town."

There was one small clearing but it was too short for a safe landing. Not only that, but on the next pass I discovered a telephone line that stretched across the center of the field!

As I swung the Cessna back toward Tilt Cove, I told Joe, "The next time we go flying, let's make sure there's a place to land. Otherwise, you'd better wear a parachute."

"Hey, that's a great idea," Joe laughed. "Then they could call me the para-doc." Based on what I knew of this free-spirited man, I have no doubt he could have been persuaded to try it.

Later that night, Dr. Joe arranged a horse and cutter to transport him over the trail to visit the patient. After much coaxing, he convinced me to accompany him on the trip. Warm clothing and some medicinal brandy made the ride less uncomfortable. Upon reaching the settlement, the local family laid on their famous hospitality and friendship. I sat in a tidy kitchen by the old wood stove, enjoying their homemade bread, partridge berry jam and strong tea. Many neighbors had gathered around the table to greet the strangers and inquire about our trip through the storm. While Joe was conducting his medical examination in another room, I asked an elderly man about their mail service.

"Well, me son, t'is not that great," he said. " Dem EPA planes pitches over at La Scie and we ave to fetch it fifteen miles wit de dogs. One time, years ago, there was one of dem Eastern Beavers tried to put down in de mesh hout back, during a starmy March Brush (easterly snow storm). The plane fetched up hin de trees cuzz she couldn't stop. Parts a she is still hout dare hin de woods! And that was afore the Newfie Tel put de cable cross she!"

That night the patient received the treatment she needed. Mr.

Connors paid for the aircraft flight and Joe and I headed back across those daunting hills for Tilt Cove without further incident.

The legendary doctor and I made many flights together. The nearest hospital or medical clinic, at that time, was at Gander or Springdale. Consequently, Doctor Joe was frequently called to visit the multitude of coastal villages between Burlington and Jackson's Arm. There were very few connecting roads in this vast area and during the long winter sea transport was not available. Joe and I made bi-weekly trips by skiplane to hold clinics in Nipper's Harbour, Burlington, Mings Bight, and Woodstock. During these aerial sorties, Dr. Joe would often challenge me. He would point to a small pond and bet me ten dollars that I lacked the skill to safely land on such a short strip."A good pilot wouldn't have any trouble," he taunted. And to his delight I would occasionally accept the wager.

The underground miners, especially the long-hole drillers working 1,900 feet under the ocean, were a rough and ready lot. They worked twelve hour shifts for seven days to gain three free days before their next work period. During their days off, many of them played highstakes poker until their healthy bonus cheques were entirely depleted. Many were hardened drinkers. After being expelled from the Copper Cove Club, a few would try to slake an unquenchable thirst with various concoctions. It reached a point when the local shop had to stop selling aftershave lotion, antifreeze and shoe polish. Needless to say, emergency flights to the Springdale hospital to have someone's stomach pumped out were not uncommon.

Seriously ill patients were flown to the larger hospital in Gander. On one occasion in early summer, Dr. Joe was escorting a pregnant lady in my Norseman floatplane enroute to Gander. She was already in labour and there were complications. During reasonable weather conditions, we would take a direct course from Tilt Cove, across Notre Dame Bay to the Lewisporte area and then on to Gander. This meant flying over the ocean for about 85 kilometers before reaching land, but it did shorten the alternative coastal route considerably.

As we were nearing shore, west of Fortune Harbour, Joe came rushing to the cockpit: "You've got to land this thing at once. There's a baby on the way and I need some help quick!"

I swung the old Norseman toward the nearest bay. Luckily, the sea was calm and there was a sandy shore on which to ground the floats. The assignment that Joe gave me as his assistant was not a pretty task, but with his competent hands, and despite my grimacing, we managed to deliver a little baby girl on the floor of the cabin and there was an extra passenger for the last leg of the flight to Gander. A week later, I picked up the lady and her tiny daughter to return them from Gander to their home at the mine. Mrs. Quenell thanked me for having assisted in the birthing, and told me that as a personal tribute to me, she had named the little girl "Jean."

During the winter of 1962 we made numerous passenger flights to Twillingate, on the east side of Notre Dame Bay. The harbour ice was very rough, so we used a small inland lake for our landing. The following spring, after the skis had been removed, I made my first floatplane charter to Twillingate. I had three hefty men and considerable baggage to deplane on arrival. The passengers were returning home so they were very familiar with the region. I asked them if they would prefer me to land in the harbour or on the pond by the town site. They agreed the pond would be more convenient and close to their homes. On circling the pond to look for rocks or obstructions, I noticed that the water was a murky sand colour.

"That little pond looks awful shallow," I remarked. "Are you sure it's used by floatplanes?"

The husky passenger sitting in the front seat beside me seemed confident enough: "Oh yes skipper, the planes uses he all year round."

With that assurance, I lined up into the wind and gently went about setting the craft down on the water. As the speed decreased, the floats came down from their step and settled deeper in the pond. Suddenly, the plane lurched forward and stopped! We had grounded on a sandbar in about three feet of water, a good 300 feet from shore. It was impossible to move or refloat the plane. I jumped in the water and assisted the passengers by wading to shore with their luggage. With the craft lightened by seven hundred pounds, I was able to push the machine into somewhat deeper water for flotation. Cautiously I applied power and with great relief the Cessna jumped into the air without further contact with the sandy lakebed.

Later, Bill Eaton, an experienced EPA pilot, laughed when I told him about the incident. "There can't be more than three feet of water in that entire pond," he said. "You're probably the first pilot to ever land there with floats."

"Yes," I said, shaking my head in dismay. "And I expect that will be my last time as well." I never seemed to learn about trusting local advice!

The Christmas season brought an increased demand for passenger charters from the various mines. Unfortunately, at that time of year we were between open water and solid ice in most areas. The salt water ice was usually not safe for ski landings until early January and float operations were restricted by the thin ice coverings. Usually, the Norseman was the last plane to be changed over to skis.

In 1962, there were a number of people in Baie Verte and Tilt Cove who wanted to reach Gander for their Christmas break. There was still open water in the Baie Verte harbour, so I made two trips to Gander on a cold December day. It was not fun flying since the minus 10C temperature was rapidly forming slob ice, and the spray on takeoff quickly covered the aircraft with ice. Leaving Gander Lake in mid-afternoon, I started to head back to base when I received a desperate call for another load out of Baie Verte. I was disinclined because of the worsening ice conditions but it was Christmas!

With seven passengers and piles of luggage, I had a hefty load on departing Baie Verte. As I struggled to climb over the hills, one of the passengers came up and said, "I guess you know that we have to stop in La Scie to pick up my husband." When I told her that we already had a full load, she became a bit hysterical. To quell the discussion, I turned east toward Cape St. John and soon landed at La Scie. The wind was blowing in through the narrow harbour. Small clumps of ice dotted the water and the inner section was frozen. After boarding another passenger and rearranging the baggage for an extra seat in the aisle, I sized up the situation for departure.

There was only a couple of thousand feet of calm water to start the takeoff. Beyond the fish plant the harbour widened to the ocean. The onshore breeze created a gradual increase in wave height as we passed the shelter of the inlet. Although extremely rugged, the Norseman had a low-lift wing and was underpowered. With my excess load and ice covering, it was difficult to gain flying speed as we roared out into the ocean swells.

After years of piloting, your hands and feet are literally part of the aircraft. They automatically respond to the feel of the air pressures against the flight controls which are transmitted through the cables, pulleys, and the control column and rudder pedals. After a long run, the aircraft felt ready to fly but then the floats would contact the crest of the next wave and reduce the speed. The further we went, the bigger the swells became! The plane bounced and quivered with every wave contact. We continued to kiss the tops for a very long distance before finally being fully in the air. At least over the open ocean there were no obstacles to obstruct our sluggish climb. An hour later I landed on Gander Lake and disembarked my happy passengers on the icy shore. The usual bush plane landing lake near the airport was frozen.

Boarding their taxis, they waved and shouted: "Gene, have a great Christmas and don't forget to pick us up after New Year's!" Pleasing one's passengers is not always the best procedure in bush flying.

In serving remote communities, we soon found ourselves performing personal favours for many of the residents. Every day we would order car parts, prescriptions, whiskey and numerous other items not available at the mining towns. Our dispatcher in Pasadena would arrange these purchases and have them ready for delivery on the next flight to the mine. This extra service boded well for public relations and did much to enhance our reputation.

Ernie Creighton was the personnel manager and flight organizer for the big copper mine at Tilt Cove. Although he was hardheaded and more blunt than he needed to be, we had to be very cooperative with him to gain the company charter work. Ernie had a passion for Siamese cats. When I would visit his home, the arrogant cats would strut on the chesterfield, snapping their tails at me with their ears folded back. Apparently we shared a mutual detestation.

Usually, on Friday evenings, I would find a reason to fly to Pasadena with some paying cargo. This allowed me some time for social activity away from the rougher frontier lifestyle at the mine. One Friday, Mr. Creighton asked for a favour.

"My big male cat has to be castrated, so I was wondering if you would mind taking him to a veterinarian in Corner Brook?"

"Sure, Ernie," I replied. "As long as you have him caged in a strong enclosure."

The cantankerous cat was sealed up in an old cardboard suitcase and placed in the rear of the aircraft cabin. The floatplane flight to Pasadena was a bit over an hour from Tilt Cove. It was a beautiful evening and as I approached the eastern end of Deer Lake, I was in a happy frame of mind, thinking of the pleasant evening ahead in Corner Brook. Suddenly, a loud screeching noise sounded from the rear cargo compartment. The large tomcat, having clawed his way through the cardboard container, leaped over my shoulder and landed on the windscreen over the instrument panel. With his mouth open and his fangs showing, he hissed and howled ferociously, hair on end, and appeared about to leap and rake my face with his widespread claws. The big green eyes twitched threateningly and his tail was rigid. I had never had a fondness for cats but this one was the "the cat from hell." He was definitely intent on doing serious damage to my features. My reaction was immediate. I slid the cockpit window to an open position with my left hand while with my right I made a lightning stroke, grabbing him by the scruff of the neck while he tried his best to claw me. In one motion, I slung him out the window.

I took a huge breath and as the blood gradually flowed back to my pounding heart at something approaching normal rate, I thought, "What will Ernie Creighton say? But what else could I do! What will I tell him?"

Then my thoughts shifted to that cat floating through the air, spreadeagled like a flying squirrel, careening at maximum speed toward the lake surface 3,000 feet below. A feeble smile grew into a grin as I pictured some old Newfoundland trout fisherman casting from the shore below. What a surprise he would have when the spiraling, free-falling cat slammed into the water by his dry fly with a giant SPLOT!

I phoned Mr. Creighton with the bad news as soon as I landed. I told him the cat had apparently freed himself from the old box as I carried him up the seaplane dock and our entire staff was now out searching the shoreline. Alas, the cat was never found. This is the first time I've ever had the courage to tell Ernie the true story of his cat.

Servicing an exploration camp

Chapter 6 The Wrinkles of Bush Flying

Changing from floats to skis (Ed Enns)

In the early summer of 1962 our company was again dangerously close to making a financial crash landing. Although we were keeping our aircraft very busy, the constant demands for capital investment were greater than our profits would allow. We needed more staff for administration and maintenance. The Ministry of Transport had issued a stern warning about the lack of adequate hangar facilities, and more shop equipment was required. We were still paying exorbitant lease rates, there was no working capital, and the banks had refused further overdrafts. As a last resort, I mentioned the seriousness of our problems to mine manager Bob Baker during one of our salmon fishing forays.

"Bob, I think we're going to close up shop. We just can't get any financing. Perhaps the mine should purchase a Beaver aircraft like Bowater Paper and Lundrigan Construction, and then hire me to fly it for you."

"We'd rather not get into that. Would cash input of $20,000 get you through? The mine has a huge exploration program scheduled over the next twelve months and I could provide your company with an advance payment for the air services that we'll require," he said, once again offering to save our necks.

I was totally surprised and somewhat speechless as I accepted the offer. This gentleman never ceased to amaze me with his almost reckless show of confidence in us. But then, all of the high level officials of Johns Manville organization, Ross Sampson, Bob Hutchenson, Karl Lindell, Tom Stephens and Josh Hulce, treated us with the same generous trust and respect that Bob showed. The vice president of mining, Karl Lindell, told me he wanted all his contractors to make comfortable profits.

"The lack of profit often leads to scams and lost loyalty," he said. "And we don't want that! We benefit by having financially stable contractors."

Compared to other large corporations, they were exceptional in their clear-cut, honest and fair dealings.

Locals from the little town of Baie Verte were hired and trained as the big mine was developed. The Baie Verte Peninsula was comprised of many tiny fishing and lumbering communities. The new employees were not accustomed to having a regular job, but were keen and eager to learn a new trade. Some mornings, I would have breakfast at the staff mess hall. On one such morning I sat at a table with Dave Straw, the exploration manager, and his office manager Piercy Budgell.

Dave seemed very alarmed: "Where are all the workmen this morning? There's hardly anyone here. Is there some kind of wildcat strike going on? There should be sixty men here. What in hell is going on, Piercy?"

Piercy responded in a casual tone: "Why it's nothing unusual, sir. The mackerel struck in the bay last night. Everyone goes fishin' when the mackerels come in. You won't be seein' many workers here for the next couple days!" The Baie Verte mining officials still had quite a bit to learn about the ways of the local baymen.

Nearly every summer there are outbreaks of forest fires in Newfoundland or Labrador. In recent years, the government has acquired its own fleet of modern water bombers which are kept on standby at strategic airports to provide the lead role in controlling the fires. Other aircraft and helicopters are often called in to transport ground personnel and equipment. In the early 1960s, the old Canso bombers were in short supply and helicopter service was very scarce and inadequate.

In the summer of 1962, a large fire erupted east of Gander and swept toward the coastal villages. Ground crews weren't able to contain the outbreak owing to the dry forest conditions and strong westerly winds. Eventually, some of the fishing communities were seriously threatened and were cut off from road access. In response, the provincial government hired a number of bush planes from EPA to assist with the emergency.

Wesleyville forest fire

We were contacted by the Newfoundland Emergency Measures Department and asked to immediately dispatch a floatplane to Wesleyville. The town's people were being evacuated by aircraft and taken for safety to the Island of Fogo. Although the weather was generally clear, when I passed to the east of Gander, the entire region was engulfed in dense smoke and the burning odors filled the cockpit. In order to maintain visual contact with the ground, it was necessary to reduce speed and fly along at treetop level. As I approached the coast visibility got even worse. Steering a compass course, I saw the small village of Wesleyville finally come into view beneath the fuselage. I took a tight turn, swung over the hazy ocean, and landed in the harbour among the fishing boats. I docked at the main wharf and secured the aircraft. Swarms of excited people were milling about on the dock. There would have been total confusion except for the orders being doled out by a tall, stately nurse. She was systematically sorting out the elderly and infirm members of the group. She then assigned them to a priority list for departure.

With great difficulty, we assisted the struggling passengers down the high wharf to the pontoons and helped them with oarding. The older ladies were very nervous and extremely unhappy about being forced to fly in these "water contraptions." Some had never been in an aircraft before. As I taxied through the harbour prior to takeoff, a large woman sitting in the co-pilot's seat next to me pleaded with me to take her back to the dock.

"For the love of God, get me out of this thing!" she bellowed. "I'd rather burn in the fires of hell than be put through this hordeal!" I tried to calm the passengers by telling them the conditions for the flight were ideal and we would only be fifteen minutes enroute to Fogo Island.

"Try to relax and enjoy the scenery," I pleaded. "You're leaving all the danger behind you."

The island of Fogo was about 70 kilometers northeast and the route was entirely over the ocean. Fortunately, my passengers grew silent, speechless with fright. However, they didn't know how bad the conditions really were or they would have been even more terrified. Visibility over the water was about 1/8 of a mile with thick smoke and haze. In order to retain visual contact, it was necessary to skim along a few feet over the waves. We passed by the town of Musgrave Harbour without even seeing it. Maintaining a careful compass course, I persevered until the bleak shores of Fogo finally emerged into view. As the dark cliffs loomed through the fog, I had to decide whether the Stag Harbour entrance was to the left or the right. Knowing that the coastline was steeper on the eastern side, and that the westerly wind would drift us eastward, I banked to the west and followed the shoreline until, with some relief, I recognized the harbour indentation. The light breeze made it possible to land straight ahead without even circling the higher ground over the townsite.

The nursing staff of the Fogo Hospital was on the wharf to receive their new allotment. As I was disembarking my passengers, my near hysterical lady co-pilot remarked: "Well, I can't believe it. The only problem with that flight was it was much too short. It sure beats bouncing around in an open dory!"

I made three more trips that afternoon and didn't see any other aircraft, either in the air or on the water. On the last pickup, I was informed that the evacuation was complete. Enroute to Gander for fuel, I wondered how so many people had been handled in such a short time. The seaplane base was a beehive of activity with seven EPA bush planes awaiting dock space for refueling. Only then did I learn that there had been twelve aircraft involved in the airlift flying the same route with minimal visibility! We'll never know how that operation succeeded without a mid-air collision or other serious incident. I made a mental note to file away. On the next exercise like this I would make sure that proper radio coordination was provided to monitor safe separation.

At our Long Pond base in Tilt Cove, we refueled the aircraft with a hand pump from 45 gallon drums. During the long storage periods it was common for condensation to infiltrate the steel containers and therefore we filtered the gas through a felt-lined funnel as we topped up the tanks for the next trip. Charters to and from the two mines and Gander were frequent so as to connect passengers with Air Canada. On one such occasion I was rushing to refuel at Tilt Cove for the one hour flight to pick up the Baie Verte mine manager. The felt fuel strainer could not be found. Reluctantly I pumped fuel directly into the Cessna wing tanks and departed from the northern coast of Notre Dame Bay.

Rather than fly all the way around the western shore, in good weather we would fly a direct course to Gander. Although much shorter, this direct route took us over considerable open ocean before reaching land near Lewisporte. Most days the sea surface was in turmoil, which precluded a safe water landing if ever it was required.

I was admiring the bright summer morning while cruising nonchalantly at 3,000 feet when the trouble began. The engine gave a few intermittent sputters, and then resumed its normal harmonics. Thirty kilometers from land was a bad place for an engine failure! The coughing became more persistent and I began to lose altitude. I knew immediately that contaminated fuel was the culprit. Continental engines don't like to burn water. An ocean landing was imminent.

The lightly loaded Cessna handled well in the glide as I swung around to face the steady, easterly draft of wind. The surface wasn't as good from 100 feet as it had seemed from 2,000, and the long swells were big, warning of the relentless might of the ocean. This was it. It wasn't ideal, but I believed she could take it since there were no rough chops between the round rollers and the tops were not breaking. I lined up parallel to the crests as the large swells rolled slowly under me, rising, sinking away, and reaching up again to touch us. I leveled her off over the tops and held her there, waiting. The ocean grabbed the keels, sizzling against the metal float skins, and quickly arrested my forward motion.

The landing had been too easy. It left me with a gut-wrenching feel of insecurity for me and my little plane. The surface calm was deceptive as the aircraft lurched steeply and slid down the swell into the deepening trough. Climbing from the cockpit with wire cutters and vice grips, I clung precariously to the wing strut in order to reach the drain valve under the wing tank. Clutching a wing support in the heaving waters of the open Atlantic is very frightening. Each time the craft careened down the slope I thought it would overturn. As each wave swelled up, the little craft climbed its face precariously with an unstable tilt to one side. Then there was a slow motion roll the other way as we pitched and slithered sideways down the crest into the next trough.

Desperately hanging on with one arm, I cut the safety wire and removed the drain plug. A volume of liquid spewed out of the drain, spraying me with a mixture of 80/87 octane and rusty water. After draining about twenty liters I replaced the bung, hoping that most of the water had been in the bottom of the fuel tank. I then clambered under the cowling to drain the carburetor. With my face only a few inches above the sea, the sound of the rushing water was terrifying. As well, the slow, lurching movement was somewhat nauseating, though we were still upright and afloat. I was certain that a capsize was inevitable as each breaker swept underneath the aircraft, tipping the wings to a dreadful angle. Strapping myself back in the seat, I held my breath, switched to the left tank and silently prayed that the engine would quickly come to life. The little jewel barked twice and then gloriously spun the prop in vibrant rhythm.

I lost no time in proceeding with a bouncy takeoff along the crest. Settling down in a smooth climb, I tried to fathom whether my drenched cap was caused by ejected fuel, salt spray or body sweat, no doubt the latter! How stupid had I been, deciding to cross the open ocean with the possibility of dirty fuel? Such recklessness is usually fatal! One becomes extremely humbled by these blunders and lives to avoid repeating them.

On reaching Gander, I carefully drained the starboard tank and refilled it with clean fuel. I certainly didn't want a reoccurrence, especially with Bob Baker on board. On our flight north to Baie Verte, Bob displayed his usual sarcasm: "What in hell have you been doing? You were half an hour late and you stink of gas!"

I countered by explaining that I'd some maintenance work to do on the aircraft that morning and had spilled a bit of fuel: "Sorry, but there was no time to change clothes. Besides, you would enjoy life more if you would slow down a bit and get your ass out of that knot. Even Nancy keeps telling you to stop and smell the roses."

Sometime later, I related this story to my elderly parents. Mother, being quite religious, anxiously remarked that no doubt I had been carrying the St. Christopher medal that she had given me when I left for Newfoundland: "That's what saved you from disaster... you did have it with you?"

"Well, the medal was in the aircraft, but when the engine stopped St. Christopher jumped out the window!" I replied.

Bob Hutcheson replaced Bob Baker as manager of the Baie Verte Mine and moved his family from Asbestos, Quebec to Newfoundland. In 1963, the mine had many dealings with government officials regarding exploration rights, mining claims, production export, and taxation matters.

Bob called me in Pasadena on December 26: "Gene, I've got an urgent meeting with the premier in St. John's the day after tomorrow. I would like you to fly me in there. We could stay overnight and return on the thirtieth. I want to be home for New Year's Eve as I'm sure you do as well."

I flew a ski-equipped Cessna 180 to Baie Verte and picked Bob up on the frozen lake near the mine site. The onward trip to St. Johns took two hours, and we arrived in early afternoon. Bob had made reservations for us at a hotel near the airport. He said he should be finished his meeting by five o'clock, and would be free to leave early the next morning.

The weather report indicated some snow overnight, so I went back to the airport and arranged to put the aircraft in a hangar. That evening, during an enjoyable dinner at the Battery Hotel, we looked out over the city as a gentle snow was ringing the luminous lights with a halo of holiday splendour. Before we returned to our rooms, the taxi driver seemed anxious about a pending storm: "There's a nor'easter comin in, boys. She's gonna be a duckish day tomorrow. If it were me, I'd be stayin where I was at."

He had that right! Over the next two days, two feet of snow fell. The wind swirled through the streets forming huge white drifts. The mayor declared an emergency to keep all traffic off the streets until the snow could be cleared. Most of the stores were closed, since neither their employees nor their customers could travel. We were stormbound in the hotel for three nights.

On the morning of December 31, we managed to get a taxi to the airport, although only a few roads were passable and the airport was closed to all traffic. We eventually found an attendant to help open the hangar doors but we had to shovel a 4-foot bank of snow to get the machine outside. I phoned the chief traffic controller and explained that with skis I could takeoff on the ramp by the hangars without any snow clearing. He was very cooperative: "I can't officially give you a departure clearance but there is no other traffic and if you were to takeoff without asking permission there should be no harm done." I wished him and his staff a very happy New Year.

It was mid-afternoon when we reached Baie Verte. Bob thanked me when he deplaned: "It's starting to snow again. I hope you don't have further problems getting home. I'll call Nina and tell her that you're on the way." He gave me a waving salute as I took off for Pasadena. But my New Year's Eve celebration was not to be. Flying west, the snowfall became heavy. I slowed down and followed along the coast of White Bay. There was no place to land if the weather worsened, since the ocean was not yet frozen. At the end of the long bay, the forested terrain rose gradually to about 800 feet. I knew that if I could reach Sandy Lake, there would be flat landscape for the last 70 kilometers. Ten minutes after passing Hampden the visibility dropped to zero! Luckily there was a long, thin, frozen lake below. I made a half-blind, sweeping turn, chopped the power, and settled the skis on the blanket of snow.

Our dispatch office was closed for the day so it was impossible to relay any message of my non-scheduled stopover. It was still storming as darkness settled in. I had a few chocolate bars in my briefcase, so I snuggled into my down filled sleeping bag and nibbled on my New Year's Eve snack. The weather had cleared by morning, and I was therefore able to reach home in time for the New Year's Day meal.

By now, some readers may have erroneously concluded that we were a careless and irresponsible bunch of redneck pilots. During our aviation exploits, when alone in an aircraft, we often took calculated risks with somewhat faulty engines, overloading, and hazardous weather conditions. In such circumstances we would always try to leave a door open should something go wrong. The pilots were all skillful at making forced landings, judging glide distance, and skimming the trees in bad weather, and we were not troubled by spending a night in the bush. However, when passengers were on board, we did not intentionally threaten their safety in any way, and we tried to avoid stranding them in the bush.

The limits placed on the aircraft by the manufacturer have a wide margin of safety. With experience, pilots learn how and when those limits can be safely exceeded. For example, the venerable Douglas DC-3 was designed to carry about 28 people. But in 1975, during the evacuation of Saigon, 98 Vietnamese orphans were safely carried on one trip.

In early years, bush planes were symbols of dangerous adventure and the pilots were considered romantic daredevils with no fear of death. In reality, most bush pilots were just ordinary people with a yen for the outdoors and some spirit of freedom. The work we did was far from glamorous. Although the job had more risks than most, crashing or dying was never part of the pilot's thoughts. There were some mechanical malfunctions and errors in judgment, but most of the serious accidents were associated with adverse weather. From 1957 to 1977, sixteen commercial pilots were killed while flying for EPA, NLAT, and other operators in the province. There were very few passengers involved in the majority of those mishaps.

Chapter 7 J. Roe -The Burning Edge

Flying Officer Jim Roe (RCAF 1953)

As boys, Jim Roe and I were inseparable companions. During my last two years of high school in Kingston I lived at his home on Bagot Street, where his parents treated me as one of their own. We both dreamed of becoming pilots and joining the Canadian Air Force and we decided to sign up together as soon as we completed grade twelve at Regiopolis College. Shortly after celebrating our seventeenth birthdays, we passed our final exams, left for Ottawa, and signed up for aircrew training with the RCAF in 1952. We had acquired false birth certificates to qualify as officer candidates and we were accepted. Luckily, we were both sent to the Centralia Flight School for pilot instruction, and eventually acquired our wings at the same graduating ceremony.

We were inseparable during our military escapades. After graduation we were transferred to Portage La Prairie, Manitoba for advanced fighter pilot and gunnery training. It was there that Jim had an unfortunate run-in with a very senior officer during a poker game. He realized in the cold light of day that his career with the Air Force was in serious jeopardy. With regret, but determined to keep flying, Jim resigned from the military and soon found employment as a traffic controller and then as a bush pilot with Eastern Provincial Airways in Gander, Newfoundland. Though separated by thousands of miles we were still like brothers and stayed in touch constantly, often vacationing together on our annual leave.

After I left the military in 1959, it was Jim who convinced me to take a flying job in Newfoundland.He was flying a DeHavilland Otter for EPA out of their seaplane base in Pasadena the same year that I started flying for Ray Wellon. His seaplane base was only a couple of kilometers from our facilities on Deer Lake. We were able to socialize together again and he even checked me out in one of EPA's Otter float planes, which I had never flown. He would have been in a lot of trouble had his company found out that a pilot from the competition was piloting one of their airplanes.

In the late 1950s, EPA was awarded a contract by the Danish government to supply two Otters and two Canso aircraft for passenger service in Greenland. Their aircraft and crews were based in Sondrestrom and Godthaab. All aircraft were amphibious, allowing them to operate from the runways at the various airports and to land in the water near the communities along Greenland's rugged coast. Jim had been assigned to the Greenland operation and was due to return to Newfoundland in the fall of 1961. Unknown to EPA, Jim had plans to resign from EPA and join my new aviation business when he returned, but fate got in the way.

On August 29, Jim was flying an Otter CF-MEX along the coast of Greenland from Sondrestrom to Egedesminde at 5,000 feet. The fitting on the high-pressure fuel line had come loose and was spewing raw, ignited fuel at the firewall connection on the front left side of the cockpit. When the fire broke out, Jim had four

Danish passengers in the cabin and crewman Harris Robinson was in the cockpit. Jim radioed an emergency call: "Mayday. Mayday. Engine on fire. Flames in cockpit. Trying to land." He then cut the throttle,relayed his position,shut down the big radial engine, reduced the airspeed, and began a quick descent for a deadstick landing on the water.

The fire in the cockpit quickly got worse and Harris was badly burned before the flames and heat forced him to escape to the passenger cabin. With his clothing on fire, Jim slid the cockpit door open enough to squeeze his lower body out of the opening and stood on the float spreader bar ladder below the door. Half in and half out of the cockpit, his hands and arms seared by the fire now engulfing the cockpit, he somehow manipulated the flight controls and managed to touch the plane down. The aircraft bounced on the water, throwing Jim forward from his perch, and then slid toward the beach. When it came to a sudden stop on the sand, Jim was pinned underneath the left pontoon. The passengers jumped clear of the burning machine, but the heat was so intense that they couldn't get to Jim right away. When the left wing fell away, after the fuel tank exploded, Harris, showing great courage, was finally able to pry the weight up from the float and drag Jim from under the burning wreckage.

A civilian helicopter, piloted by Larry Kline, arrived shortly after and flew the party to the Sondrestrom Hospital. Although badly shaken, the four passengers were uninjured. Harris had substantial leg burns, but Jim was in a critical state with third degree burns on most of his body. He was transferred to Goose Bay and then to the special burn unit at a Toronto hospital. I flew to Toronto on September 5 to visit my injured friend. He was in a terrible mess but still able and even anxious to talk. The conversation was one I will never forget.

"It was pretty scary trying to land that damn thing," he said. "It was really strange watching the skin on my arms turn black and my watch strap melt off my wrist, but I just couldn't let go. The air pressure against the door held me against the cabin, but I don't recall any feeling in my arms."

He was bandaged from head to toe, but he didn't seem to be in much pain, being heavily sedated with painkillers. He was fully conscious and clearly needed to talk.

"I felt my hair burning after my cap flew off in the slipstream," he continued. "The door sort of shielded my lower body from the flames. I can remember hitting the water hard. It wasn't a pretty landin but it was a landing! I don't remember much after that until I woke up in the hospital. If it hadn't been for the passengers, I think I would have jumped and just let her go. I guess my only thought was to get her on the water in one piece as fast as I could."

I asked him if he was aware of the severity of his burns.

"Yes, they've been very frank about my condition," he said. "They're not sure if I'll make it. I really hope they let me die. I'll lose at least one eye and I don't want to live without legs or arms. It would take a miracle of plastic surgery to fix my face, although you might say it's an improvement." Despite the bandages hiding his face, I believe he had somehow managed a smile. "I'm not sure how I ended up under the float. I guess when she hit the beach I must've flown through the prop and then was trapped as the pontoons caught up to me on the shore."

The medical team entered the room.

"I sure hope none of the mechanics get blamed for this fire," Jim said just before I left. "That's the last thing I would want. It was just one of those things and nobody's to blame. Tell those docs that they should just let me die. Gene, me son, try to comfort the family."

That was the last time I saw my buddy alive. He died with no regrets two days later, on September 8, after twenty-six years on earth.

I stayed with his family in Kingston until after the burial.They received a posthumous award from Canada's Secretary of State. The certificate and medal recognized Jim's bravery in landing his burning aircraft and expressed Her Majesty's highest appreciation for saving the passengers. The Danish government also issued a commendation for his heroic action. The Town of Gander named a street "Roe Avenue" in recognition of Jim's valour and his devotion to duty in sacrificing his life to save his passengers.

Pilots, like ship captains, are entrusted with the responsibility of keeping their passengers and crew safe and alive. I'm sure all pilots wonder how they would react if and when they were called upon to respond quickly in a life threatening situation. No one really knows until it happens. In Jim's case, the question was asked of him and he gallantly provided a definitive response. The Roe family lost a loving member, EPA lost a great pilot, the country lost a hero. And I lost my best friend.

Chapter 8 Main River Lodge

Fishing lodge constructed on Main River
for the Johns Manville Corporation (1962)

Bob Baker, the dynamic manager of Advocate Mines, had a commanding personality that matched his impressive stature. He loved traveling by bush plane, whether for business, hunting or fly-fishing. During the construction of the mine, I lodged with Bob in the town of Baie Verte. His wife, Nancy, was still in Quebec, so the two of us batched it in the large company house during the summer of 1962.

With my floatplane based in the harbour, we would often do some exploratory fishing after regular working hours. Bob's main interest away from work was the pursuit of Atlantic salmon and this provided me with a welcome perk. We fished most of the remote rivers on the Northern Peninsula and in Southern Labrador. During the early1960s, the daily limit was ten salmon and we would normally fill our quota in the evening solitude, returning to Baie Verte as darkness fell.

"Gene, we're going to have this mine in operation next year

and there'll be many customers visiting the site," Bob told me during one evening fishing trip.

"I think we should have a company retreat where we can show these clients some great fishing in a comfortable atmosphere."

I agreed that many Newfoundland companies, Lundrigans, EPA, and Bowater Paper, had such getaways for business meetings.

"OK, then," Bob said. "I want you to go ahead and make arrangements for a lease and construct us a lodge. Have it completed by year's end and we'll pay the cost."

That was how Bob did things. A few weeks later, I asked him if he had prepared any details on location and other specifications.

"For God's sake, Manion," he growled. "I 'm busy constructing this damn mine. I haven't got time to become involved with that lodge project. You're more familiar with the good locations. You choose the best remote fishing site available, get a lease in our name and build something that will be adequate for six guests and staff. Do it the way you would do it if you were building it for yourself and your customers. Don't bother me with the details. You should have had the damn thing started by now!"

Bob's dedication to his work was inspiring and he expected those who worked for him to show a similar commitment and initiative. Those who didn't were soon excluded from his circle. But if you were on his team, he responded with total engagement and support. Occasionally some large contractor, lobbying for bids, would make the mistake of offering Bob a kickback. These individuals were immediately ushered from the premises and never again permitted to bid on any contract work for the mine. Fortunately, he accepted me as a dependable friend and placed great trust in my own work ethic.

I arranged a crown lease on the headwaters of the Main River, which recently had been a favourite fishing spot for famous outdoorsman and author Lee Wulff. The site was in a pristine valley on the Northern Peninsula, just over 100 kilometers by air from Baie Verte and a similar distance from our Pasadena base. nine kilometer stretch of pools and fast water offered excellent salmon and trout fishing. The lease site was accessible by floatplane, being situated on a large, deep lake near the hilly headwaters. A 2,500 squarefoot precut house was purchased.

I had earlier met a fabled character from the area named Frank Pye. He was a hardworking extremely competent man who was famous for pulling off the most difficult jobs, often in an unorthodox fashion. That year the big asbestos mine had required the relocation of their entry gatehouse, but the owners were unable to locate a crane to lift the building onto a flatbed truck. When Frank was told of the problem, he said without hesitation: "I'll have it on the truck tomorrow morning; you just park the flatbed alongside the gatehouse."

At 7:30 the next morning, when the shift was changing, Frank blocked the mine entrance. He told the large gang of workers that they couldn't enter the property unless they gave him a hand. He gathered them around the perimeter of the building that had been jacked from its foundation. On the count of three, the men lifted the building and placed it on the truck and it was moved to the new road entrance. The shift going off duty was then drafted into lifting the gatehouse from the truck and setting it on the new cement studs. The mine manager said that Frank's ingenious solution had saved them over $2,000 in crane rental fees. So although Frank had a notorious fondness for drink, we hired him as lead carpenter for the Main River project.

Lumber, cement, roofing and tons of building materials were stacked at our base office lot in Pasadena. The airlift got underway in late June. Some of the larger items were carried in the Norseman, but most of the flights were assigned to the smaller Cessna floatplane.

The five man crew worked long hours at the site and the structure gradually took shape. When we hired him, Frank freely admitted he had a serious thirst whenever booze was available. He accepted the job with the condition that he would not drink on the work site, provided we would fly him out to civilization for a few days of leave every few weeks. We both kept our promise. His freedom usually started on Friday and he was told to be back at the base on Monday morning for the return flight. It became routine that we would find Frank passed out on our dock, unable to walk but he was always on time! Three of us would carry him down to the plane and throw him in with the cargo. His faculties were conspicuously fuzzy for the remainder of that day, but he would always have work arranged for his crew.

Late one evening, Bob and I were flying back to Baie Verte after some fishing further north. Since our route passed near the construction site at Main River, Bob suggested we drop in on the camp and say hello to Frank.

He arrived as I secured the floats to the dock cleats. After exchanging a few pleasantries, Bob asked Frank: "I don't suppose you'd care for a sip of single malt Scotch?"

With a look of yearning in his eyes that left no doubt about his answer, Frank reached without further ceremony for the bottle through the open cockpit door. Bob always carried a large flask of whiskey on his fishing trips, supposedly for emergencies. Frank pulled the stopper, raised the bottle to us in a wordless but heartfelt salute, and without further ado, thrust the shaking bottle to his lips. Like any man dying of thirst, Frank chug-a-lugged with gusto. Bob had to tell him to come up for air and grabbed back the half empty flask.

"Oh, me damn nerves! Wasn't that a treat?" Frank gasped. "You fellows should visit the job more often!" Then he went contentedly back to work.

Later that summer, the crew needed four sheets of quarter inch steel sheeting for the construction of a water holding tank. The larger Norseman was busy elsewhere, so we secured the sheets beneath the fuselage on the pontoon spreader bars of a Cessna 180. The rectangular pieces measured four by eight feet and were carefully tied to the undercarriage using half-inch nylon line.

The departure and climb to 3,000 feet was routine except for some light turbulence over the White Hills. Suddenly, there was a loud bang and shudder as the little plane lurched upward to a steep angle. Immediately, I reduced power and shoved the control column forward with difficulty. The metal sheets were out of my field of vision below the aircraft, but I knew that the load had broken free and shifted upward, hitting the belly. Just as I was regaining some control, there was a terrible rolling motion and another series of sharp vibrations. Level flight was now easier to maintain, but the craft continued to yaw sideways, trying to roll to the left, and the elevators felt sloppy.

I radioed the base with a distress call giving my position, turned gingerly toward Pasadena and reduced the speed to 70 mph with partial flaps. The controls were slack and unresponsive. Obviously, the craft had serious damage, but it was impossible to determine where and how much. Gently, I descended toward Deer Lake and carefully landed near the eastern end of the 25 kilometer waterway. Rick and another mechanic, Eddy Oake, came up the lake to meet me with the motorboat and towed the craft eighteen kilometers back to base.

Reaching the dock, we examined the damage. It was very alarming. We couldn't understand how the plane had stayed in the air. The entire left elevator had been torn away and half of the horizontal stabilizer was missing. As it tore free of its bindings, the sharp edge of the sheet metal had sliced off the outboard section of the plane's tail section.

We wondered what someone on the ground would have thought had they seen these large galvanized panes flying through the trees, shearing off limbs in their descent.

Eric Watson made many trips to Main River Lodge with the bigger Norseman aircraft. It could carry a large amount of freight, but when heavily loaded it required a lengthy stretch of water to reach liftoff speed. Often, Eric would still be zooming along on the water as he passed the EPA seaplane base, nearly a kilometer down the lake. During the evening gatherings at the Lakeland bar, the EPA pilots would chide us about the poor performance of our old Norseman compared to their high-performance DeHavilland Otters.

"What in hell is wrong with that old plane of yours?" a pilot would say. "You were still screaming along on the water when you passed our base and nearly out of sight when you became airborne!

What kind of pig are you flying?"

"It's like this,' Eric told them one night. "All of us NAT pilots have thousands of hours logged in the air, but some of us are frustrated coastal boat captains. So we're trying to rack up some more water time! It's you novices who need the air experience."

We were trying desperately to complete the lodge construction before freeze-up. The lake at the site was 1,600 feet above sea level and would normally freeze over by mid-November, but that particular year there was an early cold snap. Frank advised us on the radio that the lake had completely frozen on October 28. We expected a warming trend would follow to permit a floatplane landing. Instead, the temperature plummeted each day. Food resupply to the site was impossible and the five man crew was getting very low on staples.

Each day they gave us an ice report. The men were getting very anxious to vacate the work site. We needed at least five inches of good blue ice for a safe skiplane landing and there were no helicopters available in western Newfoundland. By November 10, there were still only two or three inches of ice, but time was running out. An evacuation had to be attempted.

We decided to use a floatplane for the recovery. Everything seemed fine as my plane came to a stop by the dock after sliding for half a mile on the glassy surface. Then, suddenly, the thin ice gave way, letting the pontoons settle in the water. It was a bad situation, but not critical. Knowing it would be difficult to get the plane back up on the frozen surface without damaging the floats on the sharp ice edge, I decided to make three trips with lighter loads. After breaking ice for about 70 feet, the floats grudgingly climbed up on the thicker shelf and we settled in to a fairly normal takeoff.

Frank took the opportunity to complain that they had been getting pretty tired of eating only meat and fish. They had shot a small caribou and caught a few spawning salmon to keep them going. He didn't mention his thirst. That was understood.

The following summer, in 1963, the lodge was sufficiently finished to accept guests. Mr. Baker had visiting dignitaries from

Europe at the new mine in Baie Verte. Andre Emsen from Belgium, who controlled the asbestos-cement cartel in Europe, was inspecting the operation. He and his entourage would be the first guests at the new lodge.

"Gene, we'll fly these men to the lodge for a few days of fishing and I'd like you to pick up three dozen live lobsters for our dinner tomorrow evening," Bob informed me.

It was a routine request, as I had been flying to the Gander Bay area all spring to purchase lobsters directly from the fishermen. No one in Newfoundland had as yet developed an export market for these delectable crustaceans and the fishermen were pleased to be rid of them for twenty-five cents per pound. But during breakfast the next morning, after discovering that the Newfoundland lobster season had closed the previous week, I advised Bob that he had better choose an alternate menu item, but he wouldn't hear of it.

"I promised these men a feed of fresh lobsters, and by God that's what they'll have! Is the lobster season open anywhere else in the Maritimes?" he fumed.

"I'm sure it's still open in the Quebec Gulf over in the Magdalen Islands," I replied. "But it would be impossible to have them shipped over in time for tonight."

His brow furrowed: "Well, can't that damn machine of yours fly to the Maggies? I didn't tell you where to buy them, I just said to get them! André is going to purchase 80 percent of our production. I think we can afford to feed him some lobster."

By now, I should have known that when Bob said he wanted something, he wanted it done, no questions asked. This was one of the few times that he ever got upset at what he would have seen as my lack of initiative. From Baie Verte to Les Iles de la Madeleine, Quebec and back as about 1,000 kilometers, and over open Gulf waters for 500 of those kilometers. Fortunately, the weather was ideal and it would make for a nice change in my flying routine. I had the live lobsters back at the lodge by late afternoon with sufficient time to make the two flights from Baie Verte with his dignitaries. The food that evening was a big hit and the cost not much different than it would have been in downtown Paris. During the after dinner discourse, Mr. Emsen thanked Bob for the wonderful feed of fresh lobster. Bob told his guests that the lobsters only cost about thirty cents per pound.

"It's not me you should thank," he said. "Let's raise a toast to Gene, our resourceful pilot. Without his vast knowledge of procurement practices, we might well have been dining on bologna this evening."

Interesting arrays of guests were invited to the seclusion of Main River Lodge. During the 1960s, we arranged many travel connections for the passengers with Air Canada in Stephenville. The station manager, Hank Holland, went out of his way to accommodate us. On a few occasions, he delayed the departure of a Vanguard in order to await the arrival of our bush plane passengers. Our feeder services, and his accommodating ways, led to a close friendship. In turn, we occasionally invited Hank and his associate, Herb Seagrim, to the lodge for camaraderie and salmon fishing. The major salmon pools were named after our early guests.

At the time, Herb was the chairman of Air Canada, and he proved to be an affable outdoorsman with volumes of interesting tales to relate about flying. Our mutual friend, Colonel Edington, base commander of USAF Harmon Field in Stephenville, usually joined this group when he discovered their destination was Main River. While fishing, he and I had lengthy discussions, comparing various RCAF aircraft with USAF interceptors. After the closure of Harmon base in 1967, I missed the pleasant annual encounter with the colonel.

On another occasion, Karl Lindell had invited a few high profile guests from Europe to join him at the fishing lodge. The chairman of the board of Swissair, Mr. Baltensweiler, was among the group. After four days of wilderness activity, their scheduled bush plane departure was delayed by heavy fog in the high country. As their pilot, I was asked to make a radio call to rearrange his travel schedule. I gave a Montreal phone number to our dispatcher in Pasadena and asked him to make a request to the Swissair operation manager:"Tell him the chairman is weatherbound for a few hours at a remote camp and will not

Herb Seagrim, Colonel Edington leave Stephenville in Widgeon
Destination – fishing on the Main River.

make his Air Canada connection out of Stephenville. We will try
to put him on their next flight which will not arrive in Montreal
in time to board your next Swissair DC-8 flight to Geneva. The
chairman requests that you delay that departure for six hours, as
it's urgent that he gets to Geneva tomorrow. Perhaps a
mechanical delay can be arranged." I also asked the dispatcher
to call Hank Holland in Stephenville to arrange a seat for Mr.
Baltensweiler on the later Air Canada flight to Montreal.

In about ten minutes, we had a confirming call from Swissair:
"Yes Sir, please tell the chairman that everything has been
arranged. The DC-8 will hold for his arrival. Please let me know if
there is any change."

Mechanical delays are not always what they seem!

The virgin forest and muskeg along the Main Valley was
excellent moose habitat. Owing to the lack of road access, the
region wasn't frequented by hunters. On our flights from Baie
Verte to the lodge it was common to see any number of animals
foraging in the lush vegetation along the river valley.

It was late September 1963, and the moose season in
Newfoundland was open. Bob decided to try getting his moose by
hunting from the company fishing lodge. On our way to the site we
flew low up the Main to take in the brilliant fall colours. As we

passed the big bog at Paradise Pool, Bob watched a large bull moose disappear into the woods.

"Can you land here on the river?" Bob asked, his blood up. "Maybe we should have a quick look for that big fellow."

There was a deep stretch of river underneath where we frequently landed to fish. I landed in the current and beached the plane on a sandbar. Bob set out through the tangle of riparian alders that led to the open bog. After crossing a large clearing, we found a wellworn game trail that disappeared into the dense forest.

"This is where he went," Bob whispered. "I'll sneak ahead slowly with the rifle and maybe we'll come up on him."

I followed a few feet behind, careful not to step on any brittle branches. I really didn't have much confidence in such a stalk. The moose's keen nose and hearing would make him well aware of us long before we would have a clear shot at him in the thick undergrowth. The path angled back and forth up a shallow incline. On each side the vegetation was sufficiently dense to block our vision. We hoped the trail would lead to another clearing on top of the hill where we would have a reasonable chance of spotting the wily beast.

About twenty minutes into our pursuit, we suddenly froze. There was a loud clamour of snapping branches ahead of us. My heart stopped at my first sight of the bull. He appeared about 100 feet ahead of Bob, storming down the narrow trail toward us like a runaway locomotive. His head and huge rack of antlers were low to the ground and he was coming right at us at full gallop. Bob stood paralyzed in front of the massive animal. He had no time to sight the rifle or jump clear. Certain that Bob would be trampled and killed by the rampaging bull, I turned and jumped in desperation from the trail into the undergrowth. My left boot caught under an exposed root, but most of my body was off the trail. I stretched frantically to be clear of the behemoth's path. I heard a sharp metallic crack and then closed my eyes, expecting the inevitable excruciating pain when his hooves crushed my trapped leg. The ground vibrated with the thumping of 700 kilos of terrified beast. I felt a brush on my leg, but was surprised that there wasn't any accompanying pain. And then all went quiet.

Shaking all over, I sat up and looked around. Apparently the moose had stepped over my leg. There was not a sound coming from where I had last seen Bob. I could only assume the worst. I tried to struggle to my feet, but fear had sapped all the strength from my legs.

"Bob, are you out there?" I shouted, as my breathing grew less ragged. No answer. "Bob, can you hear me?" There still was no answer, but I heard a slight rustling in the brush on the other side of the path.

"I'm over here," Bob finally responded in a hoarse and barely audible croak. Gradually, I was able to pull myself upright and unsteadily wobbled up the trail.

"Bob, where are you?" I shouted. "Are you badly hurt?"

"I don't think so but I can't seem to get up," he replied, his voice still quivering.

Slowly, I worked my way towards him, pushing aside the brush. He was about 12 feet on the other side of the trail, lying on his back, but still holding his rifle skyward in a white-knuckled grip.

"I froze in front of his horns," he began slowly. He was still in shock, his face blank and his eyes locked in a distant stare. "I knew there was no time to get out of the way. I guess it was a reflex. I was bringing my rifle up to shoot when his antlers smashed into the end of the barrel. The next thing I knew I was flying through the air. I didn't even get the safety off."

"Christ, I thought you were dead. Are you sure you're okay?" I asked as both our breathing began to return to normal.

"I got some good bruises and sore ribs, but I sure feel lucky to be talking. I really don't think he was charging at us particularly. He probably heard us and was just getting to hell out of there. We just happened to be in his way. Swollen hormones often create strange action."

"You're probably right. But how did he miss goring you?"

"I don't know," he said. "All I can figure is I must have had a death grip on the rifle and when his horns struck the muzzle he lifted his head and threw me and the rifle into the brush."

As he tried to get up Bob was still shaking like a leaf as the narrowness of his escape sunk in. He sat back down: "Do you think you could make it to the plane and bring me back that flask of Scotch in my duffel bag? I really think I need a good nip."

"OK, but you relax, I may be gone a while," I replied. "Give me your gun. I'll keep an eye out for that son of a bitch on my way to the river."

It was a hot afternoon for September and I was saturated with sweat when I finally broke into the clearing near the river. Stripping off most of my clothes, I doused myself in the cool water of a small stream. Before resuming my trek across the bog, I scanned the clump of trees that were grouped in an island near the far riverbank. There was a large dark mass lurking within that clump of trees. I stood still and watched carefully.

Finally the dark object moved. There, less than half mile away, stood our quarry. It would be a difficult stalk, as there was absolutely no cover except marsh grass between me and the moose. I would have to crawl up most of the way on my hands and knees. Slowly, a few feet at a time, I closed the gap. Waiting for another moose would have been easier, but after the scare he gave us, I wanted revenge to bag this particular beast.

Occasionally, he seemed to sense danger and turned his head in my direction. I froze and waited. When he calmly resumed nibbling on willow branches, I cautiously moved forward again. His swaying antlers were massive. As I got within range, my nerves were near the breaking point. Finally, I was within 50 feet and I knew there was little hope of inching any closer. As I brought up the 30.06 to firing position, I was surprised to see that my hands were trembling violently from the excitement of the long ordeal, or maybe it was just the strain of crawling on my hands and knees.

I told myself to calm down. When taking a sitting position, my head and shoulders were now exposed to view. The animal spotted me and was ready to bolt. I quickly fired and the 180-grain bullet missed the mark. Automatically, I worked the action, slamming another cartridge into the chamber. I squeezed the trigger as the moose started to run through the alders. Luck was with me. The second round struck the bull in the neck, and he tumbled on the riverbank as though a rug had been pulled from under him.

He was dead when I reached him, and probably was before he hit the ground.

I delivered the bottle of fortitude back to Bob and, after a few healthy guzzles, we walked back to the fallen moose. Bob was sufficiently recovered to assist me with the task of paunching the animal. We left the carcass open for cooling, sawed off the 48 inch antlers, placed the large liver in a plastic bag and set off back to the aircraft.

"Let's fly on up to the lodge for the night," Bob suggested. "We can pick up the meat tomorrow. I think I've had enough hunting for one day."

That evening, we sat around the fireplace reliving the hunt. Bob suggested I keep the antlers as a souvenir. For more than forty years, those splendid horns have hung on the wall of my hunting camp. Every time I look at them I still feel a real sense of danger running down my spine as I recall the vision of that huge animal bearing down on us.

Bob brought the mine into production on time and on budget. But he said he thought the challenges were over at Baie Verte, and he moved on to manage the Heath Steel mining operation in Bathurst, New Brunswick. I was sorry to see him leave, but fortunately the Manville Corporation replaced him with another great mining engineer, Ross Sampson.

Karl Lindell & Bob Hutcheson at Main River (1962)

Chapter 9 Sealing History -A Primer

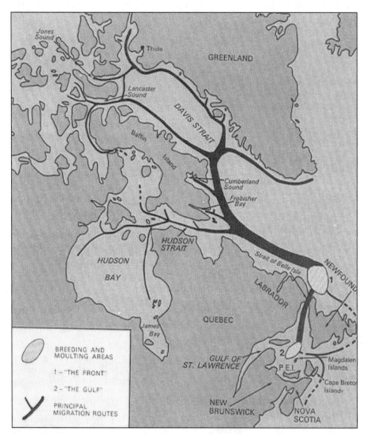

Harp seal spring hunting areas—"Front" and "Gulf"

The history of sealing is filled with tales of bravery, hardship and disaster. This hunt has long been a part of the economic and cultural heritage of Canada's east coast. Since 1960, the seal hunt has become increasingly controversial, owing to provocative measures taken by animal welfare groups in their fund raising programs.

Seal hunting off the shores of Newfoundland and Les Iles de-la Madeleine has been a tradition for hundreds, even thousands of years. The hunt began long before the arrival of the first European explorers. Jacques Cartier found Labrador Indians taking seals in the Strait of Belle Isle (between Newfoundland and Labrador) in 1534. Shore sealing probably began soon after the discovery of these lands by Europeans and continues to the present day. First, there was a fishery that captured migrating seals in nets. Later, schooners enabled the men to get to the whelping or breeding herds on the drift ice; it was the influx of these vessels that heralded the rise of sealing as a major spring industry. The harvest reached a peak in 1831, when 683,000 seals were taken, but catches varied over the following decades and were tallied at 180,000 in 1978.

In time, steam vessels replaced the schooners, but these too became obsolete with the arrival of steel ships strong enough to withstand the tremendous pressures of the pack ice. The herds were already heavily exploited by the early nineteenth century, but the newer ships provided improved comfort and safety for the sealers.

Following World War II, the consistently large harvest of harp seals resulted in a population decline from over three million in 1951 to about 1.25 million in 1960. Quotas were put in place in 1971 limiting the kill to 245,000. In 1972, the catch quota was reduced to 150,000. Since then the overall population has increased to about 5.5 million in 2007. Currently there is a dilemma: should the increasing seal numbers be kept in check by an organized cull to protect declining fish populations, or should nature be allowed to take its course?

The seal hunt became more widely based after 1949, when Newfoundland joined Canada. But although there were ships from Nova Scotia, St John's and even Norway and Russia, most of the sealers working on these vessels came from the rugged northeast coast of Newfoundland or the Magdalen Islands. The ships located the drifting masses of seals, and then sent the men out on the treacherous ice floes to hunt with bats or rifles, skin the animals and drag the pelts to their respective vessels. With the retreat of the melting ice, the swimming seals are also taken as they begin their return passage to higher latitudes.

Although seven different species of seals are found in Canada, the harp and the hood varieties are the main object of the spring hunt. The harp seal adult is about sixty-five inches in length and weighs approximately three hundred pounds. Each year, large herds migrate south from arctic waters to whelp their pups. In great numbers, they find suitable drift ice off the Labrador coast, usually east of Sandwich Bay. Being very gregarious, the females gather in huge concentrations, and give birth around March 10. This herd is called "The Front."

The young pups, or whitecoats, weighing about twelve pounds, are suckled on the ice by the cow for three or four weeks. Toward the end of this period, the females mate with the males scattered throughout the same area. The pups are born with white, silky fur that begins to shed after one week. In four weeks the molt is complete and the natal fur is replaced with dark, splotchy hair. These *Beaters now begin swimming for food and weigh sixty pounds. The front herd moves south with the wind and current, gradually dispersing south of the Grey Islands as the ice breaks apart, often drifting to Notre Dame Bay.

In the Gulf of St. Lawrence, northwest of the Magdalen Islands, another large gathering of whelping seals takes place around the same time. The Gulf herd is estimated to be about one-third the size of the Front herd. The young whitecoats drift eastward on the ice with the wind and current for three or four weeks. With the grinding and churning of the ice, the pans become smaller as the season progresses.

In the spring of 1960, there were about 450,000 seals in the front and 230,000 in the Gulf. In 1975, the combined population was estimated at 1,250,000, with pup production of about 350,000.

Immature seals feed primarily on plankton-fed crustaceans, while the adults eat both these and cod, capelin, herring and squid. Their annual consumption of capelin has been estimated at 500,000 metric tons.

Evolution has provided the seals with the unusual reproductive phenomenon of "delayed implantation." The development of the embryo will not start in the female until eleven weeks after mating. This allows the seals to mate when they are congregated on the ice floes, but delays birth until optimum ice and feeding conditions prevail the following spring.

Those with first-hand experience of the hunt consider the most humane method of killing seal pups to be clubbing with a hardwood bat. This either kills the animal outright or puts it in a state of deep, irreversible unconsciousness. Traditionally, the "gaff" was the preferred weapon and the most humane. Scientific studies indicate that the surviving mother is hormonally attached while weaning, but has no specific emotional attachment thereafter. The mothers show no sign of bereavement with the loss of their pups, unlike dogs and many other animals.

Historically, the seal hunt was extremely lucrative for the ship owners and the big merchants who outfitted the voyages and traded in seal oil and furs. The merchants managed to keep the lowly sealers in a state of perpetual servitude. They were often treated with disdain and endured horrible working conditions with barely palatable food, terrible living quarters and a cavalier indifference for the safety of the sealers – and all that with very little compensation.

Prior to WW2 the captains or shipowners paid the men only a slight percentage of their profits, which depended on the voyage's success. Often no wages were paid after room and board were deducted, and the books were not open for verification. Even in the 1960s, the sealers were subject to the whims of the shipowners and frequently spent three months on the hunt with little pay to take home. A bumper season could produce $300 to $400 per man under ideal conditions. Greedy merchants dispatched every craft they could find, seaworthy or not, and crammed them full of poor coastal men with promises of great financial rewards. In the mad drive for profit by reckless captains, many ships were lost to the treacherous sea. Hundreds of hunters met a violent death as they were hurled over the side or trapped on the surging pans and lost to the elements during the vicious March storms.

The sealers sometimes were even expected to pay the ship-owners three dollars for the privilege of being allowed to hazard their lives to win a fortune for the merchant. Typically, in the early years, they were fed hard-tack and switchel (a black, unsweetened tea). Twice each week they received "duff," often made from spoiled flour boiled with putrid water, and sometimes a bit of salt pork with raw seal meat. The swilers hunted from the ships from early March until late April or mid-May, living like galley slaves in the hope of finally receiving for their perilous labour a pittance to help in eking out a pitiful existence.

To comprehend the seal hunt is to understand an integral part of the maritime tradition that played a large part in forging the character and relentless instinct for survival of the people of Newfoundland, who faced incredible hardship.

The animal welfare groups have taken advantage of the cute, cuddly, young seal pups to publicize their propaganda campaign (especially in Europe). Erroneously, they have sermonized that the harp seal is on the verge of extinction, that the hunt is very cruel, and that the hunters are barbarians. They have an interesting dilemma. If their boycott takes place, the hunting could stop and that would dry up their lucrative base for future donations. Curtailing the hunt would eventually lead to a necessary cull to control the increasing population and preservation of fish stocks.

Traditionally, the hunt was always conducted by ships or smaller land-based boats. Ski planes had not been utilized until 1963. In 1988 and recent years, more than 10,000 people have been involved in the sealing industry. The total value of the landed catch was about $2 million. The seal fishery provides an economic base for many coastal communities. With the change in regulations, the young whitecoats are not now being harvested and most killing is done with rifles.

Sealing ships on the hunt in early April Note: the broken ice pans

Harp females giving birth on Gulf ice.

Longliners used for sealing.

Chapter 10 Seal Pelts and Skiplanes

Gene and Alphonse Doyle set up base on the Magdellan Islands

In the spring of 1962 the *North Star VI*, under the command of Captain William Moss, was enjoying a successful hunt for Gulf seals. The vessel carried a small helicopter to spot the seals from the air and lead the ship to the patch. Near the end of March, as the ship was collecting their various caches of pelts from the ice, a pair of strange helicopters was spotted landing near their flags. On closer investigation, they found that the crew of the two choppers were stealing their pelts and slinging them to shore on Prince Edward Island. Enraged, Captain Moss stationed two armed men to defend their pile of skins. Two helicopters approached and landed nearby. A scuffle broke out. The helicopter crews overpowered the ship's men and disarmed them. The chopper crews then loaded their helicopters with pelts and soared off to P.E.I. again.

The matter ended up in court, where lawyers for the helicopter crews presented a telegram from the Fisheries Department stating that sealskins must be collected within a period of three day of the killing. Dr. Mark Arsenault of Grindstone in the Magdalen Islands was the alleged instigator who had organized the helicopter maneuver. Although the RCMP impounded 3,500 pelts, the episode had occurred outside of Canada's three mile limit where the court had no jurisdiction. The matter was dropped without any final resolution.

Since my partner, Rick Richard, had lived on the Magdalen Islands for a few years, he was well acquainted with Dr. Arsenault. Hearing of the recent sealing fiasco with the helicopters, we contacted the doctor to hear his account of the incident. He sparked our interest when he told us that in his opinion, if the operation was properly planned, with good pilots and equipment, large profits could be made using aircraft instead of boats for the sealing. Eager to become involved in a profitable venture, Rick and I flew to the Magdelans for further investigation.

As both a compassionate doctor and canny entrepreneur, Mark Arsenault was a highly respected resident of Grindstone. After a lengthy discussion, we decided that seal hunting by skiplane could potentially be very rewarding. We badly needed an injection of capital to keep our company afloat. Our financial burdens were still mounting. We urgently required new and larger aircraft to service our mining customers, and the banks still considered our business too risky for a loan. The seal hunt would be at a slow time of year for us and a shot at quick cash was irresistible. Deep within us, there was no doubt a thirst for a new and challenging adventure.

Sealing with aircraft had never been done before, so this would be a pioneering operation. We were well aware of the tremendous risks involved, so we carefully planned every detail of the operation. It became evident that we would need to invest most of our resources in a go-for-broke operation. Extensive preparations began in early January of 1963.

The Magdalen Islands are a string of narrow, undulating, flattish islands stretching over 112 kilometers from Deadman's Island in the southwest to the Bird Rocks in the northeast. The main group consists of seven islands linked by sand dunes and causeways. These islands are part of the province of Quebec, and are located 60 kilometers north of Prince Edward Island in the

Gulf of St. Lawrence. They lay 210 kilometers west of Newfoundland and 320 kilometers south of Anticosti Island. The main town is near the Grindstone airstrip on Havre-Aubert. The previous isolation of these communities has been reduced by ferry service from Souris on P E.I. and air service from Charlottetown and Moncton.

The sea around the islands provides the chief source of revenue. Most of the workforce is involved in fishing, fish processing and sealing. The sea has exacted a heavy toll over the years. Marine tragedies are a major part of the oral and written traditions of this isolated corner of Canada. The inhabitants are politically part of Quebec, but economically tied to the Maritimes, with a unique and vibrant culture that is very much their own.

My next trip to the Magdalen Islands was on February 17, 1963. I departed Pasadena in our Cessna JNI and left the west coast of Newfoundland at the Port Au Port Peninsula. I headed the little craft out to sea for the long over-water flight to Grindstone. Many details had to be quickly arranged prior to the hunt, so it wasn't possible to wait for better weather conditions.

At first, the ocean was mostly ice free except for waves of spotty slob ice. As the flight progressed, the dark, overcast sky lowered and the falling snow became moderate. For the last 90 kilometers, I had to rely on my instruments as visibility was negligible over the thickening ice pans. For navigation, the aircraft was equipped with only a radio compass which points toward a beacon that is tuned to a selected frequency. In theory, by aligning the aircraft with the indicator, the resulting course will lead you to the assigned beacon. I had brought the instrument approach chart for Grindstone airport. There was no radio control at Grindstone, so I couldn't file an instrument flight plan or know the destination's weather conditions. I hoped the clouds would break up sufficiently to provide adequate visual conditions for landing, otherwise a blind let down procedure would be required although I did have the instrument approach chart with me. Flying to a strange area in such weather was somewhat nerveracking, especially with my ill-equipped aircraft. There was no safe place to land if there was an emergency and the single engine skiplane had no de-icing equipment.

My estimated time of arrival was approaching. Fleeting patches of white ice could be sporadically seen below through the falling snow. I used my thumb and forefinger as rough dividers on the map to estimate my position from the island coast. The first glimpse of land was a black, jagged, rocky cliff, not the low beach that I expected. Immediately, I descended and circled the area for a better look. It was a formidable rocky island standing alone in a sea of ice with no other land visible. For a moment, I wondered where I could be since I knew the Magdelans were relatively flat and elongated. After spotting a lonely lighthouse, I checked the chart. I now realized that I had drifted somewhat to the north and made land fall at Bird Rock Island, on the extreme northeast of the Magdelans. It was one of the most isolated lighthouses in Canada. Since 1873, many of the lighthouse keepers had died in tragic accidents or under mysterious circumstances and many ships had come to grief on its dangerous shoals. I turned left to a more southerly heading.

Ten minutes later, flying low over the frozen waters, the outline of the low north shore of Grosse Isle became visible. I was now able to follow the coast south to Fatima and make a visual landing at the airstrip.

Dr. Arsenault greeted me in his usual cheerful manner: "What in hell are you doing flying across the Gulf in this weather? When your office told me you were en route, I couldn't believe it. There's been no other traffic in here today and the airport is shut down!"

"Well," I said. "I figured I needed some bad weather experience to get ready for this hunt you've roped me into!"

We spent the afternoon going over the plan, meeting some of his friends and choosing an operating site. That night the weather cleared, so we flew to Moncton to meet with Carl Burke over dinner. Carl was the president of Maritime Central Airways (MCA), a large charter company based in Moncton. MCA had been involved in providing heavy airlift to the Distant Early Warning line (DEW) sites in the far north. Since there was no aircraft fuel available in the Magdalen Islands, we needed to arrange transport for our fuel requirements. Although Burke thought the scheme was a bit farfetched, he was still impressed by the strategy and detail of our plan. We estimated our fuel requirement at 3,600 gallons. MCA agreed to make three trips with a C-46 cargo plane that would initially provide about 2,300 gallons of drummed gas on site, with more available if needed.

Mark wanted to fly back to Grindstone after our meeting, but I refused. Having had some wine with dinner, my no-fly rule of seven hours between bottle and throttle wasn't negotiable. We arrived back in the Magdalens early the following morning.

A sturdily built, rugged looking man named Alphonse Doyle met us at the airstrip. Mark had suggested this formidable man as part of our team. The hunt required an "Ice Captain" who would be totally in charge of the men chosen as hunters and skinners. He would hire the twenty skilled sealers, be responsible for the safety of the men on the ice floes, select the site for each day's operation and coordinate all offshore activities.

Alphonse was the right choice. He was highly regarded among the fishermen of the island and had twenty years of experience as captain of a 65 foot fishing dragger. For seven months each year he successfully guided his crews throughout the Gulf and Fleming Banks in pursuit of fish. During these long voyages he had become very knowledgeable about local weather, sea currents, ice conditions and the management of his crew. We would only later discover what an exceptional individual Alphonse truly was. I constantly marveled at his energy and courage, and above all, his unselfishness.

Alphonse climbed on board my aircraft and we headed out to sea on a northwest course. I asked him to explain the ice situation.

"The seals should show up about 60 kilometers offshore around March 7th," he said, warming to a subject he knew so well. "They'll choose rafted ice for whelping as the broken slabs of ice provide some protection for the babies. Right now the Gulf is relatively smooth with large flat ice pans, but as the season progresses, the wind and current will gradually batter the area and cause the pans to get smaller. In a cold winter like this, we should find at least ten inches of ice out here now, and that'll increase over the next two weeks. But if there's less than that, we should cancel the operation because the pans will break up and be too small for your aircraft by mid-March."

Since this was only mid-February, we didn't spot any seals, but we landed in various places about 60 kilometers offshore to check the ice thickness. Alphonse told me to stay with the aircraft and keep the engine running while he chopped a few holes. On the return flight, I asked him why he had been so cautious.

"Whenever your aircraft is on this drift ice you must always be prepared for a quick departure," he replied. "Remember, the changing wind and current can suddenly cause violent pressure that can break the pans apart. I've no doubt you'll see this happen before the season is out!"

Before returning to Newfoundland, most of our strategy had been finalized. Our company would finance the operation and I would be in charge of aircraft maneuvers and act as general manager. Alphonse would be Ice Captain and Mark (Dr. Arsenault) would coordinate all land-based activity. All expenses, including those for the aircraft, would be paid from gross receipts. The twenty sealers would be paid a daily wage plus a bonus per pelt. From the remaining profits, Mark and Alphonse would be paid 25% and our company would retain the balance. Our crews would be quartered at Mark's home, the fuel would be moved from the airstrip to our selected shore base twelve kilometers to the west and portable radios would be set up for communications. All personnel and equipment would be on site and ready to proceed by March 6. We would use three skiplanes and one helicopter.

Back in Newfoundland, the seal operation would reduce our fleet considerably. In order to serve our regular customers, we would need to lease another aircraft for eight weeks. We had a Cessna at Grand Mere, Quebec, which had just finished an overhaul, so I traveled there to ferry it home. During my short stay in Quebec, I met an accomplished young pilot who was interested in some spring work for himself and his aircraft. A deal was reached with Pierre Meagher and he immediately became a new employee. He proceeded to Newfoundland with his plane in early March.

On March 4, we dispatched three aircraft to the Magdelans: a Norseman with Eric Watson as pilot, a Dehavilland Beaver with Tex Hendrigan at the controls, and I ferried the Cessna 180. Since we would need to transport the seal pelts from the rougher berthing areas to our more skiplane-accessible ice pans, a Bell G-4 helicopter was chartered for external slinging. Our always eager engineer, Eddie Oake, came with us. He brought his toolbox and numerous spare parts to maintain our little fleet and keep us flying.

Upon arrival at Grindstone, I was informed that the helicopter pilot requested a fixed wing escort to accompany him from Charlottetown, Prince Edward Island, to the islands! I pondered the matter. If that pilot needs an escort to fly eighty miles over good ice, during good weather, how in hell, I wondered, will he handle the adverse conditions we are expecting? We couldn't risk the success of the operation on the excessive caution of one timid pilot. I immediately cancelled the contract and made alternate arrangements with Northern Wings at Sept-Iles to send one of their choppers with a more inspired pilot. Two days later, a highly-motivated John Tremblay arrived with his machine and the appropriate slinging gear. We were ready for action.

During the Magdalen seal hunt, I kept a daily log of the events, so from here I will rely on that diary to tell the story of our sealing adventure:

March 5: Alphonse and I made a scouting flight and found the seals beginning to congregate in growing numbers about 80 kilometers (fifty miles) to the northwest. Checking the ice, we discover at least twelve inches of excellent ice in the area. The hunt will begin tomorrow.

In the afternoon, the post office asked if we could fly the mail to the people on Entry Island. It was only a few miles off the coast and they reported a field adequate for skiplanes. We agreed. However on locating the small field it appeared somewhat precarious. The clearing was perched on the edge of a steep cliff about two hundred feet above the shore. The far end was rimmed with trees and sloped up and away from the overhang at a frightening angle. There was little wind, so I skimmed in low, just clearing the brink of the rock face, and dropped the skis on the lip of the bluff, running uphill to stop alongside a small crowd of island folk. They were very pleased to get their overdue mail and in formed me that six students needed a ride to the mainland. After taking three of them onboard, I start the takeoff downhill toward the sea. Similar to a carrier departure, we ran out of field just as we were reaching flying speed. We were in the air and gained some extra lift by allowing the craft to sink over the edge toward the ocean.

It was not really as dangerous as it sounds, but it was one of my most thrilling departures. The second trip was less exciting, as I now was familiar with the prevailing circumstances and the aircraft's performance.

March 6: Alphonse and I were airborne at daylight from our base in the bay of L'Etang-du Nord. It was a bright, frosty morning. Ahead, stretching to the far horizon lay a broad expanse of ice glinting and throwing long shadows in the morning sunlight. This vast, featureless plain is an awesome sight. The desolate strip of beach and thin line of sparse buildings faded from sight behind us. We are humbled by the thought that we are just a tiny speck amidst this huge expanse of whiteness.

On a course of 315 degrees, we find a large swatch of whelping seals 85 kilometers out. The mothers and their newborn are among the rough, broken ice. Circling the area, it wasn't difficult to locate a large smooth pan that would serve nicely for the fixed wing aircraft. I call the shore base and gave instructions for the operation to proceed, providing the pilots with my location. Alphonse and I land on the smooth surface and spread out a black roll of roofing felt along the edge of the pan to assist the pilots in recognizing the chosen site from a distance.

Thirty minutes later, the Norseman and Beaver land beside us with thirteen sealers. Alphonse remains on the ice to await the helicopter's arrival, which is slinging two drums of fuel. Tex and I return to the shore base to pick up the balance of the hunters, a fuel pump and a portable radio station.

Eddy Oake and Rick Richard had modified the cargo cabin in all three aircraft. The messy sealskins would be slippery and without a partition they would slide to the rear of the aircraft causing dangerous shifts in the center of gravity. The cabin bins that we inserted would keep the weight forward and prevent the bloody oil from seeping into the lower fuselage. Slight changes were later made to improve the system, but it worked quite well from the first.

By the time we arrived back at the offshore strip, the helicopter had dispersed the swilers among the rough ice, about a half mile away, and had transported sufficient pelts to load the Norseman. One of the swilers hooked up the sling load on the chopper and another stayed on our pan to assist with loading of the skiplanes. Soon all three planes are engaged in carrying loads to shore and the helicopter is able to keep us supplied with full loads. Each plane can make a return trip in about one hour, except for a slight delay on every second trip for refueling.

This first day goes without a hitch. With sunshine and its reflective effect, the minus 15C temperature is quite tolerable. The conditions are ideal, although we had hoped for a shorter flight distance to the herds. Alphonse remained on the ice to direct the sealers. They had all taken a hearty lunch, but not much time is wasted during their noon meal. At the end of the afternoon, we'd retrieved 1,473 pelts. Late in the day, we carried the weary but elated ice crew to shore on our last flight. It seemed we had put together a great team. I believe that at some level we were feeding on each other's courage and energy.

Eddie and John, the chopper pilot, spent part of the night checking the aircraft and performing routine maintenance so all would be ready for the next day. Dr. Arsenault and his wife treated us royally in the comfort of their home. Too excited to retire early, we sit around euphorically toasting the accomplishments of the day and suggesting ways to improve the maneuvers.

Our hunting staff expressed their pleasure to Alphonse. They were pleased to be able to return home each evening after flying to and from work. Under perfect conditions, an experienced sealer can kill and properly skin over one hundred seals per day. However, our operating days were somewhat short in that the men don't arrive at the seals until about 8:30 a.m. and they had to finish their work around 4:30 in the afternoon in order to fly home before dark. But with the promise of a healthy bonus, they were keen to work and they performed in admirable fashion.

March 7th: Again we were fortunate in the stable weather conditions. Everything went smoothly, although high cloud cover moved in during the later hours. This overcast condition was a taste of the treacherous whiteout conditions that we would later encounter. More concentration on flying was now necessary as the dull gray sky merged with the indistinct horizon. The darkening overcast caused the ice surface to change colour and with the shadows gone it is much more difficult to locate men or equipment. From a distance the small leads of open water appear to be men or black roof paper. At 2,000 feet, the flat pans and jagged ice all blend together. We find better visibility at a lower altitude, but more attention to navigation is now required.

So far we haven't been hampered by high winds or extreme cold. The pile of skins at the shore base is increased by over 1,300. Dr. Arsenault is concerned about theft, so he hires a man to stay on guard during the night. A small trailer is moved to the site. Our crews seemed to be revved up with optimistic energy in spite of fatigue from the long hours and the exhilaration of the past few days. I phone Newfoundland to give an update and to enquire how things are going back home. Rick and Pierre seem to be coping fine without me. Bedtime comes early.

March 8th: We stirred for an early breakfast to discover that a strong wind has been blowing all night. The roads were blocked by snowdrifts and it was impossible to reach our base by truck. We returned to Mark's house where he made a few calls to locate a J-5 Bombardier snow machine. Finally, the tracked vehicle transported us through the drifting, snow-covered fields to our base. The wind chill factor was extreme and the snow, as fine as white sand, had drifted well over the skis of the planes, frozen to the ice. We began digging with shovels in the always tiresome job of freeing the skis and removing the snow from the cowlings. Eric's Norseman wouldn't start, so he draped a canvas tent over the engine and crawled underneath to apply a blowpot heater. With the wind chill, the temperature was - 25C.

This delay was frustrating for us and the gang of sealers impatiently standing by for their airlift. We moved about clumsily in our heavy parkas, mukluks and mittens that are formidable against the cold, but made us awkward and slow. The wind was still blowing from the north and we could hear it whistling through our array of equipment. The swirling grains of snow bite into our exposed faces like needles. At last, the bay came alive with the growling of engines as our three planes and the helicopter roar out of the harbor heading to the ice fields.

The desolation of the morning held a piercing beauty. The designs traced by the night storm were exquisite and complex on the ice face. This new looking world was utterly arctic and blindingly white. It was extremely difficult to distinguish the features of the surface beneath the sweeping snow. Eventually, Alphonse and I caught sight of the seal herd among the fractured ice. Dark shapes lay scattered throughout the pack ice in the blur of the driven snow. They had been pushed south during the night some 10 kilometers. The floes had been broken apart somewhat and the thin ice openings were indistinct with a snow covering, we finally found a large smooth pan nearby. We landed, marked the ice with strings of tarpaper and advised the circling planes to come on down. It was nearly noon by the time we have our first load of skins on board.

The landings offshore could be tricky as the low drift restricted visual reference near the surface. On final approach it was impossible to judge one's height above the ice. We set the aircraft up in a long, slow, blind descent, inching down from 15 feet, allowing the plane to blindly settle on the ice. When you felt the skis contact the surface, only then did you know that you had landed. On touchdown, the strong headwinds caused a slow forward groundspeed but provided extra lift for short-distance takeoffs.

The helicopter also had its share of difficulties. The loose, blowing snow whipped up by the rotor blades added to the already obscure conditions. John summoned all of his skill and attention on each descending hover when dropping his sling load. On this kind of day, our load man was vital to our safety. In these whiteout conditions we took direction from the signal man on the ice, holding powerful flashlights in each hand as he waves direction to the approaching pilots. The work is stressful for everyone.

During such windstorms the sheets of ice are churned up and pounded together. Large pans are often broken into pieces. After landing on one of my flights this afternoon, I was slowly taxiing toward the pile of pelts and the signalman. He was barely visible through the drifting snow until I was within 65 feet. Suddenly, he was jumping up and down and frantically waving me off. I had no idea what could be wrong, then a dark three-foot crack appeared in the ice with an open water lead cutting horizontally across my path. Moving at about 15 kph, it seemed impossible to stop the machine before sliding over the edge. As a reflex, I instantly applied full throttle, raising the tail ski from the surface. Helped by the strong wind and under emergency power, the empty craft responded. The gap in the ice was growing wider and just as my skis reached the edge; I eased back on the controls. The skis slid off the ice and skimmed across the open water, my speed now sufficient to lift most of the weight. What a relief to be climbing away from that watery crevasse!

It was the strong wind that had caused the ice to split and the same wind had helped me avoid a crash by providing extra lifting force on the wings. I contacted the other pilots and direct them to an adjacent pan for continued operations. Later in the evening, we praised the alert signalman who had prevented a serious, perhaps fatal, incident. Alphonse hadn't been exaggerating when he had warned us of the effects of wind pressure on the ice pack.

The Norseman was fitted with strong laminated wooden skis. On Eric's last departure from the ice field, the right ski contacted a sharp ice hummock just before lift off, shattering the ski. Although still hanging together in one piece, it was severely damaged. He managed to land at the shore base, holding the right undercarriage off the ice until the speed had decreased. A new ski was required. It has been a day of turmoil and we had only retrieved 990 pelts for our efforts.

We knew how difficult it would be to purchase a new Elliott ski. And there would be a lengthy delay in delivery if one was located. Dr. Arsenault arranged for a local cabinetmaker to assist. Eddy jacked up the aircraft and removed the damaged ski and axle assembly. Luckily, the carpentry shop was well-equipped and Henri, our carpenter, was a professional of the first order. We worked with him through the night. Three ply of cured hickory planking were artfully laminated and steam shaped for correct curvature. The axle assembly was secured to the new ski and the bottom strengthened with LDR fiberglass. Henri left the clamps on until morning to cure the bonding. It was a masterful piece of workmanship and probably stronger than the original, although not officially approved.

March 9: The strong wind had shifted to southwest, but the drifting diminished. Eric was delayed for a few hours as the new ski was fitted to his Norseman. Locating the seals was more difficult, since they had been swept southeast by the wind and current. They were now about 60 kilometers due west of our base. I was amazed at how the ice fields had changed overnight. Many of the large pans had broken apart and their edges were ringed with high ridges of broken ice smashed upward when the pans were thrust together. Banks of snow ran east from the pressure ridges and the broken areas were a chaotic jumble of ice chunks and open water. It would be a difficult day for the sealers work, traversing the dangerous disorder of heaved and crumbled ice. No doubt some of the seal pups had been killed as their ice beds ruptured and tumbled during the night.

To our surprise, many small skiplanes arrived in the Magdelans that afternoon. Word of our success had been greatly exaggerated and spread throughout aviation circles. Anxious to make their fortunes, many pilots with little ski experience were en route from the mainland to join in the hunt. Some of the crews had never seen saltwater ice before. Their aircraft were small and poorly equipped; they haven't arranged for fuel, seal hunters or boarding places. Much chaos was expected.

On my way to shore with a full load of pelts, I noticed a red flare on a distant pan. Upon investigation, I found two men frantically waving as they stood beside an upended skiplane. I took note of the position and returned to the site after delivering my load and landed on the smallish pan where they were stranded. They were from Quebec City and were attempting to land when their new Cessna 185 overturned after ground looping from striking an ice hummock. While flying them to shore, I learned they were working for a small charter company that sent them to the area with the unlikely prospect of retrieving some seals. They weren't injured in the upset. Their aircraft had been new only three hundred hours ago, and they were adamant about paying me for the flight to safety. They also asked if I would fly their insurance adjusters to the crash as soon as they arrive from Montreal.

Overturned Cessna 185 from Quebec

They had been lucky. That same afternoon a large Vertol Piasaki twin rotor helicopter landed on the ice some thirty miles from shore. The two crewmen were examining the ice with a view to becoming involved in the sealing endeavor. One wheel of the heavy machine had become lodged in an ice crevice upon landing and would not release for a takeoff. The two pilots, dressed in city attire, had tried in vain to chop the wheel free. Tex, our Beaver pilot, saw their dilemma and landed to see if he could help. By this time, they were completely chilled and their boots soaked. They had had enough of the -10C temperatures and hitched a ride, leave the freeing of the helicopter until the next day. During the night, the ice shifted, the crevice widened and the big, expensive machine sunk to the bottom of the Gulf. Our tally for the day is two sets of aircrew and 1,190 sealskins.

March 10: We had a fairly uneventful day. The weather was much milder with the temperature reaching plus five around noon. The ice surface became slushy in the afternoon, considerably lengthening our ice run on takeoff.

We had checked with a legal firm in Grindstone regarding the status of the abandoned aircraft left on the ice yesterday. They advised us that the wreck is in international waters and the law of the sea applies: an abandoned vessel in offshore water can be taken into possession by anyone for rightful ownership. Reluctantly, Eddy agreed to be left with the wreck to strip the machine of valuable parts. That evening I made three trips airlifting the detached assemblies. Finally, I got back to pick up Eddy at the scene. He was extremely pleased to be whisked away from that lonely post.

"Was I ever glad to see you," he said. "God, I thought I might never be found! Thought I might just be slowly carried out to sea. That's the most eerie place I've ever worked, you know. The silence was just devastating, and then a loud crack thundered under the ice. It scared me out of my boots! I just pray to God that you don't ever discover another crashed plane to salvage! I just don't want to go out there ever again."

Although I didn't transport many seals this afternoon, we did salvage a few thousand dollars worth of aircraft parts. Most of the hunting activity was completed for the day when we reach shore and Eric runs over to meet me.

"All the men are in, but there's still one big pile of pelts on the ice. Do you think we've time to make one more trip?"

"Sure we do, I'll go with you in the Norseman to help you load," I reply.

Eric insisted that I take the controls as he climbed into the bucket seat on my right. He had had more time on the Norseman than I, but he was quite happy to relax as a passenger on this particular flight. We had a pleasant chat on the way out. The pan where the seals were stashed was only three thousand feet in length and rimmed with a four-foot wall of jumbled raft ice. If we loaded the entire stack of pelts, it was evident we would be substantially overweight, but it seemed wasteful to leave a few hundred pounds behind. I taxied through the slush to the extreme eastern end of the pan before turning into the dying wind for departure. The heavy weight on the skis made turning difficult and as we were rounding the corner, Eric hoarsely whispered a warning.

"You'd better get her to hell out of here, the ice is sinking!"

As I applied maximum power, hearing the snarling response of the big radial engine, I glanced out the side window. There was over one foot of water above the skis and it was quickly rising up the pedestal. We were going uphill while the ice was rapidly bending beneath our weight. Saltwater ice has an elasticity that allows it to bend before breaking, whereas fresh water ice is more brittle and will quickly crack apart under pressure. With the hefty load, sticky slush and an uphill angle, the old Norseman was laboring to move forward. The whole machine vibrated under maximum throttle as I worked the elevators back and forth to free the adhesion. There was no time to throw out some weight. It was now or never!

Eric rocked his body forward and back against his restraining harness, patting the dash and coaxing the plane.

"Come on baby, come on, you can do it, you can make it!"

The seconds felt like hours as the big machine slowly inched uphill, climbing sluggishly out of the deepening water. Soon we were free of the sinking slope and roaring down the surface hoping for sufficient lift-off speed to clear the fast approaching wall of heaved ice debris at the end of the pan. The plane was slow gaining momentum owing to the sticky slush on the ski bottoms. At 70 knots, I eased back and the tail lowered, but we didn't lift off. When we reached 85 knots, I tried again. The plane shuddered, but felt a bit more responsive as the skis skipped along over the slush. It was now too late to abort and there was little runway left. Dead ahead is a four-foot barrier of steep ice. I wonder for a moment if it's all over. Instinctively I pushed on the throttle "but it was hard against the forward stop. At the last second, I pull back on the stick and slowly coax the lumbering load into the air. Straining and pulling our bodies up against our harnesses to help the plane, we clear the icy barrier by inches.

Eric muttered "Yeah baby" as he patted the dash. "Nice job Skipper," he sighed. "I knew she'd make it, but I think maybe we were only a hair's width from becoming another write up in the crash reports."

I knew the accident account would have correctly stated: "Pilot error in loading an aircraft well beyond the manufacturer's limitations during adverse runway conditions with a non-compliant ski assembly."

"Not much to it really," I lie. "Just another routine takeoff." But the dark sweat stains on my shirt and my wet forehead told the real story. The ordeal had given us both a generous injection of fear inspired adrenaline. Our escape owed more to luck than skill. Sometimes stupidity kills. Sometimes it doesn't!

With this last trip we recover 1,060 pelts for the day. It is incredible how much weight these little seals have gained in four day, about five pounds per day.

March 11: Not wanting to take a chance on another skiplane, the insurance adjusters coaxed us to transport them to their client's

A frosty morning at our Magdalen Island base

wrecked Cessna with our helicopter. Had they enquired we would have told them of our salvage operation but they didn't ask. We calculated that the chopper was so vital to our operation that it would cost us over $2,000 per hour if it wasn't productively slinging sealskins. Without blinking, they happily agreed to the price and made a full advance payment. However, after discovering we had stripped the wreck, they were furious, vowing to see us in court. I was confronted with many choice French Canadian swear words that were new to me, but I did understand the sentence, "Vous etês des voleurs, sales et ecoeurant! (You are filthy, disgusting thieves)." Other phrases were less polite and difficult to translate. However, their legal efforts would prove futile since the marine law was in force, and in our favour. We would later learn that Lamoline Air Services was fully compensated for the loss of their Cessna 185.

As the day progresses, the irregular cloud layer began to produce a light snow from the southwest. We had continually been checking the weather forecast with Moncton Terminal but, as usual, their forecasting was not too reliable, especially over the Gulf ice. Tex and his Beaver were grounded for maintenance at noon with an oil leak, but Eric and I continued slogging. At two in the afternoon, Eric and I landed. During unloading we discussed the worsening weather.

"I had a bitch of a time maintaining visual reference on that last flight," I told Eric. "I think I'll try one more trip and see how this storm progresses. We may have to bring the men in and call it quits for the day."

Eric was nonchalant as usual: "It's supposed to be only intermittent snow showers and they don't report any frontal weather. This snow stuff will probably blow over in a short while. The cloud layer doesn't look to be very thick. I'll take on some extra fuel just in case we have trouble locating the site."

"OK then," I agreed. "I'll talk to you on the radio."

We tried to contact Alphonse by radio, but without results. Eric is still refueling as I depart the bay. The storm has turned ugly during our brief stop. The only visibility was straight down. All around everything was completely obscured by heavy snow. I lowered flaps, reduced speed and descend to about twenty feet above the ice. It was now necessary to use the instruments in order to maintain level flight. In ordinary circumstances, I would have returned to base. I pondered the deteriorating state of affairs: there are nineteen stranded men awaiting transportation to safety, it will be extremely difficult to find them in these conditions, and If I do locate them, it might be impossible to land with no forward visibility.

After holding a steady course for ten minutes, I call on the radio: Oscar. Uncle Juliet. This is JNI."

Eric responds immediately: "I'm just airborne. Where are you and how are the conditions out there? It's practically zero-zero here at shore."

"I'm on the dials at one hundred feet," I told him. "There are no breaks. I'm returning to base since my fuel is pretty low. Hopefully, I can find land. I'll refuel and return as soon as things improve. Suggest you return to shore."

"OK, Gene," Eric acknowledged. "No sweat, I've got two hours fuel, so I'll head out on the dials and try to find a break."

I tried to contact Eddy on his base radio, but there was too much static on the single sideband frequency. I realized the urgency of my situation. The ceiling and visibility were much too limited to attempt a beacon approach at the Grindstone Airport. I hesitated to go below one hundred feet on the altimeter in case the pressure had changed, causing a faulty reading. At this altitude, I couldn't make any visual contact with the surface below. Everything is a white blur. Slowly, I eased the aircraft around, turning back onto a reciprocal course. Knowing that there were very few identifiable features on the flat, white shore ahead, I watched the time carefully, realizing I now had a tailwind. I decided that if no visual contact was made within eight minutes, I would climb up and head for Charlottetown, although my fuel would be chancy. A beacon letdown would not be precise in this weather, but there might be no other choice.

A few miles from shore and stretching between the headlands, there is a prominent division between the fast ice and the moving mass. The fast ice was a solid layer formed earlier in the winter and held in place by the erratically indented coastline. Outside this thicker ice, the floating ice field moves by, powered by the forces of wind and tide. For months these moving ice sheets clash up against the battered fringe of the stronger fast ice. The tumultuous collisions created a clearly defined boundary of reared-up mounds along the outer wall of the stable ice, a visible border, very prominent at its crest, then with a smooth unbroken surface running to shore. On the ocean side, the mass of moving ice is jaggedly interspersed with irregular dark bands of open water.

Occasionally, I had a fleeting glimpse of the surface below and it now appears flat and unbroken. I surmise that I must have crossed the boundary and am over the motionless shore ice approaching land.

Tex calls me on the VHF radio from his grounded Beaver: "The weather here on shore is completely shitters in heavy snow with zero visibility. I repeat zero visibility. Wind northwest 25 gusting to 40."

It was a long five minutes. I was about to pull up when an obscure shape appeared suddenly in front of the windscreen. To avoid collision, I threw the Cessna over violently on its wingtip. As I regained control, the dim outline of a sandy bluff is vaguely visible, then disappeared below. I lowered the plane and watch the dark patches of exposed soil on the jutting headland brush by the port wingtip. An indistinct shape of a house on the cliff top is momentarily visible through the blowing snow. "What in hell?" I think. This must be the high ground on the north side of our bay, if so, it should quickly slope down to the flat sand bar behind our cache of fuel drums. The blurred line of the shore is difficult to follow as it blends into the drifted cove ice. Straining my eyes, I followed blindly along the oblique shore until I spotted the dark shape of our Bombardier parked on the ice. With immense relief, I turned into wind and felt my way down. As the parked Beaver flashed by, I reduced throttle, lowered flaps and slowly allowed the aircraft to sink while intently watching the vertical speed indicator. With no altitude reference in the complete whiteout, I caught a glimpse of our dark fuel drums, then lost them. It was impossible to judge my height above the surface in such conditions. I held the wings level. I shut my eyes momentarily, but realized quickly this was a senseless and possibly fatal reaction to impending doom, and I force myself to watch the dials, eased further down and waited for contact. The skis bounced hard as they hit the surface and I pulled off the power. There was another sharp jolt, and then I was firmly skiing on the bay ice. My breathing began to return to normal as my nerves unclutched.

It never ceases to amaze me how that necessary shot of adrenalin gets into the bloodstream at just the right moment. Without it, I've no doubt the results would be very different on flights like these. I slowly turned the plane and taxied back toward the depot, steering on the compass since the shoreline still wasn't visible. This brief 35-minute flight had been extremely unnerving. In fact, in retrospect, it was the most demanding experience I had ever encountered in all my hours of flight time. The vivid memory, after forty-five years, still gives me the scary shudders!

I then tried to call Eric on the VHF radio. We're too far apart for recognizable communication, although I hear his unreadable response crackling in my headset. Perhaps he can hear me, I thought, so blindly I transmit the impossible weather conditions here at the base.

We waited for some improvement, but to no avail. The wind had shifted to the northwest and reached gale force. The snow swept about us in a frenzy, riding with the gusting wind blowing off the frigid Gulf. We become even more worried about Eric's safety as darkness sets in. Finally, after securing the airplanes to some fuel drums, we return disheartened to the village through the sweeping snow and relentless wind. We sat down for a hot dinner and silently pray for Eric's safety.

Mark brought us up to date on the local news. Three of the small Super Cub planes from Quebec had crashed on landing as a result of overloads and bad weather. No one was injured. Another three planes were reported to have sustained substantial damage.

The wives of the sealers were called and Mark advised them of the situation. They were assured that their men would be retrieved as soon as the storm abated, but no one could say when that would be. We sat around the Arsenault living room trying to disguise the extent of our concern.

The sealers were dressed lightly for working and would be extremely cold with the extra chill factor at night. The drift ice would be somewhat flooded and prone to break up in the high wind. The men weren't carrying food for a prolonged stay. There was no shelter on the open ice and no place for the men to sit without getting wet. Our only consolation was that Alphonse was with them, and he undoubtedly would summon up sufficient doses of courage and leadership to see them through.

Eric had about two hours of fuel at 2:15 p.m. and would have had to land somewhere by 4:15 in the afternoon before his fuel was depleted. The weather 60 kilometers offshore must have been similar to what I experienced otherwise the helicopter would have returned to our base camp before dark. I tried to put myself in Eric's position. Using time and compass, he would have flown to the working area on instruments hoping to find a break in the storm. With zero visibility, he would probably circle the area for some time looking for an opening. He would know that an instrument approach to Grindstone would be out of the question in such weather and by this time he would still have had insufficient fuel to attempt a diversion to Charlottetown. Although he could cope with the basics of blind flying, he had never had an instrument rating or practiced airport approach procedures. The Norseman was not equipped with an Instrument Landing System (ILS), but did have a rudimentary radio compass that would make a blind airport landing possible. Difficult, but possible. During the course of the day, we had noticed that the weather seemed somewhat better to the north and he knew that the ice pans were generally larger in that area. If he attempted a blind letdown, he would probably choose the region to the north.

For the past few days, we had noticed a large steel ship, which we took for the North Star, working the seals some ten miles south of our hunting area. I decided to call the captain of the North Star via marine radio. Explaining the predicament to the skipper, I ask if his crew had heard an aircraft circling in the storm that afternoon. His terse reply was in the negative, his manner abrupt. I further explained that perhaps our missing pilot had made an emergency landing on the ice a few miles north of his present position.

"Would you consider making a few wide arcing circles to the north to search with your ship," I asked. "If he's on the ice, he'll shoot some flares when he hears your engines?"

The captain's response is loud and clear.

"We're out here on a sealing voyage and we've no intention of wasting our time in searching for a missing plane! They've no business being out here."

I thanked him and, without attempting to conceal my disgust, wished him a bountiful trip. The sarcasm was probably wasted on him.

I tried to catch some sleep but it was pointless. Eddy and I took turns walking the floor and peering outside at the weather. The wind continued to shudder the room and howled against the window, showing no sign of moderating. We tried to convince each other that the visibility had improved slightly.

Just as I began to doze, Mark woke me in a state of excitement. John, the chopper pilot, had just arrived at the base.

"He brought two sealers in with him," Mark told me. "They're cold and pretty shaken up, but they're OK! They'll be here at the house shortly."

Anxiously, we questioned John while he wolfed down some eggs.

"It was the worst storm I've ever seen," he said, between bites. "Some of the pans have been broken apart, but the one where the men are huddled was still in one piece when I left. They're cold and their feet are wet, but Alphonse keeps them marching around and punching at each other to stay warm. It was pretty wild out there. I had one hell of a time coming in. You know, I don't have much night experience. The snow has let up some, but I still had to hover all the way in. We crept along at five-feet with the landing light on, trying to avoid the hummocks. I can't tell you how happy we were when the shore lights appeared out of nowhere."

I finally asked the question we all wanted answered, afraid of what the answer might be: "What about Eric?"

"We didn't see any sign of Eric," John replied. "But the sealers said they heard a plane circling overhead in the storm around 3 o'clock."

March 12th: I reported the missing aircraft to Search and Rescue at Halifax. Eddie said some stars were faintly visible through the overcast. It was 12:45.

Eddie and I slipped into our heavy winter clothing and headed for our shore base. During the twenty minute drive in the Bombardier, I explained to Eddie how I would attempt a night rescue of the stranded sealers.

"If all goes well, I should be able to make a return trip every fifty minutes. Stay on the radio and leave your headlights pointed toward the wind."

As I takeoff into the dark sky, the brunt of the storm has passed. The overcast is thinning, with only occasional wisps of falling snow. The breeze is still coming from the northwest, but has slackened in strength. The outside air temperature is now -13 C. Meticulously, I hold a course of 260 degrees at fifteen hundred feet. I feel as though I am flying into an uncharted dark void; it was a small taste of what those early fliers must have felt as they winged out over the Atlantic in hope of reaching Europe. After twenty minutes, I stare into the gloomy vastness trying desperately to pick out some evidence of life below. My eyes are strained, scanning this crater of darkness. It seems the dreadful night has swallowed whole all living creatures. Despite my fear, mingled with a creeping despair, my mind is totally focused on the goal of reaching the stranded crew. I make blind calls on the radio in case Eric is sitting out there in his Norseman waiting for daybreak. No response.

My thought can't escape the image of Eric stranded on an ice pan somewhere, waiting. Then suddenly I am jerked out of the brief painful reverie by the unmistakable flickering of a light on the pitch black surface. It is about one mile ahead and slightly to my left!

Immediately, I cut power, flash my landing lights and direct the craft toward the welcoming beam. For a moment the light disappears, then is quickly replaced by a brilliant string of dancing fire that runs into the wind along the edge of a large ice pan. I have sufficient time to dump full flaps and ease down to a smooth landing parallel to the dying flames. As I stop my craft, the dark huddle of men appears, ghostly in the flickering illumination.

Alphonse opened the cabin door with a big smile lighting up his face:"I knew you'd make it. How do you like my runway lights? How many men can you take?"

Wasting no time, I load four men, powering up the machine for departure. The fire has burned out, but my own wing lights are adequate for takeoff. The snow is slushy and soft, so the heavily loaded Cessna gathers speed slowly, and then lifts off.

The cabin heat is at maximum to warm up my chilled to the bone passengers. One man sits on the floor since the Cessna is only fitted with three passenger seats. The pungent stench of seal oil is overpowering as the heat in the aircraft frees the smell from their wet, greasy clothing. The men explain that Alphonse had pulled the bung from the helicopter fuel drum when he saw my light and then had the men roll the drum along the ice, spilling fuel as it rolled. As I approached the landing site he torched the fuel, providing a few minutes of wild flames that lit up the entire area. An ingenious plan!

Although I had considerable apprehension concerning these particular night flights to the ice, they quickly became somewhat routine and proceeded without incident. My pressing concern for Eric's safety was diverted by the intense concentration required. The weather continues to improve. Before daylight, I had completed four trips, with Alphonse lighting the ice with gasoline for each landing. All the men are successfully returned to shore. On the last trip, Alphonse throws a few sealskins into the cabin before climbing aboard.

"Let's make this a profitable trip, at least" he said.

At my request Eddy had contacted Mark Arsenault. He agreed to meet me at the airport at 6:30 and join me in a search for Eric and the missing Norseman. Before proceeding to the airstrip, I canceled all sealing operations for the day and filled the fuel tanks to capacity. As I arrived at Grindstone, the doctor is already on the ramp with a few sandwiches, coffee and emergency medical supplies. While eating my breakfast sandwich, I became acutely aware of the exhaustion creeping over my body after so many hours of stress and no rest. I remind myself to be alert. My exhausted muscles and aching mind could cause carelessness on the rescue flight.

We lift off the asphalt, passing over the dreary cluster of gray buildings that blend into the monochrome landscape. I turn west and head out over the stark ice pack, empty and glistening in the sun. The rising sun and clear blue sky are a brilliant contrast to the savage storm that we had so recently endured. It seemed as though I had flown into a different world although, I felt the entire Gulf to be grim and inhospitable, a place of torment and disaster. The Cessna climbs smoothly in the cold air. At three thousand feet, we scan the endless plateau of ice, straining our vision to the limit. We cross the distinctive border of rafted pinnacles on the jutting edge of the fast ice; then we are over a kaleidoscope of patterns looking like a giant jigsaw in their multitude of shapes and sizes surrounded by dark, forbidding water. The sun throws long shadows from the lofty crests that encircle the battered perimeters. The world below is an enormous splintered mirror reflecting the sunrays like a million fractured ice candles.

Forty kilometers out, I begin a square search pattern. We are about fifteen miles north of yesterday's operating patch. Eric was aware of the larger pans to the north and if he had been forced to attempt a blind letdown, he would no doubt have chosen this area. After only ten minutes into the search we spot a dark object on the distant ice. Circling overhead, our worst fears are confirmed. It is the scattered remnants of the Norseman and a dark shape lying motionless on the ice in front of it.

After landing, as the doctor rushes to the Norseman, it becomes clear what has happened. The Norseman had touched down at the far end of a small pan and ran along on the smooth ice for about 90 feet before crashing into a twenty foot vertical barrier of rafted ice. The touchdown imprint of the ski tracks had not been totally obliterated by the drifting snow. The skis and landing gear were ripped off as the plane cartwheeled over the heaved ice. The fuselage was torn apart and the jumbled wreckage lay in a twisted pile of debris beside the drift. Time had run out for this highly professional pilot. Eric had been thrown forward through the windscreen on impact. His broken lifeless body partially covered in snow, lay frozen on the ice about forty feet in front of the wreckage. There has been no fire and there is very little sign of gasoline by the ruptured fuel cells. Pieces of the engine and fragments of the fuselage and wings are scattered along the rim of the fissure.

I move my aircraft closer to the body, which Mark has wrapped in a blanket. After a quick examination by the doctor, we struggle to lift Eric into the cabin for his last earthly flight in a skiplane. While taking a few pictures of the tragic scene, I locate Eric's watch, torn off in the cockpit. The time stopped at 16:33. He had, as expected, flown around for about two hours hoping to find a break in the storm. A few minutes prior to fuel depletion he had set up a blind let down trusting to touch down on a smooth ice pan. His chances of a successful landing were extremely remote in this deadly maze of broken plates, but he had no other option.

Mark and I have little to say on our return flight to the airstrip, lost in our own thoughts and mourning our dead brother. I watch the dancing shadow of our plane skimming gracefully over the expanse of ice, following us to shore. I could vividly visualize and relive all the details of Eric's final moments in his blind approach to that fatal ice field. My descent in the storm yesterday could have had a similar ending. Or if I had extra fuel, as did Eric, there is little doubt that I would have continued offshore instead of returning to the base. Is our destiny predetermined by fate or a toss of the dice I wondered?

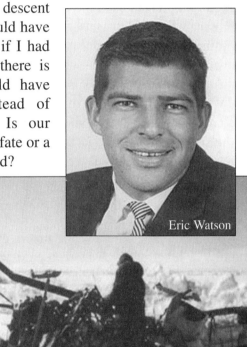

Eric Watson

We recover Eric's body from the Norseman wreckage.
Note: Cessna in background

My thoughts drift to the great times that Eric and I had together: the delight of flying and its tribulations, the celebrations, our laughter and the camaraderie that when you are young and invincible you think will last forever.

Landing back at Grindstone Airport, the reality of the nightmare sets in as we feel the full impact of this dreadful ordeal wash over us. The strain of personal bereavement, the stunning loss of this close friend and colleague only intensifies as we taxi to meet the anxious friends running toward our plane. Immediately, we contact Eric's parents and friends. We keep busy, mechanically making plans for shipping the body to Kingston and confirming travel arrangements for Hugh Atkinson and Dr. Mark, who had agreed to represent us at the funeral. Adrenalin has kept me going full out for over twenty-eight anxious hours. My mind is swimming in a sea of confused thoughts. My body is bone weary and burned out. I collapse with exhaustion into a dreamless sleep.

A few hours of rest is helpful in regaining some composure, but we all remain in shock over Eric's tragic death. This episode is the cruelest blow in my aviation career; however, decisions have to be made. The phone keeps ringing and questions need to be answered. Above all, will we continue with the sealing operation?

There are many sobering facts to consider: we have twenty-six men relying on us with high expectations of substantial financial rewards. Canceling the hunt now will place further financial strain on our company. There's not much we can do for Eric or his family. A lengthy discussion is held with Eric's parents and my associates. The conversations result in a decision to continue with the operation tomorrow. There would be no further time to openly mourn the loss of our comrade, a courageous man who met his death in a gallant effort to rescue his fellow workers. This tragedy has cast a gloom over the entire party, but the exigencies of the day are upon us. I find it tough, replaying the accident in my head with all the what-ifs.

When tragedy strikes, we are forced to reevaluate our personal perspective. We spend our career honing our piloting skills and accruing expertise in the associated fields. When we are riding the edge, unconsciously we know that there is a thin margin between good and bad luck. Luck can emerge at any time to tilt our fate. Other trades have difficulty in comprehending what force drives the passion that makes fringe flying so rewarding. Even among pilots, these sobering thoughts are seldom discussed.

Wild thoughts probe my mind: it would be nice to walk away from the planes, the smell of sealskins, the cruel ice pans, and the treacherous weather. I have a fleeting thought about going home or taking a trip to a sultry Caribbean Island to put this behind me but I know better. We have to take a grip, set it aside, and carry on.

Eric Watson 50 kilometers from shore,
two days before his death

Gene's Cessna & Eric's Norseman,
day before tragedy

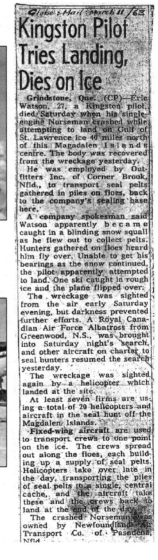

Globe & Mail March 11 /68

Kingston Pilot Tries Landing, Dies on Ice

Grindstone, Que. (CP)—Eric Watson, 27, a Kingston pilot, died Saturday when his single-engine Norseman crashed while attempting to land on Gulf of St. Lawrence ice 40 miles north of this Magdalen Islands centre. The body was recovered from the wreckage yesterday.

He was employed by Outfitters Inc. of Corner Brook, Nfld., to transport seal pelts gathered in piles on floes, back to the company's sealing base here.

A company spokesman said Watson apparently became caught in a blinding snow squall as he flew out to collect pelts. Hunters gathered on floes heard him fly over. Unable to get his bearings as the snow continued, the pilot apparently attempted to land. One ski caught in rough ice and the plane flipped over.

The wreckage was sighted from the air early Saturday evening, but darkness prevented further efforts. A Royal Canadian Air Force Albatross from Greenwood, N.S., was brought into Saturday night's search, and other aircraft on charter to seal hunters resumed the search yesterday.

The wreckage was sighted again by a helicopter which landed at the site.

At least seven firms are using a total of 20 helicopters and aircraft in the seal hunt off the Magdalen Islands.

Fixed-wing aircraft are used to transport crews to one point on the ice. The crews spread out along the floes, each building up a supply of seal pelts. Helicopters take over late in the day, transporting the piles of seal pelts to a single, central cache, and the aircraft take these and the crews back to land at the end of the day.

The crashed Norseman was owned by Newfoundland Transport Co. of Pasadena, Nfld.

Chapter 11 We Carry On

Transferring a payload 50 kilometers offshore

March 13: For the previous two days the wind has been from the northwest, but today it moved around to the southwest. It finally feels like spring, with the sunshine and warmer air. The seals have moved considerably closer to land, but the smooth landing pans are smaller and less numerous. Although the pelts are becoming quite heavy, we don't have as far to fly for their recovery.

These sunny days threaten us with snow blindness, and dark glasses are a necessity in the sharp glare. But today, even with the glasses, my tears are streaming, the lids blinking in irritation from the sand grit that seems to be lodging in the retina.

The pilots of the small Piper Super Cub planes that arrived a few days ago are badgering us to sell them aviation fuel from our cache. We probably have more than we need since the Norseman is no longer with us. They are quite desperate in even making their request since they know they shouldn't be using ordinary automobile fuel and that is all that is available. Mark doubles the cost and agrees to sell ten drums. Tex and I each make 13 trips, accounting for 890 pelts.

March 14: Windy and turbulent weather. I log seven hours and forty minutes in the air. We collect another 770 pelts. More small aircraft are severely damaged, but there is no report of injuries.

March 15: Low gray ceilings, wet snow and rain combine with a high wind to cancel all flying today time to catch up on maintenance and rest. Mark receives a call from a man named Roger Felting, the curator of the San Diego Zoo. He arrived here to arrange for the capture of five live seals to be transported back to their aquarium. We agree to assist him with the snaring of two harps and a family of three hoods.

March 16: This morning the helicopter slung a large quantity of pelts to keep Tex and his Beaver occupied. After lunch, John follows me with his helicopter, carrying special nets and slinging equipment. Alphonse and the curator accompany me in the Cessna.

We find a good patch of harps about ten miles west of Le Corps Mort Isle (Deadman's Island) and land nearby. Around us are hundreds of pups, white-haired, with large mournful eyes. Their whiskers droop as they suckle the richest milk on earth. Some of the mothers slide silently through the crevices into the deep water as we intrude in their domain. Roger expertly throws a net over a large female and we quickly roll the 115 kg animal into the open spread net. A leather lanyard connects the net to the sling mounted to the belly of the helicopter. The young whitecoat is easily captured, wrapped in wet muslin and secured to the skid of the chopper. John lifts off and heads to shore with the live mother seal dangling underneath and her baby lashed to the skid cover. We make a westerly circle with my Cessna, attempting to locate a family of three hood seals.

Alphonse isn't long in directing me to an area of scattered hoods which are separated into solitary family groups. The large bull seals are often aggressive in protecting their pup so the men ask me to stand guard with a rifle directed on the male in case he reacts violently and gets out of control during the capture. As

Alphonse and Roger approach the animal, he inflates his nose bladder and lunges toward them. The nylon net is skillfully thrown over him and he becomes entangled and immobilized. He barks and snorts in defiance, but helpless, he is soon secured by ropes and net wraps.

It was somewhat easier to enmesh the female and the youngster. While we wait for the return of the helicopter, we photograph each other astride the bucking mother.

"The Calgary Stampede has nothing like this," Alphonse laughs, bouncing, rotating his arms skyward while brandishing an invisible lariat. John makes two trips slinging the heavy adults to shore.

Unwisely, owing to its apparent docile nature, I think it will be okay to stow the pup in the rear cargo area of my Cessna, without restraints. On the inbound flight with Alphonse and Roger, the little seal stealthily crawls through the rear bulkhead into the rear of the tail section. Without much concern, I notice a gradual change in the trim of the aircraft. Suddenly my rudder pedals start to twitch and the elevator control becomes partially jammed! We immediately discover that the seal has disappeared into the rear fuselage, where all the control cables are routed through a series of small pulleys. With some gentle maneuvering, I land on a nearby pan. Crawling through the battery bulkhead, I am able to delicately remove the pup's ensnarled flippers from the cables. We then secure him properly and return to the base. Whatever can happen usually does!

Roger, the curator, came well prepared. His crew had their DC-3 modified with a system that would keep the seals cool and moist during their long flight back to California. Later in the week, the curator calls to report a successful transfer of the seals to the comforts of their new home in California. On this most interesting day, the hunt and capture had provided some diversion from the usual routine and our other worries. Tex recovers 495 pelts.

Young hood seal and mother

Cuddling a beater

Transporting live hood seal for San Diego destination

March 17: We were off to a good start this morning, but on my fourth trip the aircraft engine develops a roughness of sufficient concern to ground it for maintenance. Eddy thought it would take a few hours to troubleshoot the magnetos and carburetor for malfunction. Our loader/signalman isn't able to work with a sore throat, so I decide that I could be of more help to the operation by replacing him on the ice. When Tex drops me off on his next flight, I look around at the desolate surroundings and wonder if this is really such a good idea.

A bizarre feeling of despair engulfs me as the smooth purring of the Pratt and Whitney engine fades away and the barrel-shaped fuselage of the Beaver disappears to the east. Every fifteen minutes the helicopter drops a fresh sling load of steaming, dripping pelts beside me. I quickly unfurl them and place the empty sling to one side. The chopper pilot departs to get another load from the sealers on the rough ice. The swiling area is of sufficient distance from me to make the sound of his machine inaudible.

There is such a thing as a deafening silence. It's an eerie feeling of absolute isolation, and now I am there, alone in an empty world of ice. The open sky is vast and stretches as far as I can see, with nothing to obstruct the view of the boundless, frozen world. I am a mere dot in a vast plain of soundlessness. The small patches of open water have frozen over and all is still and quiet as death. The grayish sky merges with the limitless ice field stretching in all directions. It feels as if I am the only living creature on a sterile planet; there is no movement, nothing but dry cold air and a desert of whiteness. Never have I been so overwhelmed by anything as by this humble feeling of desolate solitude and spine-tingling insecurity.

A terrifying, loud crack suddenly shatters my dream-like state as a small breach streaks across the ice beneath me. A cold chill travels up my back; suddenly it jolts me awake and I am aware of my surroundings, just as I hear the unmistakable and welcome wump-wump of the approaching rotor blades.

My afternoon is spent helping to load the Beaver, unraveling the nets and pumping fuel into the chopper. At least I have a better understanding of the work offshore and now I can somewhat relate to the lonely travails of the early arctic explorers. We take 540 pelts on this day.

March 18: All work ceases at noon as another beastly storm sweeps the Gulf. Although we secure the aircraft wings to fuel drums, the planes quiver and quake under the southwest gusts, which drives a column of wet snow and rain across the bay. The short day adds only 340 sealskins to our growing pile.

March 19: The Gulf "Clipper" has passed and the day turns fairly warm, with occasional sunshine. It takes Alphonse and me thirty minutes to find the seals. They have moved to within four miles of Deadman's Island. The ocean currents are very strong in the region of these rocky islands.

Alphonse explains the situation to me. The land mass of the Magdalen Islands acts as a partial barrier to the eastward flow of water from the large St. Lawrence Gulf. As the water is forced around the southern part of the land formation, it speeds up with the venturi effect. A low pressure area in the water on the east side of the island further accelerates the current as it passes the end of the land barrier. Deadman's Island and the other smaller rock structures are situated in the region of fast moving water. They cause further disturbance, resulting in unpredictable sea movements from various directions, especially during tidal change. It can be quite a dangerous area in a small motorboat or sailboat. As the ice shield reaches this region, it becomes an even more treacherous mass due to the erratic forces at play.

The driving wind has churned the ice, making the pans considerably smaller than they were yesterday. Our payloads are therefore reduced. The broken ice harbouring the seals is a jumble of small, disorderly chunks, making the sealers' work more difficult and dangerous. While loading our planes, the rapid movement of the ice is easily discernable against the stationary island background. On each successive trip our loading pan moves noticeably further to the southeast. Early in the afternoon, Alphonse takes over as signalman. Above the noise of the idling engine, he fills me in on what has just happened.

"When the tide changed at noon, all hell broke loose," he shouts above the roar of the engine. "The entire area where we were skinning became a tumbling mass of pitching ice. The pans all around were crumbled and crushed and tossed around. We had to scramble like hell across that pack-ice to find a safe place to stand," he says. "The lunch boxes and all the men's stash of heavy parkas were lost to the sea before they could get to them. One sealer, in trying to recover his winter coat, lost his balance and fell into the frigid water. Luckily his buddy was able to reach him with his gaff and haul him up on solid ice. Although he got soaked, he wants to continue *sculping, but you should carry him ashore to at least get some dry clothing. We were lucky no one was lost through the broken hummocks, but the men are all good at *copying on loose ice."

Things have settled down, so Alphonse thinks it is safe to carry on. He isn't much for showing emotion, but he does finish with a warning." You can bet there'll be more of the same this afternoon as the ice floe gets tormented in the faster current by the islands. Keep an eye out, and tell the other guys to be on a sharp lookout for sudden fractures. Don't shut down your engines out here."

Every day I am more impressed by the leadership, calm knowledge and composed nature of this stoic man of the sea. The balance of the day proves to be uneventful, and we retrieve 893 pelts. The distance to shore is now only a few kilometers.

March 20: The ice conditions are becoming worse every day, with the large pans breaking apart. The weather stays warm, making our landing areas very slushy. It is great to feel spring in the air and to be able to work without our cumbersome parkas. Some of the sealers even have their shirtsleeves rolled up.

The seals are close to the southern shores so our trips are very short. We carry 595 pelts.

March 21: There isn't much doubt in anyone's mind that our operation is nearing an end. The ice has become very loose, with large patches of open water. We don't have far to transport our loads as the seals are close, but the pelts are becoming very heavy. I am also concerned about the roughness of my Cessna engine, which seems somewhat worse. We add 760 skins to the pile.

Two groups of seal skin buyers arrive from New York and appear to be very impressed with our cache. The weather forecast for the next day is unfavourable and the battered landing areas on the ice are getting dangerously small. After a quick discussion with Alphonse, we decide to terminate the operation.

In the evening, we have a wrap-up party with all the crew and try to show our admiration for their truly professional work. As the happy celebration continues, it becomes a mutual admiration society the sealers say the pilots are their heroes.

March 22: Although only three weeks in real time, it seems we have been at the hunt for six months. Everyone is anxious to go home, so the day is spent in gathering equipment and preparing the three aircraft for departure. Eddy has a problem finding the cause of the engine trouble in the Cessna. Tex and the Beaver and John and his helicopter are ready to leave as soon as the weather improves. The spare parts that we recovered from the crashed Cessna are crated for shipment and the remaining drummed fuel is sold to the airport manager.

March 23: Tex and John leave the island in early morning. I conduct two test flights on CF-JNI, but the rough engine prevails. Mark and I spend the afternoon negotiating a better price for our pelts. We notice the fierce competition between the buyers as they sort through our stack of nearly 13,000 pelts. We decide to hold out for a better price, since the offers have increased every day.

March 25: The sealskins are sold in the morning and Eddy and I fly out of the Magdelans in the afternoon. The weather over the Gulf is good, but with our uncertain engine, I choose to take the long way home, over as much land as possible.

We cross Prince Edward Island and follow along the north coast of Nova Scotia and Cape Breton at seven thousand feet. From Cape North, near Sydney, we have 120 kilometers of water to traverse before reaching the south coast of Newfoundland. The view is majestic, and disturbing. The Gulf is dotted with ice remnants, but there are no pans that would be safe for an emergency landing. There are always disconcerting engine sounds and vibrations when one flies a single engine plane far from land. It's called "automatic rough." We are no exception and the engine problem seems to worsen as we leave the land mass. I ask Eddy what he thinks about continuing the flight: "Do you think it's foolhardy?"

"That sound seems more erratic, but maybe it's just our over the water imagination kicking in," he says. "All the dials are normal and the power output seems OK. But if I wasn't so anxious to get home, I'd probably suggest a diversion to Sydney Airport."

*** (End of actual diary entries) ***

As we approached the Newfoundland coast, we could see low ceilings looming ahead. The entire range of higher terrain was shrouded in a low scum of cloud. We were now in radio contact with our base in Pasadena and were receiving weather information from the USAF base at Stephenville. The news was not encouraging. Low cloud and poor visibility in heavy snow was reported throughout western Newfoundland. I veered to the east, where the sky looked brighter. We intersected the coast near Rose Blanche. The land sloped up steeply away from the coast and there was no visible opening through the barrier of hills to the inland plateau. I turned further east and followed the rugged shoreline to La Poile Bay. With little forward visibility, we scouted the inlet, but couldn't find passage to the interior. Further east we entered White Bear Bay and followed the frozen river valley inland toward the highlands.

As we threaded our way uphill the weather worsened, but in the cabin, there was warmth and security, and we were reassured by the light of the instrument panel and the fairly rhythmic purr of the engine. But occasionally, our serenity was interrupted by the return of that nagging, irregular engine noise. Below there was a hostile rocky gorge. The propeller brushed the bottom of the stratus cloud and our wing tips barely skimmed above the snowy treetops. Eddie made a rapid gesture downward at the frozen stream. I peered out the side window and caught a glimpse of prancing caribou disturbed by our intrusive, low flight pattern.

Although the weather was of great concern, we were delighted to be back over land. The Newfoundland terrain was familiar and charts weren't necessary. Along our route there was nowhere to land in this rocky river valley and I knew the most difficult passage would be the height of land south of White Bear Lake.

"There's a comfortable hunting cabin on White Bear, belongs to Bill Newell, about ten miles up the ridge," I said to Eddy. "If we can make it over the hump, we'll land there and await some improvement."

The barren ground was mostly obscured by the whiteout as I circled around the higher hills searching for an opening between the ground and the sky. Flying half visual and half on instruments is not a prescription for a long life. Disorientation can creep in. We were more than a little relieved when the large lake suddenly broke through the cloud cover into view below us. The ground ahead was forested and laced with a series of waterways to follow. I decided to continue to our base.

The remaining 95 kilometers was much less demanding. We passed over Victoria and Caribou Lake. Anticipation mounted as Grand Lake came into view below. We entered North Arm Gulch, leading us downhill to our base at Pasadena. I even seemed to feel the eagerness of the aircraft as she slid down the final turn over the street houses and toward our field at Green Acres Farm. I watched the smooth, solid surface of the pasture come up to kiss the skis. I eased off on the power; she floated a bit and then our landing gear contacted the sweet ground of Newfoundland.

Stopping the craft in front of our little hangar, we were enthusiastically welcomed by our entire staff. Ahead there was that delicious period of ease and relaxation; a good tiredness already started to wash over me. The challenge of those treacherous ice fields seemed far away, almost as if it hadn't happened, unreal. It was like waking from a particularly distressing dream. During the short drive to my home in Steady Brook, I savoured the sight of highway traffic, the green coniferous forest rolling up and away from the lakeshore, the quiet homes along the Humber River, with everything so civilized and so unlike the white, inhospitable gulf ice that I had just left behind. After consigning my sealing clothes to the garbage, there was the luxury of a shower, a shave, a few drinks and the pleasant prospect of a quiet, undisturbed rest. Sleep did not come easily at first. I lay on my bed and all the demands of flying played upon my uneasy mind. Yet I viewed them with a kind of pleasant detachment, till they drifted away and I succumbed to the warm comfort of my bed.

A few days later, I was ushered into the manager's office at the Royal Bank in Corner Brook. He motioned me to the leather seat in front of his desk: "I haven't seen you lately, Gene. I suppose you're still looking for a loan?"

"Yes, Jerry, I am. I've taken your advice and I'd like a loan for $87,000." I let my certified cheque float onto his desk. "You've been telling me all this time you'd match our cash position. Well, our cash position is in front of you. I assume you'll keep your word."

His mouth opened, but at first no sound came out as he gaped at the note: "Where in hell did you get that?" he finally blurted out as the size of the cheque registered. "I haven't heard about any bank robberies around here lately!"

"No," I replied. "This was a mainland job! They treated me much better in Quebec."

By the end of the meeting, I had deposited the draft and the loan. Our account now held over $180,000. We could now arrange to purchase some aircraft and cancel the leases that had been sapping our progress. We were back in business.

And again, I gave a silent vote of thanks to the now late Ches Crosbie for his pompous, drunken, yet inspiring threat to wipe out our business and chase us out of his province.

The following year we were inspired by a thirst for adventure and profit to conduct a similar seal hunt. However, on checking the Gulf ice in late February, we found only an 8-inch thickness. On the advice of Alphonse, we reluctantly cancelled the hunt. However, many small planes with inexperienced crews descended on the Magdalen Islands to make their fortunes. The thin ice broke up quickly in the early March storms and a large number of aircraft were involved in accidents.

Excerpt from the *Financial Post*, March 14, 1964: "The hunt has all the characteristics of a gold rush. Inexperienced sealers are rushing to the scene. About 150 planes are taking off, flying around and landing without much planning or regulation. Men are going out on the drift ice ill-equipped to survive... the waste... is reported to be fantastic and sealers grab for more than they can actually bring to shore for processing."

After that fiasco, the Ministry of Transport, in their concern for safety, ruled that sealing by aircraft would no longer be permitted.

Two years later, Alphonse Doyle went down in the Gulf in his iced-up fishing dragger, losing his entire crew.

Capturing live seals

The competition

Approaching our base on Magdalen Islands
(Deadman's Island in foreground)

Young harp seal that got tangled in control cables

Chapter 12 A New Era

Some new equipment and new docks

The profit from the seal hunt provided the necessary boost to our financial situation. Bank loans became possible, aircraft financing evolved, credit was reestablished with suppliers, and some funds were available for upgrading base facilities. Prior to purchasing the new planes, I investigated the new Canadian manufactured "Found Brothers" bush plane. The FBA-1 was designed specifically for the north country and had many pleasing features. However, after flying it and pushing it to the limits I thought that the engine was underpowered and that it might prove unsafe in tight situations due to lack of wing lift at low speed. The aircraft had great possibilities with a few modifications, but such changes would not be made in time for our needs. A much improved version was finally produced by Robert Beamish and Tony Hamblin in 2007.

We purchased two new Cessna aircraft, another Beaver, and a Twin Beechcraft 18 (on floats). The ground staff also received improvements: a new office, docks, and maintenance building at our Pasadena seaplane base. We also constructed a new maintenance hangar and office at Deer Lake Airport.

There were still many difficulties in the business but at least we had better equipment and the working conditions were improving.

Although the mine at Tilt Cove was phasing out, the asbestos mine in Baie Verte continued to expand and had increasing aircraft requirements. Tourism was growing rapidly, large hydro and other construction projects were underway, roads, bridges and wharves were being built, and the survey for Gros Morne Park began. Generally, the province was a beehive of activity, attempting to catch up with Canada.

The Bowater Paper Company began a large wood harvesting development on the south side of Grand Lake. That region had no road access as it was separated from the populated areas of Deer Lake and Corner Brook by the expansive 130 kilometer lake. The paper company used tugs and barges to service their main depot. Their loggers were isolated from society during their work periods and fed and lodged in an array of company buildings on the south side of the lake. From our Pasadena base, the flight to the logging camp took only ten minutes and so was not an expensive charter. The loggers soon made an arrangement with their employer which would permit them to go home on weekends on a rotational basis.

This new development created substantial work for our floatplanes on Friday evenings and Monday mornings. For the next two years we transported 60 or 70 workmen back and forth to work every weekend during the harvesting season. Some of the men hung out at the local bars during their two-day break and would show up in pretty bad shape on Monday. A few would pay for their return trip when they came out on Friday, knowing that all their money would be spent on more pleasurable activities. A few were incapacitated to the extent that their buddies had to carry them on board and strap them in on their way back to the depot. No rowdiness ever took place in our aircraft. They were just a hardworking bunch of young men who also played hard on their free time. This diversion also served as a break in routine for our pilots.

There was a flurry of mining exploration throughout Newfoundland in the 1960s. Since most of their interest was in the interior, bush planes and helicopters were a necessity in supplying their camps, moving drill rigs, and transporting core sample. We conducted large scale magnetometer surveys for Noranda Mines on the Northern Peninsula, and had servicing contracts with the government geophysical mineral assessments. Brinex, Little Bay Mines, Rambler Mines, Newfoundland Zinc Mines, Buchans Mine, and Cominco, were all searching for new metal finds with an influx of survey camps.

The Baie D'Espoir Hydro development created considerable work for both our planes and those of EPA. Water systems were diverted from White Bear Lake and Spruce Lake to flow through Crooked Lake to the new reservoir north of St. Albans, on the south coast. An airstrip was constructed near the generating station but most of the work required float planes.

Beechcraft 18 on floats

The Newfoundland Power Commission had our Beechcraft and a Cessna on charter to transport a number of their executives around the area and return them to St. John's. It was late in the evening when Pierre Meagher and I finally got them all on board and headed east for the 200 kilometer flight. Brian McGrath, the general manager, asked us to arrange ground transport for his group on arrival in St. John's. "Where do you plan to land?" he asked.

That was a good question since we had been advised that the usual lake for floatplane operations (Quidi Vidi Pond) was out of

Glover Island on Grand Lake

Huge boats could be carried on the Beaver

bounds due to "Regatta Day" preparations. As we circled the city, darkness had set in. Both Octagon Pond and Paddy's Pond were too small for a safe Beechcraft departure. I contacted the control tower on the radio and advised them that we were landing on Windsor Lake, the only other lake in the city.

There was an immediate response: "Oscar. India. India. This is St. John's tower. There is a Notam (Notice to Airmen) that floatplanes are prohibited from using Windsor Lake, as it is the city's water supply."

"I acknowledge your message, but owing to darkness and the lack of other suitable areas we are now landing on Windsor Lake," I replied. "Would you kindly arrange ground transport for our nine passengers?"

It was completely dark except for some flashing red lights when we backed the two planes up on the shore by the highway. The flashing lights were from the three police cars awaiting our arrival. Two uniformed officers met us on the beach with a haughty reprimand: "You can't land here. This is our water supply!"

We ignored the police as we helped our passengers up the bank to their taxis. "Sir," I said. "We couldn't land at Quidi Vidi, Octagon Pond is too small, the harbour is crawling with ships and we are not allowed to operate float planes after dark. I'm sorry but this was the only option."

After considerable private discussion they issued us a violation notice and said they would see us in court. On returning to base the next day, I wrote an explanatory letter to the city council with copies to the St. John's Constabulary, and the Ministry of Transport. The infraction was changed to a warning.

Water supplies were beginning to cause aggravation at various locations. Skiplanes had used Welsh Pond extensively to serve La Scie and a number of small communities on Cape St. John. It was a large lake situated two kilometers up the hill from the village. In 1963 we received formal notice from the town council that planes were forbidden to use this as a landing site. They were concerned about contamination from oil and fuel leaking from the planes. In late May of the same year we had an urgent call to conduct a medivac flight to pick up a patient in La Scie and transport him to the Gander or Corner Brook hospital. The patient had a collapsed lung and was the son of a councilor.

The harbour ice in town was unsafe but the fresh water lake at the higher altitude was still fine for a skiplane. "But we are prohibited from landing on Welsh Pond," I reminded them. Eventually, when they realized that it was the only option, the restriction was lifted, and we conducted the flight.

Following that event, we wrote a letter to the council explaining the cleanliness of an aircraft compared to the continuous, black string of horse droppings that accumulate on the ice every winter. Welsh Pond was the route used by the logger's horsedrawn sleighs in carrying their pulp sticks to the roadside depot!

After having recently purchased a Grumman Widgeon amphibian in 1965, Pierre and I had an unusual trip that fall. We were enroute to Wabush to pick up a group of businessmen. The direct route for this 880 kilometer flight took us over the desolate interior of Labrador's vast landmass. We were still over an hour from our destination when the weather began deteriorating. We dropped lower and lower over the bleak barrens, trying to stay visual with the ground. Instrument flying was rejected since the cool temperature was conducive to wing icing, had we chosen to proceed in cloud. Fuel was also a concern in threatening weather, especially at low altitude.

We knew from the chart that a remote weather station was located in the area, but we didn't know if the site offered a suitable landing strip. I called Eon Lake on the radio and they informed me that there was a dirt strip at their station which the military planes used for resupply. Pierre turned starboard a few degrees and soon we sighted the narrow strip in the middle of the boondocks. The 3,000 foot sand runway was more than adequate for our landing. Pierre parked near the cluster of buildings to await better weather.

To accommodate the five personnel, there was a comfortable staff house, dining area, games room, and kitchen. The cook cordially invited us in for coffee and muffins. He seemed delighted to talk with us since they didn't see many strangers during their one year stint.

"Most of us can take it, but there's the odd one who's not cut out for isolation." He pointed toward a small building behind the kitchen. "That's the radio shack, where all the weather equipment is located. You'll see what I mean when you meet Douglas, He's harmless, though, and supposed to go out before freeze up. Just been here too long."

The building had a formidable appearance, with all its assortment of wires and antennae reaching skyward. We were anxious to see the new hourly forecast, so we walked over, only to find that the door of the meteorological station was locked. Soon we heard the security device being turned and a safety bolt sliding away. A tall, thin young man, neatly attired, swung open the door and addressed us with a gaunt stare.

"I presume you are the crew of the arrival aircraft. I expect you are aware of the high security measures in place here. We have an array of highly restricted equipment with hourly printouts of classified data. Being in charge of this Command Post, I am obliged to give you proper warning." He acted like the captain of a secretive spaceship.

Douglas then let us enter the building but cautioned us not to look at anything except the weather report. He locked the door behind us and turned off all the lights except for a small spot lamp focused on the telex spitting out weather data. Standing behind us, he gave me a spooky feeling, but I couldn't help feeling sorry for him.

The weather was reported to be improving toward Wabush so we climbed back in the Widgeon, very glad to make distance from the bushwhacky commander.

Bush planes are operated by VFR rules. The Visual Flight Rules mean that the pilot shall control the direction and stability of the aircraft using visual reference to the ground and horizon. These single engine planes are not equipped with sophisticated instrumentation to permit safe flight while in cloud and usually the pilots have not been trained for blind flying or the complicated arrival procedures where a precise approach technique is required. Without proper instrument flight training and simulator practice, a VFR pilot becomes completely disorientated when outside visual reference is lost. Continuing the flight usually leads to spells of dizzy vertigo and disastrous loss of control. Studies have found that the majority of fatal VFR accidents are caused by the pilot losing visual contact with the terrain.

Additionally, in Canada it is illegal to carry commercial passengers under instrument flight conditions unless the aircraft has more than one engine, dual radios, dual navigation equipment, dual instrumentation and an instrument landing system (ILS). To retain an instrument license the pilot must be recertified every year by a demanding MOT check ride. The pilot must show proficiency in all aspects of blind flying, including an aborted landing with one engine inoperative.

Of course, these regulations are necessary since there are no navigational beacons or instrument letdown procedures at most bush plane destinations. Even if the pilot is capable of flying his small float plane on instruments, he has no way of knowing when he has reached a wilderness mountain lake, or how to penetrate the cloud base without slamming into the higher terrain. Bush pilots are therefore forced to fly low during inclement weather in order to stay in visual contact with the ground. They gain an intricate knowledge of the terrain: the low winding valleys, the notch in the mountain range, regions of less turbulence, winter whiteout areas and special landmarks like a broken tree or a bald cliff. After a period of familiarity, a map is not required for the chart imagery is firmly etched in the pilot's awareness file. His senses are alert to every detail that is visible.

We operated a twin engine amphibious Grumman Widgeon and a twin engine Beechcraft on floats, both equipped for instrument flying. However, it was not feasible to fly without visual reference unless the pilot was certified and the destination a major airfield. The single engine planes and helicopters were not so equipped.

Fog is a formidable enemy. The weather in Newfoundland and Labrador continually challenged the pilots in their attempt to stay visual on their flights. The island, with 9,600 kilometers of shoreline and surrounded by ocean, is notorious for moist air, low cloud, poor visibility, high winds and rapidly changing conditions. The Long Range Mountains extending along the west coast cause upslope stratus formations and strong turbulence near the fiords. Probably the trickiest and most frustrating flying area is the 25 kilometer stretch of water separating northern Newfoundland from Labrador, where the weather can be grand one hour and zero-zero the next. Even in the fine summer days, a shroud of fog lies in wait off the southern shores, ready at any moment to be carried inland and obliterate the land.

Weather forecasting was never very successful for the low altitudes where we flew. The forecasting center in Gander placed most of their priority on high altitude conditions to assist the Trans Atlantic carriers. We usually depended on the Harmon USAF base in Stephenville for general weather information but the experienced pilots became very knowledgeable in predicting local conditions.

Our company was called on numerous occasions to transport passenger and freight for the 130 kilometer flight to Burgeo and the offshore island of Ramea. They were relatively large fishing communities without road access. A coastal boat service operated along the southern coast and connected them to Port aux Basques, but it was slow and uncomfortable. The Lake Group, who owned the fish processing plants, was one of our more frequent customers. Spencer Lake and his wife and her three dogs often traveled to Corner Brook or Stephenville in our float or ski planes.

Ramea Harbour

One of my more memorable charters took place in June 1964 during some labour strife at the fish plants. I picked up the Lake family in Stephenville after their arrival on Air Canada. The flight to Ramea was uneventful in my Cessna 180, although a southerly breeze was beginning to form some fog banks along the coast and the temperature was only two degrees above the dewpoint. After I disembarked my passengers in Ramea Harbour, Mr. Lake asked me to wait while he prepared a package for delivery to Corner

Brook. During the one hour delay I became concerned as the misty fog was rapidly settling around the island. Condensation takes place when the temperature and dewpoint reach the same values. Had there been passengers involved no doubt I would have stayed overnight in Ramea as more caution is used when people are on board. As well, there is the old bush pilot dilemma of "get-home-itus," something which has caused many fatal accidents.

I took off toward the harbour entrance, running her out along the increasing swells. The sunrays were still visible overhead although my forward vision was only a few hundred yards. I thought the fog would dissipate once I reached the main shore at Burgeo, fifteen kilometers to the north. Unable to see anything near the surface, I climbed through the occluded layer. It was a nice sunny evening on top. On my recent flight south the weather inland had been clear and I falsely assumed that the whole area would open up once I got a few miles inland but that didn't happen. The carpet beneath thickened and stretched as far as I could see.

The flight time to Pasadena was about one hour and ten minutes. Turning back to my foggy departure point was out of the question and there was no option except to proceed, hoping for an opening in the clouds further north. I called the base on the company radio to get their current conditions.

Thankfully, Rick's voice came in loud and clear: "That low stuff has moved in here and everything is shitters with fog. How are you doing?" I told him of my predicament at 5,000 feet with a total undercast layer. He knew that Cessna CF-JNI had no navigation equipment not even a directional finder. "What's your plan?" he asked.

"Call the Sheppards in Lark Harbour and see if a letdown over the ocean would be doable," I said. On a previous occasion I had done a blind cloud-breaking descent over the Gulf and then proceeded visually into the Corner Brook Harbour, skimming along the ocean surface. Soon Rick called back to advise that the gulf was also blanketed with fog and both airports at Stephenville and Deer Lake were below instrument landing limits. Things weren't looking good.

I had no passengers to worry about and fortunately I was very experienced in instrument flying, although not current. That, however, didn't solve the problem of a safe letdown at Pasadena in the soup. I was well aware of the fact that instrument skills deteriorate rapidly if not used, and vertigo can become a deadly factor. These are the tortuous moments when a pilot's mind strains to determine the best choices.

Our seaplane office was at the western end of a 25 kilometer lake. There was a width of nearly one kilometer between the high hills that bordered the lake on both sides. If I began a slow descent on the centre of the lake, I should be able to break cloud over the water surface. It was a plan: "Rick, I should be somewhere overhead in about thirty minutes. If there are no breaks you'll have to line me up by sound and I'll try an easterly letdown over the lake." I kept a careful compass course, dropped down 3,000 feet and eagerly waited his report as my ETA approached.

At 8:48 Rick's confident voice crackled in my headset: "I hear you now. You just passed the base but you're a couple of miles to the west. Turn right to about 095." I quickly made the turn and reduced speed to 80 mph. "OK, that sounds good. You're just coming by the dock. Suggest you take up the lake heading and start descent. Latest altimeter 101. Wind light easterly. Good luck."

I automatically tightened my seat belt, eased off on the power, reset the directional gyro to the compass, swung left on to 083 degrees, pulled on partial flap, checked the fuel selector on "both" mixture full rich, carb heat "on," adjusted the altimeter knob for sea level pressure, and a quick glance showed all temperatures and pressures normal. I had one last look to the north, where the ominous top of Gros Morne Mountain was protruding through the cloud tops. It was time for descent. Carefully monitoring my artificial horizon, I gently eased her down into the wispy whiteness holding a slow, consistent rate of descent to let her settle to a long, straight approach.

My world was now reduced to the luminous dials on the instrument panel, descending blind and not knowing the height below when I would see the water or the trees.

There was a tight suspense with the invisible closeness to the earth as I watched the altimeter unwind toward the 80 foot elevation of Deer Lake. 1,000 feet. 500 feet. 300 feet. And no sign of anything outside! I slowed my rate of descent and let her inch down further. If there was still nothing at 100 feet I had decided to pull up and try again. The air was dead still and void of reference as I sank steadily toward the invisible surface of the lake. I checked the accuracy of my heading, knowing there were hills on both sides. When the altimeter needle showed 200 feet, I slowed the speed slightly and dropped another fifty feet. Suddenly a darker mat loomed up from below and soon I felt the cushioning effect of the air being squeezed between wing and water. A touch of power held her off as I waited for the secure feel of sizzling water on the float keels. There was a small bump and then we slowed gently but firmly, with the gratifying sound of music rippling and tinkling against my aluminum pontoons. Closing the throttle, the Cessna fell off the step and settled gently into the sanctuary of the lake. I dropped the water rudders for steerage and wiped the perspiration from my forehead. It had been quite a while since I had concentrated so intensely on the dials! The ground controlled radar approaches (GCA), with RCAF jet fighters in zero/zero weather, had been far less challenging.

The outline of the shore was not visible until I turned and taxied to the south. I radioed Rick with an arrival report: "Down and happy just below Maxwell Cabins. Be with you shortly."

Rick's response was cheerful: "I'll buy you a drink at Skinners and strongly suggest it's high time you renew your damn instrument rating!"

The year 1965 brought a new era to my business life as well as to my personal life. Nina Nord and I were married that year. Nina, who was born in the Ukraine, came to Canada with her family after WW2 and settled in British Columbia. She became an accountant and went to work for the McCulloch Corporation. She first came to Newfoundland when the company sent her out to set up the books for local chainsaw distributors. Like me, she immediately fell in love with the province and, dare I say it, with me too. With her accounting background, Nina fit well into our business, taking over the administrative supervision.

Office personnel: my wife Nina Manion (left) and Joan French

To again supply planes for seal fishery

Outfitters, Inc. Ltd. of Corner Brook will again prosecute the seal fishery this year, using aircraft chartered from Newfoundland Air Transport Ltd. at Pasadena.

NAT aircraft have not been converted to skis for the winter season.

For the prosecution of the seal fishery, planes probably will be based in the Magdalen Islands.

Meanwhile, NAT officials reported on the year's activities. The firm operated three Cessna 180 single-engine planes, and a twin-engine Beechcraft a n d carrid 2,642 passengers and 434,200 lbs of air cargo during 1963.

The charter air service has been in operation for three years serving Newfoundland and Labrador.

The transport of passengers and cargo to construction and mining centres, airlift of hunting and fishing parties, exploration and hospital flights form the bulk of the company's work.

During 1963 NAT took delivery of a float - equipped Beechcraft. This modern nine - passenger aircraft is the first of its type to be placed in use in the Maritime Provinces. T h e new type bush aircraft was extensively proven in Central and Western Canada for similar use.

The management of NAT

Gene Manion and Rick Richard of Pasadena, outlined plans for additional expansion in 1964. This includes construction of modern passenger and hangar facilities at Deer Lake airport. Permanent base facilities are being constructed at Baie Verte and additional Air Transport Board licences have been applied for to improve the class of service for this new mining centre.

Application for licences to add helicopters to the fleet may be forthcoming in 1964. The West Coast of Newfoundland has never had a helicopter service permanently based in the area, although the demand for this special service is steadily increasing, they said.

Grumman Widgeon with Clayton and maintenance crew
Front row: Tommy Caines - Ace Caines - Denis Bursey -Derek Oates
Eddie Oake - Jud Bursey and Clayton Pilgrim (behind)

The best workhorse in the bush – DeHavilland Beaver

Our Cessna 180 aircraft provided excellent service

Chapter 13 Hunting Activities

Caribou and moose antlers at Pasadena Base

It took me some time to become familiar with the way things worked in Newfoundland. The Wildlife Regulations seemed to be open to different interpretations depending on with whom you were dealing, and often on who you knew. My first introduction to the somewhat arbitrary ways of bureaucracy and the flexible interpretation of regulations came shortly after I arrived in the province in 1960, when I took a job as pilot with Wellon's Flying Service.

Reg Coombs was one of the first in Newfoundland to get involved with fly-in hunting camps as a tourism venture. Wellons flew hunters and guides to his two wilderness camps, one at Peter Stride's Lake and another at Spruce Lake. In the late fall of that year, after flying primarily supply runs to the mines, the manager of Wellons, Frank LeDrew, reassigned me near the end of the hunting season to go down to Peter Stride's Lake to transport a number of caribou carcasses from the Coombs camps to a frozen storage facility in Corner Brook.

After I arrived in my Cessna 180, the guides met me at their wharf and asked how many carcasses I could take. They had a whole rack of them hanging in the meat house. I told them to start loading and I'd tell them when we were at the weight limit. It turned out that four caribou made a good load. They told me to hurry back because they had enough carcasses for several trips. After three more flights, I stopped for a late lunch at the camp with the guides. They explained that they had had a bit of a problem. Someone had broken into Dunphy's Storage facility in Corner Brook and made off with all the meat that had been stockpiled there during the season. Coombs found himself facing many angry customers who were waiting for their meat to be shipped, but it was no longer in his possession. Luckily, the guides said, they had a bunch of unused hunting tags and Coombs had ordered them to make up the shortfall by going out the last day of the season and killing enough caribou to replace the stolen meat. The illegal tags had not been assigned to them and their use was a serious violation of the game laws.

I had done some hunting in Quebec and I knew in that province a pilot transporting illegal meat would be in the same trouble as the hunter. I'd just assumed the rules were the same in Newfoundland. I could be heavily fined and have my license suspended if they happened to check my cargo. It was definitely a risk that I wasn't willing to take. I had an uneasy night of confusion, knowing I had to go back to take out the guides and another load of meat the next day. In the morning, after much pondering, I called Captain Harry Walters, who was in charge of the Wildlife Enforcement Branch in St. John's, and reported the incident to him. I then flew down to complete the closure of Stride's Camp.

I had never met Walters, but when I told him I didn't want my name involved with the report, he assured me that he would keep my name confidential, and he thanked me for reporting the infraction as a good citizen should. A few days later, Mr. Coombs shipped the illegal meat by refrigerated truck to the Port Aux

Basques ferry going to the mainland. The wildlife people were on site and promptly seized the cargo of meat.

Within a week I had a call telling me I was to appear in court to give evidence against Mr. Coombs. That call was shortly followed by another call from my enraged boss, Frank LeDrew. He informed me that I had just been fired.

"You stupid son of a bitch," he shouted. "Coombs is our best fall customer and you've just got him in a pile of trouble with the law. You just can't treat a customer like that. He could be put out of business. You've got everybody in deep shit. The guides will lose their licenses, and you are the chief witness being called to testify. I thought you were smarter than that. You just can't do that to customers!"

He continued to rant along those lines, but I quickly realized the implications for the company and for me. I hung up without argument. They had a small customer base and they had probably just lost one of their best clients. So I was unemployed. What have I done now I asked myself?

As it turned out, Frank was being unduly pessimistic. I talked to a lawyer and told him there was no way I was going to testify. I had acted in good faith and Walters had not. My lawyer assured me that since I had only been asked to appear in court over the telephone, and had not actually been officially subpoenaed, I could just stay home.

Coombs was a well known character in the Corner Brook area, notorious, among other things, for his fondness for drink. He was said to seldom be sober, even when flying his small floatplane. It was common practice when he would land at our seaplane base to move all of our planes to give him a wide berth at the main dock. But as it turned out, Coombs was also the head of the Liberal Party Association for Western Newfoundland. He and Walters were close friends, and Walters was also a force in the Liberal Party. Given his position, it was no surprise to learn that Coombs had many friends in high places. So when he went to court he just blamed the whole poaching operation on the guides, saying he had played no part in the matter. The guides lost their licenses and received a fine while Coombs got off with a warning to keep closer control over his staff.

Three days later, I got a call from Ray Wellon, the owner of Wellon's Flying Service, asking me to meet him at his lounge in Corner Brook for a drink.

"Gene," he said. "We're in a bit of a bind. We can't find another pilot on such short notice, would you consider coming back to work for us?" So all was forgiven and I even got an apology and some free drinks, although Reg Coombs and Harry Walters went on my watch list!

In 1965, I found out I still had a bit to learn about how things worked in Newfoundland. Our company got a sizeable contract from Shawmont Engineering to transport hydro crews, building material for cabins, food, wire, insulators and other supplies for power line construction between Buchans and Glover Island. The line went right by one of my hunting camps at Rainy Lake, in a prime moose area.

In early August, after I unloaded the freight at their dock, one of the cooks invited me to sit down for a meal after the work crew had finished eating. He insisted he had lots of food left over. I was amazed to find myself cutting into a huge, tasty moose steak. It was mid-summer and the moose hunting season wouldn't open until September. I asked the cook where he got moose meat at this time of year.

"Why, there's moose all over the damned place around here," he said. "The lads have been living off moose meat all summer and they love it. We've got a freezer full of the stuff and it saves the company money."

I was well aware there were lots of moose in the area. But the problem was, at the rate they were being consumed, there would soon be a major reduction of animals in that area. Apart from conservation considerations, each of those moose killed out of season had a dollar value for my business and there would be a lot fewer moose, if any, for my customers to hunt when I flew them in during the fall. I struggled with the matter on the flight back to base, and finally decided I had no choice but to report the violation.

I made a phone call that night to the wildlife department alerting them to the fact the hydro camps were killing large numbers of moose out of season. Once again, I asked that they leave my name out of it and once again they assured me that they would. The next day I got a call from the Shawmont project manager informing me they no longer required our services.

It was a big blow to a small company still struggling to grow, but there was no one to complain to. Fortunately for us, after a couple of weeks the construction company became dissatisfied with the service they were getting from EPA and reinstated our contract. Would I ever become sufficiently clever to avoid these conflicts?

There was a vigorous boom in big game hunting activity during the 1960s and early 1970s. We leased extra floatplanes from Bradley Air Service, EPA, and the Bowater Power Company to meet the fall demand. There were more than twenty big game outfitters, with sixty remote camp locations. We were servicing all those commercial sites and flying many local residents in their annual pursuit of moose and caribou. When the weather was flyable, our sixteen aircraft were in the air from daylight until dark. The maintenance crews worked all night and the entire staff pitched in to keep things moving. The pilots refueled their planes as the dock crews unloaded and assembled the next consignment.

The logistics were enormous in that at times we had over 500 people in the wilderness camps, and tents scattered throughout an area of 30,000 square kilometers. Most of the commercial camps had radio contact and we were given instructions by their management. The local resident hunters relied on us to select a good unused site for their destination and to pick them up on specific dates that they provided on their departure. Huge piles of building materials, food and supplies were transported from late August until late October. Tons of quartered animals were unloaded on our docks during this assault. One day of inclement weather created a large backlog and all the schedules had to be reorganized according to priorities. Prior to the highway being built across the central part of the province from Corner Brook to Burgeo in 1976, the workload during the hunting season required three Otters, one Beechcraft, one Widgeon, four Beavers, and four Cessnas. As well, our other customers had to be looked after; the mining industry continued to need aircraft, our scheduled service between Deer Lake and Labrador was maintained, we had contractual obligations with the USAF to provide regular shuttles between Stephenville and their radar station in St. Anthony, and we were sporadically called upon to fly medivac missions to St. John's and Halifax.

The weekends were the busiest, with everyone anxious to be the first to get going. The parking lot was jammed with pickup trucks and trailers, many from the United States. The pilots' wives brought lunches or cooked a scoff at the base as their husbands had little time to stop for a full meal. The dispatcher would have three plane loads waiting on the dock to avoid delays in loading. Another crew carried the incoming gear from the docks to the awaiting vehicles and the offloaded meat was clearly marked for the owner. While the ground crews were servicing the planes, others would be unloading the incoming gear and loading for the next trip. In this way, the dock time was reduced to less than ten minutes. You could see that the staff enjoyed this hectic pace; it showed in their spirit. They were proud to work long days because they cared. Many nights Pierre and I laboured till midnight, arranging maintenance and working out the next day's schedule. Some nights we would sleep at the office since we had to be there again at six in the morning to get things rolling again.

There were very few dull moments at our dispatch office. We monitored all the aircraft, arranged the priority of charters, passed on weather information, and relayed messages from the remote camps that were on our radio frequency. An assistant dispatcher would be on the telephone arranging groups to meet our tight schedule and passing food orders and camp messages to the owner. Bizarre incidents were quite frequent.

On one occasion we received a morning radio call from Center Lake Camp, which was operated by Jim Carey. In a panicky voice the head guide advised us that one of their German hunters had died the previous evening while stalking a moose: "We couldn't reach you on the radio til now. We don't wish ta touch he so he be still hout there in the woods where he dropped." We contacted the camp owner and the RCMP and they suggested that we fly in to bring out the body and they would notify the next of kin and make forwarding arrangements.

I asked Tommy Caines to go with me in the Twin Beechcraft 18. Thirty minutes later we landed on Center Pond and tied up to the camp wharf. Excitedly we were greeted by the staff cook and head guide. Tommy swung the big cargo door open as I asked the staff if they needed help carrying the body to the plane.

The guide sheepishly responded: "He's not ere. We left he hout back cuzz we thot it bestest we dare not touch he." It was not too surprising since we knew that many coastal people feel uneasy about death and the associated supernatural myths. Actually, they were afraid of touching the dead.

"Where's he to?" Tommy asked.

"Ee's a big man an the walkin is rough, probably bout six spells back a de camp." (A "spell" is a guide's term for an estimate of how far one can carry a load, depending on the terrain and the weight, before needing a rest) "I'll go wit ya ta show ya where he be at," the guide said.

Following the guide, we set out through the brush carrying some rope, blankets, and an axe. It was a thirty minute trek, along the wellworn game trails, before we reached the camouflaged body. I wrapped the elderly man in a blanket while Tommy constructed a wood frame stretcher. Together we rolled the heavy body onto the carrying device and secured it with rope lashings. All the while we were going about our chores, the guide stood back watching but didn't offer any assistance. It became obvious that he would not come near the corpse. "When they's dead, they don't urt hanyone," Tommy muttered. The guide had been quite accurate in his "spell" estimate, in that we stopped eight times for a breather before reaching the aircraft.

Some days the weather appeared very good, but with strong

southerly winds we would have to stop all flying due to severe turbulence. Most of the deep valleys and fiords run east and west, and therefore, with the wind blowing across the terrain, the ground effect created severe turmoil in the low-level air currents. On a few occasions we had aircraft momentarily flipped beyond ninety degrees while flying over the Grand Lake Canyon and over the Long Range fiords. At such times the waiting hunters become very restless and critical since they did not see any reason why their flights had been suspended.

On such a day, Pierre and I were servicing the camps on the Northern Peninsula from our base at Parson's Pond. The camps were located beyond the high ridge of hills about 15 kilometers from the flat coast land. After attempting a flight to Four Ponds in the Beech 18, Pierre returned with his load of passengers because of severe turbulence over the mountains. We waited around all morning, hoping for a decrease in the 50 kilometer wind. Uncle Ang (Angus Wentzell) had a store and motel in Parson's Pond and was operating three hunting camps in the high country. It was his sixteen clients that we were trying to transport to their respective camp sites. They could not understand why we wouldn't fly since there was no low cloud and along the coast the breeze was steady and not too severe. Of course, bush flying was a new experience for these American hunters.

Old Angus came to have a talk with us: "I knows you know what yer doin but these guys are getting ostile with me. Would you take some of they up fer a short flight. Shake the shit outa them and perhaps it'll cool them down? I'll gladly pay for the trip."

There was no real danger in the proposal, since the aircraft are built to withstand the turmoil and the pilots don't mind the rough ride. Landing and manoeuvring on the water can be tricky in such conditions, but mainly we don't wish to have scared, sick passengers, and there is a chance they could get badly banged around, resulting in a contrived insurance claim. In any case, I agreed to take the three most boisterous hunters for a ride in my Cessna 180. They were delighted to get going and were quite happy and talkative during the takeoff and the first ten minutes of the flight. As I climbed out over the low country there was some bumpy air but nothing too uncomfortable. Approaching the high ridge, I asked them to tighten their seat belts and to expect some turbulence for the duration of the trip.

I could see the frothy water in Portland Creek Gulch and knew the wind was ripping across the gully, bending the trees and whipping up the wave crests. The little plane was soon caught in the furour and lashed about the sky as though being shook by a vicious dog. I did very little to subdue the violent motion and let the fierce air currents have their way with our vehicle. The passenger in the co-pilot's seat had a death grip on the arm rests. Happiness had left his ashen face. One rear passenger was using the sick bag and the other guy pleaded with me to turn back. Granting his request, I turned toward the coast and we were soon back on the water with old Angus and his other customers standing on the sea plane dock.

He greeted us with a demure smile: "How come yous are back? Did ye have some trouble?" For the rest of the day, his sixteen big game hunters were quiet and very content to stay in the security of the motel bar.

Another memorable flight took place on a wet, scuddy Sunday afternoon. We had cancelled all flying in the western region when a hysterical voice came through on our dispatch radio: "Pasadena. Pasadena I bin shot. Send a plane. Send a plane!" Our dispatcher repeatedly asked who was calling: "Please identify yourself." But the caller would not say the camp he was calling from. He would only repeat the original message: "Send a plane. Send a plane. I bin shot. I bin shot!"

Desperately we tried to determine who was calling for help. There were about twenty camps with our frequency and it could have been from any of them. Don Bonia, one of our dispatchers, came running from the coffee lounge saying he recognized the voice: "That's Frank Hahn at Cross Pond. He's the only one with that gut wrenching voice!"

All the other pilots had been flying in the morning so I elected to attempt the trip. Knowing the area well, I edged the Cessna through the scud and down the Humber River, behind the Marble Ski hills, across the valley to Pinchgut Lake, and then followed the highway towards Stephenville. Manoeuvring around the shrouded hills east of St. George's Bay, I finally landed on Cross Pond. Brimming with extreme panic, Frank met me on the dock. In his terror stricken voice he explained that his young camp helper had shot at a blue jay and the shotgun pellets had penetrated the kitchen window – behind which he had been washing dishes. A number of the small pellets had hit him in the chest. He thought he was going to die of the wounds. I opened his shirt and on close examination found the shot had barely penetrated his skin. He wasn't even bleeding. With great difficulty he finally quieted down and began to believe that death was not necessarily at hand. Lead poisoning became his next concern. I agreed to fly him to the hospital in Corner Brook for a second opinion.

"But for God's sake Frank," I said. "The next time you're shot, when you call us on the radio please identify yourself and tell us who in Hell is calling!"

We also operated our own set of remote tourist camps. Each site had a staff of one cook and four guides. One guide was appointed camp boss. The cooks were normally the most troublesome, with their unpredictable ways. In the fall of 1966 my cook at Saddler Lake became ill, and an immediate replacement was needed. Most cooks were already employed and it was difficult to locate someone on such short notice. In my search, there was no time for interviews or quality selection. Louis Brechette was small with a French accent and he'd worked in the logging camps. He was available so I hired him and flew him to Saddler the same evening.

The following afternoon, the head guide, Maurice Caines, called on the radio to advise that both himself and another guide, Jack Hewlin, were quite ill and had to get out. There were four American sportsmen at the camp who needed all four guides and replacements were not available. On further questioning, Maurice would not say what their problem was. He just wanted out! I told him that there were no aircraft available to do the flight and he would have to stick it out.

The next day he called with the same request. Knowing Maurice well, I could tell by his voice that something very strange was happening and it probably wasn't sickness. Reviewing my options, I called our handyman, Tommy Caines, to the office and quickly briefed him about the trouble. I could always depend on him for enthusiastic assistance, whatever the job. He agreed to go in to the camp for an overnight investigation. The guides at the camp were all either relatives or close friends with him, although the new cook was a stranger.

Sure enough, Tommy called out the next day: "I's got de glitch figured hout, but you best get ere soon and set dis cook adrift, or dare's gonna be worster problems!"

I took one of the Cessnas and picked up Hal Cross, the cook from Rainy Lake, so he could switch camps with Louis Brechette. After exchanging cooks I retrieved Tommy from Saddler Lake. On the way home he told me about his investigation. Louis must have quickly surmised that some of the guides were superstitious and quite involved with haunting legends. Mischievously, he had rigged some fine wire around the pans hanging on the cookhouse wall and led it through the floor and back up in the next room beneath his bunk. He would awake during the night and jerk on the wire, which caused the pots to dance and jangle on the wall in the adjoining room. Maurice and Jack, sleeping in the same bunkhouse, would hear the pans bouncing and convinced themselves that the place had been struck with puckish ghosts.

Tommy said, "By de Lard liftin Jasus, ad dose Portland Creek men found hout dat it were Louis's wire who caused de grief day would a killed he on de spot! Ave no fear bout dat. As fer me, I tinks Louis should be put in de mental. He's loony as a cut cat."

There was never a dull moment during the hectic hunting season. On one charter, Harold Oake, a very competent senior pilot, was transporting six hunters and their gear to the Blue Hills Lake in an Otter.

The dispatch office radio came to life: "Pasadena. This is Nancy, Alpha, Tango. Engine failure. Ten south Lloyds Lake.

Putting her down!"

I acknowledged his transmission and waited anxiously for a further report. Visions of a tragic crash rippled through my mind. The next five minutes seemed like hours. Finally we heard Harold's confident voice:

"Pasadena, this is Nancy Alpha. Everything OK. We're on a small lake just south of hill 949. Send a mechanic when available. No damage other than a dead engine!" Harold had skillfully glided the heavily loaded plane to land on a small pond without power. The DeHavilland Otter was a great bush plane but was somewhat prone to having problems with broken push rods. With one cylinder inoperative, unlike the Beaver, the aircraft would not stay in the air.

Within an hour Pierre flew south in a Beaver with mechanic Eddy Oake and spare parts. He found the disabled group, made three light trips from the undersized lake, and disembarked the hunters at their original destination. With a new cylinder assembly in place, Eddie had the Otter ready for flight in a few hours. Now, that it was practically empty, Harold had no problem lifting out and returning to base for his next assignment.

Austin Bugden had a similar cylinder failure in southern Labrador with his Beaver. Rather than send for a repair crew, he tried a short test flight and found that the aircraft flew fairly well except for considerable engine vibration. Using reduced power he was able to ferry the machine 240 kilometers back to our base for maintenance. All around, the rugged 450hp Pratt & Whitney piston engine was one of the best radials ever built.

While going into many unfamiliar lakes, it was fairly common to encounter minor float damage. The pontoons had a number of separate watertight compartments. Should the aluminum skin become ruptured in one section, the other cubicles would adequately float the aircraft. Clayton Pilgrim had three compartments ripped open on a rock shoal in Osmond Lake while landing a group of hunters. Clayton was a rough and ready bushman, coarse but competent. He preferred to follow his own set of rules than follow those made by others. His character is best explained by some of his remarks: "After finishing my annual medical, the doctor said they would need a urine and stool sample so on me way out I gave my shorts to his nurse!"

After reporting the problem on his radio, he added, "Guess I'll be here for tonight. I got her up on the shore. Send a repair crew in the morning." It was too late in the day to consider such an extensive repair job. From his description, the big Otter would have to be jacked clear of the water and a new six foot casing would need to be fitted and riveted in place to sheath the three right front compartments. It would be a tricky and lengthy ordeal in the bush. The Otter was heavily booked for the next few days so the mechanics began preparing their equipment for an early morning departure to the remote lake, which was 80 kilometers north of our base. All of our other planes were finished for that day but there was still lots of activity. The pilots were securing their workhorses to the buoys for the night, some were completing their flight logs, and the mechanics had begun their evening shift at the docks.

Our dispatch radio was still crackling evening static when we heard Clayton's composed voice: "Just off the water at Osmond Lake. Should be landing base in 30 minutes. Put some lights on the beach. I'll keep her on the step as long as possible and run her up on the sand." He had stuffed the damaged sections with life jackets, fiberglass fuel cans and bunk mattresses to prevent water from filling the float during takeoff. However, the water forced its way in, and he barely managed to struggle into the air with hundreds of pounds of water in the right front float: "I think she'll nose over if I try to taxi. The water has drained out now but it won't be long filling up when I land."

Complete darkness had settled in when we heard the rhythm of the radial engine and saw his flashing lights over the hills on the north shore of Deer Lake. The wind was calm, allowing Clayton a straight in descent toward our docks. His lights grew brighter near Park Point as we were clearing other aircraft that had been parked on the shore. By now our entire staff was watching his approach with bated breath. The landing was smooth and the floatplane careened rapidly toward us with considerable speed. When about 80 feet from shore, he cut the power and the big beast settled off the step and quickly lowered itself into the water. The right float was sinking heavily on the front but a short burst of throttle thrust her forward to a secure stop on the sandy beach.

"Clayton, you crazy ass, what in hell are you trying to do at this hour of the night?" I scolded.

"Well, it's a nice night and I sure as hell didn't want to be stranded up there for a day or two," he replied.

Eddie and his tireless sheet metal crew worked all night with the compressor and rivet guns. Clayton, with his serviceable Otter, was back in the air transporting more hunters at daylight the next morning.

Float repair on Clayton's damaged Otter

The Grumman Widgeon was a versatile flying boat. The two engines had been converted from the old radial type to modern, inline Lycomings. Many of us enjoyed flying this relatively fast six-passenger machine. However, it was difficult to pry Harold Oake or Pierre Meagher from the cockpit. Late in October of 1966, the first year we acquired it, Pierre was dispatched to a hunting camp on Rainy Lake to pick up Mr. and Mrs. Lindell and their group. They were to be flown to the asbestos mine in Baie Verte. When a flying boat lands and settles in the water, an enormous quantity of displaced water momentarily smothers the fuselage and wings with heavy spray. The temperature had fallen to minus 5C and, upon landing the enveloping drench immediately froze on contact with the airframe. The entire aircraft was cocooned in ice. Only by opening the side window was Pierre able to see sufficiently to manoeuvre the plane to the camp dock. It took hours of scraping and scratching to remove enough ice from the wings and elevators to permit a safe departure. It is by such an experience that pilots learn of these perils.

Many curious sightseers visited our base to watch the flying activity and they always had questions. While I was helping to strap a large boat to the Beaver pontoons, a bystander asked why in the world the wide boat stern was attached facing forward with the pointy end to rearward. Clayton always had a ready answer. "Well, sir, take a good look at any aircraft. You will notice that the blunt end is forward and the sharp tail is aft. It's called aerodynamics." Should the boat face forward, the wide stern would create severe drag and air disruption over the elevators.

On another Sunday afternoon, ttwo young Evangelist ministers, dressed in immaculate black suits, were traveling the coast, handing out religious pamphlets and trying to spread their Gospel. They stood on the dock at Parson's Pond and watched Clayton in amazement as he unloaded the dripping moose meat from his Otter, his coveralls stained in blood.

"Do you know this is the Sabbath, and why would you be working on this holy day?" they asked.

Clayton continued his bloody work as he responded, "It seems you fellas are also working on the Sabbath. Is that not true?"

The younger gentleman replied, "Yes, but we are doing God's work. We work for Jesus Christ."

Clayton reacted with his usual sharp wit, "Well, it's about the same for me. I'm doing Angus Wentzell's work, and I work for Gene Manion!"

Leaving the dock, they probably thought it was a waste of their time to try to save Clayton.

*****

Incredibly, all of our planes had managed to make it back to base except Beaver CF-GBD. I glumly listened to the marine weather forecast. But looking out the dispatch window I did not need to hear the weatheman tell me an ugly mid-October cold front had rapidly moved over the entire western region. It was bitterly cold, with a savage northwest gale screeching down the lake, frothing up whitecaps and lifting the tops off the crests and spewing water in the air. The snow laden clouds skimmed the lake and shrouded the ridge, shutting down the visibility. Although it was late October, there were rumblings of thunder over the hills.

I called Alain Guindon on the radio: "Golf, Bravo, Delta. How are you making out?" He was returning to base empty, after dropping his hunting party at South West Pond.

His response was calm but anxious: "Not good. Just passed Buchans Mine, trying to come down through Hinds Lake valley. Very high winds and not much vis."

Some of our other crews had had difficulty returning to Pasadena and the landings were very challenging because of the urbulence and the four foot waves. As the afternoon progressed, the storm worsened. It had turned into the most violent tempest of the season.

There was now desperation in Alain's transmission: "I've been circling Hinds Lake but there's no opening down the brook to Grand Lake. I've gotta put her down. Lost all visibility." There was major apprehension in the dispatch office as we waited for his next report. The normally chatty pilots left the crew room and stood silently around the base radio, listening for a favourable report. It was as if we were piloting the Beaver and trying to cope with his quandary.

Hinds Lake was a large body of water, some four kilometers long by two kilometers wide, and surrounded by high hills except where the river flowed out at the north end. Here it plunged down more than 600 feet though a hydro turbine and emptied into Grand Lake. At that higher altitude the winds would be even stronger, making for a possible capsizing on landing. The DeHavilland Beaver had high lift wings allowing it to become airborne at a relatively low airspeed. The extreme gusty wind, coupled with the huge waves, could easily pick up one wing after landing and flip the aircraft over. Should that take place, would the pilot be able to swim to shore in the cold water? These were our concerns during the long period of silence from his radio. Tensions ran high as we realized what a perilous situation it was.

During the hush, Alain had ratcheted his seat belt, lined the Beaver up into wind, pulled on full flaps and eased the plane down into the raging breakers. The floats slammed hard and bounced on every successive wave. Each impact, together with the high wind, slowed the forward motion until it lurched to a full stop. The crests of the rollers broke over the floats and threw spumes of spray through the prop and over the engine cowlings.

Finally, with an overwhelming sigh of relief, we heard Alain's voice: "On the water. The swells are huge. Will try to sail backward to the shore. There's rocks all over this place. That could be my next problem."

"OK, Alain," I replied. "Keep her into the wind and keep us posted."

Pierre immediately alerted Ace and Tommy Caines to start gathering tools and equipment, since at the very least, major float damage was expected: "You'd best prepare a tent, stove, groceries and sleeping bags in case we can fly you in there tonight."

About twenty minutes later, Alain reported that the pontoons had been badly ripped open on the rocks and the Beaver was upright, but pounding on the bottom in six feet of water some distance from shore. He would be fine but was very cold and wet after struggling in the water and trying to guide the bouncing plane to the shore through the congregation of rocks.

The occluded front moved by quite rapidly. About an hour before dark the wind abated to less than a gale. Ace and Tommy had their huge pile of gear all ready on the dock when Pierre decided it was worth an attempt. The two engines snarled as they took off through the waves in the Beech 18 for the 60 kilometer flight. Upon landing at Hinds Lake, Pierre was able to manoeuvre his aircraft to a more welcoming beach area for quick unloading.

Wet and bedraggled, Alain was a happy camper when he climbed into the warm cockpit with Pierre, leaving the dangerous site behind.

We knew from experience that even under adverse conditions, Ace and Tommy could accomplish temporary repairs. The job before them would call on their hardiness and uncanny abilities. We expected a two or three day ordeal and their likely call for additional equipment. However, to our surprise, Ace called the base the next afternoon on his portable radio: "Best send in a plane and extra pilot. We's finished up ere and ready to be hout of it."

The previous night, when they arrived at the site, the Beaver was in a precarious state, rising and falling with each passing wave and pounding on the lake bed. The seething whitecaps rushed against the protruding rocks and were thrown skyward by the wind. They had worked most of the night, cutting timbers for a skidway, gradually pulling the aircraft backwards up the trestle with a chain fall, and pumping water from each float compartment as it surfaced. Using a hydraulic jack, they temporarily riveted metal patches in place to enclose the ripped aluminum bottoms. After they replaced the drenched carburetor, the aircraft was then skidded back into the water so they could check the soundness of their repairs. Their incredible salvage work had taken place as they stood in the frothy water, using a generator light shining through the falling wet snow, with waves breaking high against their clammy chest waders. The repairs were not particularly complex, but under such tortuous conditions the job was tedious and time-consuming.

At 3 a.m. with the craft secured to the ramp, they crawled into their soggy tent for a bologna sandwich and some badly needed rest. By next morning the storm had passed and the sun cast a brilliant glow on the snowclad surroundings. With renewed vigour they completed the final sheet metal repairs and test ran the engine. The side of the left float had a compound rupture that was difficult to mend, so they hauled a piece of canvas smeared with roofing tar under the belly of the ripped pontoon and secured it taut with rope lashings. Coastal fishermen had devised this method to temporarily prevent leaks in a ruptured boat hull. For Ace and Tommy, adversity was a natural, temporary thing, an opportunity to use their skills. They had grown up accepting that courage and tolerance were basic requirements for survival and success. Most coastal Newfoundlanders of that era shared the same creative ingenuity and impressive work ethic: "Don't be whining, me son. Just get the friggin job done."

We picked up the mechanics and their gear and Alain flew GBD back to Pasadena. New float skins were permanently installed and the Beaver was put back into regular charter service the following day.

The fall hunting season was always hectic. Each day brought new challenges and adventures.

"At Days End"

Now our flights are over,
And we are safe and well;
We finish in the pilot's lounge
To write our logs that tell.
Then to Skinners for a glass or two
And we'll make their rafters roar.
We laugh about the day's ordeal
And look forward to some more.

GM

Ready for the hunting season

Don Bonia, our dispatcher

Gene and Angus Wentzell, a colourful outfitter

Gene with Austin Bugden and Grumman Widgeon

Chapter 14 Searching for Otto

Otto Fuehrer transporting supplies to hunt camps

The Cessna floatplane piloted by Otto Fuehrer could not be contacted by radio. All of our other aircraft had returned to base due to a severe November storm. Although the forecast had warned of light snow showers, the day had turned into a tempest of snow.

Most of the hunting camps were closing down for the 1964 season and our heavy activity of air charters was slowing down. Otto Fuehrer had departed before noon with Mr. and Mrs. Henry Laukka and Mrs. E. Power on a four hour reconnaissance flight to look at a prospective hunting camp site on the Crabbes River. Our dispatcher in Pasadena was in radio contact with the pilot at 2 p.m. During that conversation, Otto advised that he was encountering very poor visibility in heavy snow and that they were trying to reach the lowlands on the western coast by following the river valleys. Further attempts for radio contact were made without success. The plane did not return!

The Search and Rescue Squadron in Halifax was alerted to

our missing aircraft and thus began one of the most intensive search operations in the history of Western Newfoundland. The Search Control Center, being headquartered at the USAF base in Stephenville, sent out an A-16 plane the same afternoon, November 12. Its success was hampered by adverse weather. An RCAF Albatross aircraft made a night sweep of the region hoping to sight flares or a signal fire but the four hour flight was unproductive. The next day, military planes arrived from Greenwood, Halifax, Argentia, and Harmon. The RCMP helicopters were already involved. The Control Officer designated a rectangular pattern that measured 50 by 80 kilometers from the west coast at Codroy to the headwaters of the Robinson River. We also sent three company aircraft to scour the valleys and lowlands that Otto most likely would have taken in bad weather conditions. There were no results.

The Cessna 180 was a fairly new aircraft and was well equipped with emergency rations and adequate survival gear. Both the pilot and Mr. Laukka were experienced woodsmen and very capable of coping with vagaries of the outdoors. In the 1960s, it was not normal procedure to equip aircraft with Emergency Locator Transmitters (ELT) unless operating in the far north. The result was that no automatic signals were transmitted in the event of a crash. We hoped that they had landed on one of the many lakes where there were established hunting camps and that they would continue homeward after the weather improved. However, had that been the case, we should have had a radio message from the plane explaining their situation.

For the next week, an average of fourteen planes were involved each day, with as many as sixteen engaged in the operation. Every few days the search area was considerably widened. Expectations were heightened when two USAF jet fighters heard a garbled radio message on the emergency frequency. The source was traced to a region near Spruce Lake that was located about eighty kilometers east of the original vicinity. That region was carefully scrutinized on the following day with no results.

The search received wide publicity and since Otto was a well known pilot, we received many phone calls from well intentioned people who were trying to be of assistance. One lady from Rocky Harbour said her husband had seen a number of ravens flying out of Bakers Brook Fiord with sandwiches in their beaks.

"They must have crashed up in that ravine where the birds come from," she said.

Some of the hunting guides called from Portland Creek to self consciously report that they had been asking the "Ouija Board" to show the crash site. Repeatedly the magic board, without hesitation, directed them to a spot at the headwaters of Robinson River. Messages were received alerting us to some smoke that had been seen in the Anguile Mountains and South Branch Hills. Of course, as remote as it sounded, all of these tips were followed up but to no avail. The November weather complicated the operation, grounding the planes frequently with low cloud, snow and freezing rain. The search center spokesperson reported: "All hope should not be given up as we have been engaged in similar matters before and have seen the missing parties walk out of the woods after longer periods."

The official search, having covered over 260,000 square kilometers in three weeks, was eventually discontinued. However, our own aircraft continued looking whenever they were in that area. After the official 90 day period, the four persons were declared dead but still missing. It was a difficult period for the next of kin, their friends,and our entire staff. Heartbreaking conversations were held with Otto's parents, who lived in Switzerland. My wife and I took in Otto's fiancé, Valino Brinston.

The following year, I was entertaining some officials from the Johns Manville Corporation's mining division at our Saddler Lake hunting lodge. Ivan Sabourin, their elderly corporate lawyer, was among the guests. Ivan was a humorous intellectual who delighted in demonstrating his supernatural powers while providing evening entertainment.

"Give me a small personal item that you normally wear or

carry with you," he said. "After I examine it I will retreat to the other cabin while you carefully hide it. Place it anywhere inside this large building and I will use my Magic Wand to quickly find it."

True to his declaration, he continually discovered the hidden articles. He used a small silver bracelet as his divining rod, saying it was the same principle as divining for water. As a nonbeliever in black enchantment, I found his magic quite intriguing but not totally convincing.

One evening, I told Ivan the story of our missing aircraft. He was very interested and said if he had an object that had belonged to one of the missing persons he could locate the crash site with concentrated effort. He became very intense, unlike his usual jovial self. He requested a large map of Western Newfoundland. "Please leave me alone in my cabin without distraction," he asked.

Eventually, Karl Lindell, Ross Sampson, Bob Hutcheson, the staff and I retired to our beds. Ivan joined us for an early breakfast the next morning and eagerly spread the Newfoundland chart on the kitchen table. "I've little geographical knowledge of this island since this is my first trip to your fair province, but here's where your plane crashed," he said, pointing at a red "X" he had marked on the map. "The four people on board were killed instantly on impact! I have no doubt."

Although impressed with his sincere declaration I set the remark aside, being a skeptic of such flights of imagination.

In August of the following year, a timber survey party found the wreckage of the aircraft that had been missing for two years. The RCMP investigated the site and recovered the bones that were scattered in the woods. They said it appeared as though a wing had struck a high tree which tumbled the aircraft into the ground, with the occupants being violently thrown to their death upon impact. A pathologist made positive identification of the human remains and it was agreed to have a group burial at a memorial park in Corner Brook.

On examining my flight bag, I found Ivan Sabourin's tattered chart still in my possession, the one that he had marked the previous fall. He had placed his "X" between the Crabbes and the Barachois Rivers, about 20 kilometers east of the coast at Jeffreys. The search planes had scoured that wooded region on many of their missions, but that was precisely the location of the crash!

When I eventually was able to contact Ivan by telephone in St. Jean, Quebec, he was not at all surprised: "I told you that my powers were infallible! Perhaps you will give me more credence in the future. Do you have any other mysteries to be solved?"

Ivan Sabourin at Saddler Camp (2nd from left)

Chapter 15 Ross Sampson

Joe Eby and Ross Sampson at favourite sport
(Arctic Char -1969)

Though he was about fifteen years my senior, Ross Sampson and I became very close friends over the years. We first met in 1962. He was the senior mining engineer for Johns Manville when they opened the asbestos mine in Baie Verte. I was doing all the flying for the mine, moving supplies, servicing exploration groups, and transporting visiting dignitaries and contractors. The operation grew to 700 employees and transformed the tiny town of Baie Verte into a thriving community.

Ross, being an ardent fisherman, was instrumental in expanding the Main River Lodge and used the facility extensively to entertain the Manville clients. During our long association, he tried to hone my business skills by providing me with fatherly advice and guidance. Ross loved the outdoors and we often fished together, flying to favourite spots all over the island and in Labrador. It was while we were hunting for moose that I was forced to try an unusual manoeuvre to get us out of a tight spot.

We had flown up to the high ground south of Grand Lake by floatplane for some moose hunting. We put down on Alex Lake at the headwaters of the Shanadithit River. After a long walk and stalk, Ross shot a moose in some rough country on the side of a hill about three kilometers from the plane. In that rough terrain, it was a very long way to carry the meat so I sized up a small, nearby lake for a closer place to land. We walked back to Alex Pond and took off in the Cessna. After circling the small lake several times, I wasn't at all sure if there was sufficient distance to safely takeoff with the heavy moose meat on board. The shape of the lake being more round than long, it would be difficult to clear the trees on departure. But there appeared to be no rocks or shoals to contend with. There was a stiff breeze from the west and we had a light fuel load. I landed without incident and taxied to shore. Once ashore I realized just how small the lake was. It would be a tricky takeoff with high rising hills on the far shore. I decided to lighten the load by skinning the 200 kilograms of meat. But while we were skinning the carcass, the breeze died out completely. Now there was no way I could get both the meat and Ross into the air so he volunteered to walk back to Alex Pond.

I still wasn't very optimistic about getting the plane safely airborne with such a short run on the tiny lake. I taxied out and with half throttle, I made wide circles to create some wave action to help break the surface tension for liftoff. After much soul searching I thought it unlikely that I could work up enough speed in the few hundred yards available to get the floatplane up and over the trees. It was then I remembered reading about a technique that another pilot had used in a similar situation. I decided to give it a try.

I told Ross to tie one end of a nylon rope to a tree while I fastened the other end to the tailskid of the plane. I then revved up the engine and when it reached full power, I signaled to Ross with an elevator movement. Ross then chopped the tether on the tree with a hatchet. The plane shot out the blocks like an Olympic sprinter and quickly gained speed. The far shore was coming at me rapidly. I rolled left aileron and pulled back to lift one float out of the water and the little darling leaped into the air. With a careful climbing turn the big hill in front receded from view and I was on my way down to the valley to pick up my partner.

Ross went on to become manager of the Baie Verte mine, but by the mid-1970s he was very ill with diabetes and kidney disease. Despite his determination to continue working, he finally had to retire for health reasons. His slot at the mine was filled by two very competent managers, Jack Cole and Eddy McKenna. Ross had been my mentor and close friend for many years, so I was elated when he followed my suggestion and moved to Steady Brook, near my home,with his wife Joan and three children. I helped him out as much as I could in getting around, but his health continued to fail and it became obvious in 1982 that he didn't have long to live.

I visited him almost nightly. Now practically a prisoner in his chair, he would sit fondling his salmon flies and rigging and rerigging his fly reels. In the winter I tried to cheer him up by planning a fishing trip we could take in the spring, but he didn't think it was likely to happen. "I sure would like to, but look at me, I'll never use this stuff again," he said, pushing the gear on the table in front of him away in sad resignation.

"Ross," I told him one spring evening, "I sure would like to take you fishing. I know where we could pull in some big sea trout this time of year. But I guess you're in such damned bad shape, I'll just have to come back and tell you all about it. It's a shame you're not up to it."

His eyes lit up at the mention of trout fishing, and then he slipped back into resignation. "I would really like to go with you," he said. "But I'd just be a nuisance."

I had tremendous respect for this man and I wanted to find a way to get him fishing one more time. I said he could sit in the chopper and watch even if he couldn't fish. That would be better than just sitting at home and hearing about it later, I said. After a lot more cajoling, he reluctantly agreed to go for the ride.

The next morning, before he could change his mind, Ralph Collier and I loaded him aboard the Bell Jet Ranger and flew to Baie Verte to pick up Jack Cole, now the mine manager. We crossed over to the northeast coast to the Cat Arm River, where I knew the sea trout would be plentiful. We landed on the rocky shore where the river emptied into the Atlantic. Ross watched from the chopper as Ralph, Jack, and I waded into the water with our chest waders. In no time we were hauling in some fine sea trout, but I kept wondering how to get a rod in Ross's hand.

There was a big flat rock about 300 feet from shore where we were having a lot of success. We told Ross we had to move the chopper because of the rishing tide.With Ross's okay, Ralph moved the chopper over to where we were fishing and set her down on the protruding slab. I waded over and told Ross that if he would swing his feet out and perch on the edge of the door, he could easily do some roll casting from his seat. Ross gave it a try and before long he was reeling in trout along with the rest of us. His eyes beamed and he came alive as he pulled in those scrappy fish. He was his old self when we flew inland to a pond near St. Paul's for a shore lunch of trout and boiled potatoes. It tasted better than any shore lunch I've ever had, before or since. Ross was a real man among men whom I had admired for years. The helicopter outing had made his day. That was Ross's last fishing trip, and the last time he had a fly rod in his hand. Shortly afterwards, he was buried in the Wild Cove Cemetery near Corner Brook.

Chapter 16 Finding Tom Farrell

Rocky Ridge Lake

Dr. Tom Farrell was a well known Irish doctor, a prominent Corner Brook citizen, and president of the Humber East Progressive Conservative Association. In the fall of 1967 he booked a flight with our company to take a party of four to his camp on Rocky Ridge Lake for a week of ptarmigan hunting. Farrell was the general practitioner who handled my aviation medicals and we were on good terms. For several years, Farrell had used our company to take his hunting buddies to the cabin he had built on a small lake just over 100 kilometers south of our seaplane base in Pasadena. On this particular occasion, we were scheduled to pick them up six days later, but there was a sudden change of plans.

Three days after dropping off the hunters, Austin Bugden was returning from a flight to Burgeo and happened to fly by their campsite. Spotting one of the hunting party frantically waving a white sheet as a distress signal, Austin landed to find out what was wrong. He was told by one of the hunters, a Dr. King, that Dr. Tom had left the camp alone shortly after arrival to scout the area for ptarmigan and had not returned. He had neither food nor proper gear and had been gone two nights and was presumed lost in the bush. The weather had turned foul. The wind, blowing from the south and fed by the cold ocean currents, had brought fog and drizzle up the slope from the ocean. An immediate air search was pointless under the severe weather conditions, so Austin headed back to base, where we could organize a full scale rescue effort. After we had notified his family and the RCMP, the popular doctor's plight became front page news in the local media.

Our company had been successful on a number of search operations. We had an intricate knowledge of the country, and we had a good understanding of how people reacted when faced with troubling circumstances. Previously, we had been able to find a number of hunters who had gone astray: We had located the fatal crash site of Ralph Parsons in Labrador, and we had discovered the place of impact where a small aircraft from Quebec flew into the mountainside near Parson's Pond during bad weather.

We had planned to begin assisting with the search early the next day, but the weather wouldn't cooperate. It went from bad to worse, so we were still on the ground by late afternoon. Finally, there was a slight clearing, at least in our region, and I decided to take a look using a Cessna 180 floatplane. I took some emergency equipment, a sleeping bag, some food and, knowing Tom, a bottle of Scotch as a restorative. The weather didn't let up and the flight was difficult, but I was familiar with the terrain and could see just enough to follow the lakes and rivers to the camp.

After an hour's flight, I arrived at the Rocky Ridge camp to find two helicopters already parked on the shore, one chartered for the search and another sent by the RCMP. Neither of the pilots intended to search that day since they had barely made it to the camp in the thickening fog and driving rain. They had decided to wait, hoping the weather would clear the next day. I had come from the north and knew that there was still a possibility of looking around the lowlands, where the weather was somewhat less forbidding. Tom had left the camp with only a shotgun, and no food or rain gear, wearing short boots that would be of little use in the bog and muskeg. I figured that wherever he was, he was in serious trouble and his chance of surviving another night, as the temperature dropped, was not good. I didn't express my feelings, but I was extremely disappointed with the helicopter pilot. It is much safer and easier to fly low and slow in bad weather with a chopper than it is with a fixed wing aircraft.

The terrain in that area is a myriad of small ponds nestled between the scrub covered hills. There are no mature forests, just a tangle of stunted black spruce and low scrub protruding from the rocky muskeg. I knew there was little chance of success, but I felt that someone should make an attempt to find this desperate man before nightfall. After takeoff, I began by circling the lake in an ever widening radius, but the fog and the drizzle bouncing off the windscreen made for poor visibility. After 25 minutes of circling over the rugged tundra, I decided it was pointless to continue. As I turned back towards the camp, I thought I saw a movement of something on the ground. I turned back and dropped lower and caught a glimpse in the mist of what something waving in the tuckbrush. It was Farrell, standing on the edge of a small lake, with only his head and shoulders visible above the tangled spruce scrub.

Getting to him, however, was not a simple matter. Landing on the lakes in this part of the country is always a risky business, even in good light. Before landing on strange water, the pilot circles the area several times to try to ascertain where the shallows are or if any rocks are beneath the surface, a common hazard in the small ponds. In the duckish light, with the fog and drizzle blurring my vision, it was useless to carry out that procedure. It was a tough decision. I couldn't just leave the man there. But I couldn't be sure the plane would survive a landing on this tiny lake that was dappled with boulders. Again, I cursed the helicopters, which could have safely landed on the shore to complete the rescue. I decided I had to take the chance. Holding my breath, I sat the plane down, waiting for a crunch. Luckily, no rocks were encountered so I gingerly taxied to shore. Tom was a desperate looking man. Wasting no time, I helped him climb onboard. He had a three day growth of whiskers. He was soaked to the skin and shivering, his feet were wet and numb from wandering through the bog, and his eyes were hollow with exhaustion. Hypothermia was taking its toll. I cranked up the heat and gave him the bottle of Scotch. A few medicinal slugs took the edge off his haggard face. I didn't mention to him that our takeoff could be more threatening to his well being than leaving him another night. I just gritted my teeth and hoped for the best as I eased on the throttle, trying to stay in the same path where I had landed. During the takeoff run I waited for the floats to bang on the rocks and could only breathe again when the plane lifted off and cleared the far shore.

Tom had become disorientated the first evening after leaving camp. The fog had rolled in, shutting out his view of any recognizable features. He fired off a few rounds from his shotgun but heard nothing in response. On the first morning of his ordeal he had been able to light a fire and cook two ptarmigan. After that his matches became soaked, preventing further warmth. During the next two days he wandered aimlessly through the bogs, hoping for some sign of direction. Unprotected from the harsh wind and continuous drizzle, he slept fitfully at night, huddled among scrub brush between some boulders. Weary from the lack of food and rest, he shivered uncontrollably in his wet clothing. Hypothermia is a gradual and insidious sort of trauma. I thought he was on the verge of a serious onslaught when I found him. His responses were sluggish, his hands trembled, and he seemed disorientated. It was crucial to get him to some warmth and some dry clothes quickly.

Fortunately we were only five or six kilometers north of the camp, so we were up and down in a few minutes, with little conversation along the way. Back on the shore by his camp I helped him out of the airplane. His elated friends surrounded him immediately, hugging him and shaking his hand, thumping him on the back, congratulating him on his narrow escape. There was an hour of daylight left, so I decided to head back to base. Their camp only slept four and with the helicopter crews it was already overcrowded. After Tom had a change of clothes and a bowl of soup by the fire, he declined my offer of a lift home, deciding he would be better off warming up at the camp and returning with one of the helicopters the next day. Following the lakes and valleys, I flew back alone to Pasadena with considerable difficulty in the fading light and wispy rain.

Tom recovered quickly from his ordeal and returned to work. But, much to my surprise, he never called me or spoke to me again about his rescue. It was odd behavior, I thought, considering the risks involved in finding him. Though I was somewhat puzzled, after a few days I didn't give it much thought. But several years later I had another encounter with him.

In the late 1960s, the Liberal government of Joey Smallwood, in power since Newfoundland joined the Canadian Confederation in 1949, was in disarray. Frank Moores led the Conservative Party to victory in the 1971 election and we were elated. We had backed the Conservatives, hoping that a new administration would be more equitable and would end the EPA stranglehold on government aviation contracts. That is what Moores and his team had promised during the election campaign. Dr. Tom decided to give up his medical practice and enter politics, running for the Conservative Party. When he and his party won, it looked as if it might be a break for our still struggling operation. We became even more optimistic when Tom was appointed Minister of Transportation and followed through by opening a few small aviation contracts to public tender for the first time. Soon after, we bid on and win a helicopter contract. The contract was only for two months, but it was the beginning of a new period.

Pierre Meagher and I flew to St. John's to sign the contract at Confederation Building. All the ministerial offices were on the fifth floor. In the hallway we bumped into the new premier. We congratulated "Frank the Man" and shared a few laughs before being ushered into the office of the Minister of Transportation. We shook hands with Dr. Farrell and wished him well in his new career. He wasted no time in getting down to business.

"Here is the contract, gentlemen," he said. "All you have to do is sign it and give us a donation of ten percent."

I was more than a little taken aback: "What do you mean, ten percent?"

"The campaign cost us a lot of money and the party needs funds," he replied coolly, leaning back in his chair. "From now on, this is how things are going to be done. Everything up front and in the open."

Perhaps I shouldn't have been surprised, but I was caught offguard. I pointed out that this was a very small contract and we had bid low to be sure to get it. We couldn't even be sure that we would show a profit. But we needed the contract and we were anxious to show our caliber of service.

"If it works out for us, at the end of the contract we'd be happy to make a donation to the party," I said. "We've already contributed substantially to your party by supplying aircraft during your campaign. We've been among your strongest supporters."

However, the minister wouldn't budge. It was money up front or the deal was off and that's how it was, he told us. I continued the discourse, which gradually became a bit heated. I told him this was not why we supported the Conservative party and there was no way we would pay any money up front. But he still wouldn't budge. No money now, no contract. Finally, I could no longer control my temper. I grabbed the contract off his desk, ripped it to shreds, tossed the pieces on his desk, told him he could shove his contract and stomped out of his office.

That was the last time I had any dealings with the good doctor. He probably had no idea of the risks I had taken to save him from possible demise in the bush. I confess I have occasionally asked myself if his rescue from that forlorn bog a few years earlier had been worth my effort.

A few years later, Tom's position as Minister of Public Works came under scrutiny. In 1976, the auditor general's report drew attention to a number of public tender violations. The Supreme Court Justice, John Mahoney, was asked to conduct a public enquiry into the affairs of that department. The evidence alleged that Farrell had made a list of preferred contractors. A witness reported that Farrell had said, "Don't worry, the civil servants will take the heat." In 1978, documents were tabled alleging that Farrell, then Minister of Industrial Relations, had been involved in various corrupt shenanigans and a police investigation was initiated. The police report implicated Farrell in possibly setting fire to his apartment to destroy evidence. To complete the file, further investigations were ordered. Three months later, under heavy public pressure, Minister Tom Farrell resigned. At the completion of the Mahoney enquiry, Farrell was formally charged with having set the apartment fire. A further hearing determined there were no grounds for the charge and the case was dismissed. However, Tom's political career had dissolved.

I was saddened to think that Frank Moores and his team had defeated Smallwood in order to rid the province of political corruption and the scandalous sleaze that had prevailed. But, in spite of my little fracas, I believe that Moores and his colleagues did accomplish much in ridding the government of extravagant handouts and advancing many policy reforms. Perhaps my experience was an exception.

Chapter 17 Winter Airlift

Hauling winter groceries to the Labrador coast (Forteau, Labrador)

In 1965, the fishing villages dotting the coast of Labrador were still cut off from the island of Newfoundland for a good part of the year and were only accessible by plane. The winters were long and brutally cold. The harbours froze up in December and remained icebound until May or late June. There was usually only one general store to a village and they were unable to supply fresh meat or vegetables during the long winters. The villagers made do with preserves of whatever they could find on the land, mostly berries, salted meats, and canned rabbit. They had dried fish and dried meat, but fresh eggs, milk, meat and vegetables were not available. Even tinned fruit was a rare luxury, beyond the means of most outporters except on special occasions. There was airmail service. But it was too expensive for the merchants to pay the airfreight tariff and recover it since the villagers could not afford the mark-up.

For some time we had been lobbying the Smallwood government to provide a subsidy for regular airfreight service to the Labrador outports. We argued that it was a disgrace that those livyers*, in a country as rich as Canada, were still unable to get fresh meat and vegetables for months on end. The provincial government finally agreed to subsidize food shipments to the coast, to cover a portion of the merchants' regular cost of transportation for about six months of the year. We immediately took advantage of the new financial support to provide a resupply airlift by stationing three ski planes near a warehouse in Flower's Cove on the northern tip of Newfoundland. The pilots were rotated every two or three weeks from this isolated base since it was an arduous task, flying groceries every day through the adverse weather conditions that prevailed in the Strait of Belle Isle.

The traffic, of course, was one way and we usually flew back empty except for the occasional passenger. So I was surprised one day to get a phone call from old Mr. Edgar Hicks, the store owner up in Port Hope Simpson, inquiring about the cost of making a large shipment to St. John's. Port Hope Simpson was about 80 kilometers north of the Strait of Belle Isle. Unlike most of the villages on the Labrador coast, it wasn't a fishing community. There were some fur trappers, but most were employees of a pulpwood operation run by the Bowater Paper Corporation. The only thing shipped out of the village was the pulp sticks that went by ship to Corner Brook after the spring breakup.

In the 1960s, there was some phone service in the Labrador, although it wasn't very reliable. They were the old handcranked apparatus, often located in the general store. When they did work the lines were noisy and often unreadable. The food orders from Labrador were usually placed with the warehouse in Flower's Cove or at our main base. Mr. Hicks shouted his unusual request to me over the crackling phone line at my office in Pasadena.

"Mr. Manion," he said. "I hunderstands you've got a shipment comin ere fer we next week and I's wondering what kind a plane you'd be sending. Suppose hit be one of dem beamers?"

"You mean a Beaver," I said.

"Whatever de ell you wants to call em. How much can dey fetch anyhows?"

"Depending on fuel, we can carry about 1,500 pounds of cargo."

GENE MANION

"Well, dat's not near nuff," he said. "I honly got near a tousand pounds of food comin in, but I got a whole bunch of hother stuff ta ship south."

"Ship out!" It struck me as kind of funny because as far as I knew nothing much was ever shipped out of Labrador in the winter, and not a whole lot in the summer. I couldn't imagine what he'd be sending south.

"How about one of them Hotters?" he asked. "How much would one of dem big Hotters shoulder?"

"You mean a DeHavilland Otter," I said. (In some places in Newfoundland and Labrador, there is a tendency to drop the "H" from where it should be and add it in front of a vowel)

"Ya, ya. About ow much would dey fetch?"

I told him they would carry about 2,500 to 3,000 pounds.

"Well, I guess that's what we got ta ave," he said. "Give me some prices den on what dat would set me, iffin we were to ship a bunch o' stuff hout to St. John's."

St. John's was a long way away. At $2 a mile it was a substantial amount of money and when I told him the cost there was silence on the other end of the line while he did some calculating. "No, no," he said. "I can't take heasy ta dat." Then, after pondering the matter some more, he asked, "How's bout St. Anthony? Ow much fer ta take me stuff hover dare? We could ire some trucks to take dem on down ta Tarbay. What better twoud dat be?"

I told him the price to St. Anthony and he said that would be doable. "Now I wants yer pilot ta put hon as much as she can suffer," he said. "We gots a big load a stuff ere."

I didn't want to appear to be too inquisitive about what he was shipping, but by this time my curiosity was hard to contain. What could he possibly be shipping from that remote outport during the winter?

"How are you going to ship this out?" I asked. "Will it be in boxes? What the hell are you shipping anyway?"

"Rabbits," he said. "We gots a sale fer ar rabbits."

"Rabbits!" It seemed to me that five thousand pounds of rabbits is a lot of rabbits. I knew the people of Labrador usually snared a few rabbits, but I couldn't imagine catching anywhere near that number. My customer hung up without further explanation. I had my answer and had to make do with that since the negotiations were concluded. It was still a mystery when I made the flight to Port Hope Simpson the following week. After landing the Otter I went in to talk to Mr. Hicks to find out what was going on. As I walked by the store there they were frozen solid and stacked like fire wood against the side of the shed. More rabbits than I had ever seen or ever will see in one place in my life. I needed an explanation.

"I've been wondering about those rabbits," I said. "I know you guys snare some rabbits in the winter, but how the hell would you ever go about catching that many?"

In a way, the rabbits were there because of a storm, Edgar said, giggling with pleasure. He explained that the big blow a year earlier during the fishing season had wreaked all kinds of havoc. Ships were tossed up on the shore, docks were smashed, and countless fishing gear was destroyed. It was a storm from which the fishing industry along the coast could not hope to recover without some help from the government.

"You member when de guvment sent we all dem fishin nets last fall? You should, cuzz hitt was you fellas what flew dem in."

I remembered it well. We had flown in hundreds of crates of nets to communities all up and down the coast which were supplied by the government's Gear Replacement Program. But like any government program there were all kinds of forms to fill in, asking, among other things, how many feet of fishnets were actually lost. Some non-fishermen thought it fair game to imply that they had lost considerable equipment during the violent storm.

"Well, we got ar share," he said.

"Now why would you folks get any nets?" I asked. "You don't even fish."

"Well, day nare hasked dat question!" he said.

"So dare we was wit strings a nets, so ad ta figure hout what in ell we gonna do wit em. Finally one of de lads says, dey should work fer de rabbitts and de mesh looks bout right. By damn, dat's what we done."

His face was all lit up with pride at the thought of their ingenuity.

"You should've seen em. We strung dem nets hall through the woods. We'd run de dogs tru de trees, and put de scatter on dem critters something fierce. They'd run right smack hinto dose gill loops. You wouldn't believe de rabbits we'd catch in dat tangled mesh. Never saw de likes of she. Best ting hever made fer catching rabbits. Twas some wunnerful ta watch. At times, dose guvmint arseoles does we good you know!"

Although grounded many days by poor weather, the winter airlift was very successful. It provided work for us and our planes and coastal communities with fresh food, car parts, snowmobile repairs and many other essential items that otherwise were not obtainable during the long Labrador winter.

An agent, Graham Hancock, was set up in Forteau, on the Labrador side of the Strait, to dispatch the aircraft and coordinate deliveries. We also established a landing strip on the shore near Forteau to allow deliveries during poor ice conditions. Garland Patey acted as our agent in St. Anthony.

The pilots enjoyed the extra winter work but at times the flying conditions were hazardous during the crossing of the treacherous Strait. There were no hotels in the area and the boarding houses left much to be desired. It was, however, quite satisfying to know that we had lessened the winter struggle of isolation for many communities from St. Paul, Quebec to Cartwright, Labrador.

Port Hope Simpson, Labrador (1964)

Chapter 18 Prominent Passengers

Lee Wulff demonstrating the art of fly-casting

The passengers we carried in our small planes were a varied lot. Many were of the middle class, others were poor coastal men looking for work, and some were stretcher cases. There were pulpwood workers, miners, tourists, doctors, fisherfolk, and politicians. Occasionally we would have local dignitaries on board with a wide diversity of interests. We became quite familiar with our passengers in that some would sit up front in the cockpit, and we frequently shared the same dinner table and lodgings with them. As well, there was usually a great deal of conversation during the flight. In the early 1960s, Albert Martin was the general manager of the Bowater Pulp and Paper Company. Bowater was a huge corporation with a large pulp mill in Corner Brook, vast land holdings, hydro projects, hundreds of employees and substantial political influence. It would be no exaggeration to say that the entire economy of western Newfoundland was dependent on the Bowater empire. I had the opportunity of flying Mr. Martin from Corner Brook to Gander on several occasions. During one of these charters, we were forced to land on the Gaff Topsail Plateau to wait out a violent snow storm. For three hours we were immersed in constructive conversation while stranded on the bleak barren ice. He was very inquisitive about my vision for our little company and seemed seriously interested in the many problems we were struggling with at the time. He told me not to hesitate to contact him if he could be of assistance. Over the course of the next few years, he leased us land for our seaplane base in Pasadena, invited me to use their corporate skeet range, gave me political and financial advice, and leased some wilderness holdings for our tourist camp expansion. He showed an aura of fatherly consideration.

His son, Leonard Martin, served us extremely well as our lawyer for a few years before being appointed to serve on the Federal bench in Ottawa. I had very high respect for both Albert and his son.

****

Helge Ingstad and his wife Anne were my Norwegian flying companions for three days in 1960. They had been on a lifelong quest to find a Viking settlement in North America. Mr. Ingstad sat up front with me to look at the land formations and to instruct me on where he wanted to go. They continually showed glowing enthusiasm and optimistic determination during the encounter.

"Gene," he said, peering through the windshield of my Cessna 180, "My studies have convinced me that the Viking sites of Helluland, Markland, and Vinland correspond exactly to Baffinland, Cape Porcupine (Labrador), and someplace in Northern Newfoundland. Today we should fly down the coast of Labrador, toward Belle Isle, at a low altitude as though we were standing under a square sail in an open boat, looking for the ideal place to establish a winter haven."

It became exciting for me as they included me in their search. Maps and drawings were painstakingly referred to as they snapped pictures of the coastal terrain. The nights were spent at a motel in St. Anthony, where the conversation about the Viking voyages continued. The second day, we toured the coast between Red Bay and Tabusintac (Quebec) at various altitudes and angles. We felt like early explorers.

"We're looking for an indent on the coast with shelter from the winds. There should be timber nearby with a fresh water source, and some grassland would be nice," Helge said.

On my last day with them, we zigzagged back and forth across the Strait of Belle Isle and scoured the shoreline from Flowers Cove to Conche. I left them at the Grenfell Mission and wished them luck on their endeavours.

Shorty afterwards, their luck and perseverance paid off. The old Viking settlement at L'Anse Aux Meadows was discovered near St. Anthony on the northern tip of Newfoundland. This historic place,which had been undisturbed for about nine hundred years, became a National Park and World Heritage site. It is now visited by thousands every year.

Perhaps it is wishful thinking, but I like to think that my three days of flying with the Ingstads might have played some small part in their eventual discovery.

****

Chester Dawe was a wealthy businessman who owned a large building supply outlet in St. John's and a sawmill operation in northern Newfoundland. He had an air of nobility whether at his lavish office on Topsail Road, his sawmill in Rodickton, or on his yacht *Hemmer Jane*. Over the years, he often chartered a floatplane to take him between his summer home on Roaches Line and his various enterprises, and a keen respect and friendship developed between us. On occasion, I even stayed at his home, where he provided stimulating conversation in his luxurious library as we sipped fine brandy. I listened and learned from this remarkable businessman who told me he enjoyed having me for a pilot, especially on some harrowing flights over the ocean on the northeast coast. His pompous appearance was in stark contrast to his generous and kind nature. His top hat, silk gloves, and ebony walking stick made him distinctively flamboyant. He and his trademarks are fondly etched in my memory.

****

Author Farley Mowat was well known throughout Newfoundland. He and his wife Claire lived in Burgeo for a few years, but their travels were mostly by boat since he had a deep attachment to the sea. But the sea caused him grief in January of 1967 when a huge fin whale became stranded in an ocean lagoon near the fishing village of Burgeo.

A few local scalawags used the whale for target practice, which caused open wounds that soon became infected. Farley tried desperately to save the whale by organizing a team to feed it. They tried in vain to tow it out to the ocean but an extreme high tide was needed to tow it through the shallow entrance. While all these efforts were being made, the infections worsened. The plight of the whale received national attention and Premier Smallwood officially declared Mowat "The Keeper of the Whale." As guardian, Farley was promised one thousand dollars to arrange herring food to sustain the whale.

The media went into a frenzy with the story. Mr. Bob Brooks from the *Toronto Star* chartered one of our skiplanes to access Burgeo. The sea ice was unsafe, so we had to land him on a small lake situated three kilometers from the community on the frozen barrens. By the time he reached Burgeo by walking, snowmobiling, and boat, he thought it would be easier to get to Baffin Island. Other newsmen from across Canada and the United States called us to gain information on how to reach the outport whale area. They couldn't understand why there was no airport at Burgeo. For the next five days there was no way of reaching the coast owing to a severe winter blizzard with winds gusting to 100 kilometers per hour.

Finally, a shipment of special penicillin and other antibiotics arrived in Stephenville by Air Canada's priority express. A veterinary surgeon called our dispatch office: "Those drugs must be kept cold, so they are in a special container with dry ice. Please meet the shipment with one of your ski planes and get them to Mowat as quickly as possible. Call Burgeo with your ETA and they'll meet you on the landing pond."

We knew it would be a very difficult flight for our pilot Pierre. With the low ceiling and poor visibility in snow squalls, we would normally have cancelled the charter. However, the urgency of the matter had reached a crescendo by all the press coverage and it seemed that the fate of the poor whale was now in our hands. Pierre reached Burgeo that afternoon. The drug delivery put the "Keeper" and his followers in high spirits. However, the injections arrived too late. The whale had died in the lagoon overnight! Farley, extremely upset with the outcome, made a few scathing remarks about the ruffians who had unthinkingly shot at the stranded animal. Many of the coastal residents mistakenly thought he was reprimanding everyone in the area and they took offence to his remarks and the national publicity he had allegedly caused. Unfortunately, Farley's quiet life in Burgeo became uncomfortable. He eventually moved to the mainland and wrote a book about the incident, *A Whale for the Killing*. Prior to this unpleasant event, he seemed to enjoy the Newfoundland country and had a great passion for its people, and a craving for the surrounding waters.

****

Arthur Lundrigan was a gentleman of exceptional quality. He was finely groomed and impeccably dressed. He and his three brothers were successful in building a diverse group of thriving enterprises during the Smallwood era. They constructed hospitals, banks, culture centers, schools, hotels, and government buildings throughout the province on a lease-back structure. Most of the roads and bridges throughout the province had the Lundrigan stamp. At the peak of their expansion, over 3,500 people were employed by their ten large, diversified business operations.

Their commercial activities required considerable travel. At their head office in Corner Brook, they used a Beaver floatplane with a full time pilot, Ernie Moraze. By 1965, with more airstrips being built, they procured a Beechcraft 18 that would speed up their travels and permit night and instrument flight. As their pilot was not instrument rated, they hired me to fly their new plane for the winter months.

Although I enjoyed the change of pace, executive flying was not really my cup of tea. While the businessmen are having their meetings, the pilot is obliged to hang around the airport terminal, not knowing when the decision makers will show up. Often the departures are delayed well into the night or even to the next day. Destinations change frequently and there is always unrelenting pressure to meet their schedule regardless of weather conditions. Art and Harold Lundrigan were the most frequent travelers. They treated me with great respect and never questioned my judgment.

During those wintery flights to St. John's, St. Anthony and Labrador City, Art and I developed a friendly relationship. He usually kept his shrewdness and wisdom to himself but occasionally would offer advice especially in the area of political insight. The following year, as their business surged, they upgraded to a jet aircraft and hired Colin Phipps as their full time executive pilot.

In 1983, I invited Art to join me on some salmon fishing trips with my helicopter. I easily convinced him that his fishing adventures would be much more satisfactory and productive if he had a helicopter instead of a Beaver. The next spring he purchased a Bell 206 and hired Austin Garrett as his permanent chopper pilot.

After the fall of the Smallwood government, or perhaps due to excessive international expansion, the Lundrigan empire underwent a considerable meltdown. Arthur passed away in 2000 and Harold was grounded by a series of strokes.

****

Don Jamieson was another renowned Newfoundlander who migrated from broadcasting to high places in the federal government. On his frequent journeys from Ottawa to his home in Swift Current, he would hasten the trip by using our aircraft after deplaneing from Air Canada in Stephenville.

Similarly, we had the occasion to transport Jean Chrétien (Minister of Parks and Northern Affairs) when he officially opened the Gros Morne National Park in 1968. Pierre Meagher, being fluent in French, was the obvious choice to pilot Chrétien's group from Stephenville on that important event. They expressed admiration for the performance of our Grumman Widgeon as it wound through the rugged mountains and splashed down on Rocky Harbour Pond by the new park office.

****

The Irving brothers ran a large family empire in St. John, New Brunswick. Arthur looked after the oil refinery and its outlets while the other brothers took care of their forestry and real estate holdings. I had the opportunity to fly them around the remote coastal communities in their search for new oil customers. They were intense, quiet men. Arthur, with his inquisitive mind, had many questions about the Newfoundland people, its unique wilderness, the wildlife, and especially the waterfowl. I later found out that he was an enthusiastic duck hunter and a great supporter of Ducks Unlimited.

On one occasion, I had an overnight stop with Arthur in St. Anthony. During the evening, I walked across the street to the Irving Service Station to purchase some cigarettes. On entering the convenience store, I noticed the glass in the main door was badly shattered. Someone had taped the pieces together with duct tape. After paying the young attendant for my purchase, I jokingly remarked, "You're gonna get in trouble for that broken door. Mr. Irving is in town and I'm sure he will make you a visit."

Dropping my change on the floor, the young man was obviously startled: "You mean Arthur Irving himself is in town? Holy shit, we got a new pane shipped in. I best get hon to it."

I knew that Arthur had a reputation for always making a casual inspection of any Irving Station that was nearby. Many of the attendants did not recognize him other than as an observant customer who needed to use the washroom. Shortly thereafter, the station would receive a biting report outlining the urgent need to repair the list of deficiencies that had been recently discovered.

The next morning, I stopped at the Irving Station and was warmly greeted by the same young man: "Don't know how ta thank ya. You sure saved me ass last night. When the big boss dropped in hat 10:30, I ad the glass fixed and the whole place sparklin. I thinks I even got more points fer callin him Mr. Irving, cuzz he looked some wonderful surprised when I knowed his name."

****

Whenever I hear the tinkling of a bell, I immediately think of a memorable night in Ramea. The Lake Group of Companies frequently used our planes for access to their various fishing enterprises along the southern coast. Their main processing plants were situated in Burgeo and the island settlement of Ramea. Spencer Lake's wife, Margaret, was the daughter of Marie Penny who had firmly established herself as the Queen of the south coast fishery, with a fleet of fishing boats, a number of general stores, numerous fish plants and a distribution center in Boston. After Marie's passing, Spencer and Margaret moved their main office from Burgeo to Ramea and they took residence in the big Victorian house called Four Winds. On a Sunday afternoon, after delivering Mr. Steve Neary, a local politician, the thickening fog prevented my return to Pasadena. Spencer Lake insisted that I stay overnight at his house.

After I secured the aircraft, Mr. Lake took me up the road to their gracious hilltop house and showed me to a small, well-appointed bedroom on the lower floor that had an outside entrance. He invited me to dinner around seven: "Come up early and we'll have a cocktail." I thanked him and said that I would rather decline since my flying suit was somewhat soiled and not presentable attire: "I'll just go over to the local restaurant for a bite."

Spencer insisted: "You're just fine. We all know you're a grounded pilot, so don't fret about your clothes."

Upon entering their prestigious reception room and seeing the guests, I was utterly embarrassed, but it was too late to withdraw. Before me, all in formal attire was a gathering of the coastal elite: Spencer's brother, the mayor, nephew Kevin Smart, the local doctor, the fish plant manager, Mr. Neary, the local minister, and all their wives. They greeted me warmly, handed me a glass of wine, and we stood around the room exchanging pleasantries for about half an hour. These wealthy merchants seemed superbly happy in their outport fiefdom. Shortly, Mrs. Lake announced the serving of the meal in the adjoining room.

The long mahogany dining table was covered with white embroidered linen. It was graced with a sparkling array of cutlery, bone china, crystal wine glasses, monogrammed napkins, and a fresh display of cut flowers. The walnut sideboard displayed an assortment of homemade bread, partridge berry tarts, a variety of French wine, and decanters of port, brandy and Madeira. Following the minister's solemn grace, where he asked God for plentiful fish, there was a clinking of glasses with a toast to the providers. Mrs. Lake, seated on the kitchen end of the long table, tinkled a small brass bell. Everyone's chatter stopped as two neatly dressed servants wheeled in a cart from the kitchen. The maids were attired in white starched blouses and pleated skirts. They had rosy cheeks and shy, bright eyes, and the heavy fabric they wore could not hide their youthful legs and attractive hips. They hastily served a smoked mackerel appetizer. It was a ceremonial, five course banquet that I endured in my scruffy attire. Each time the next course was needed, Mrs. Lake jingled her little bell and with that sound, the maids came rushing in to clear the used dishes and serve the next round. I was quite amused by the bell chimes and the quick service that always ensued. After returning home, I purchased various bells and tried ringing them at the table. None of them have ever worked! Some 25 years later, in 2001, my wife Nina and I visited Ramea. The

Lakes were gone, but their aged home was still prominent in the town. It had been converted to a Bed and Breakfast. Although we found it clean and comfortable, the old aristocratic charm and social grace was missing, and so was the little bell.

****

Bruce Page was unexpected when he dropped in at my wilderness camp on the Buchans Plateau with one of our Hughes Helicopters. "You're wanted down at the Star Lake Camp. Apparently they killed a big caribou and need it measured," he said.

It was mid-October and I had set up a tent on the barrens to spend a solitary week photographing caribou on their migration route. Bruce joined me for a morning coffee before we took off for the 40 kilometer flight. Prince Abdorreza Pahlavi (the Shah of Iran's brother) was on a big game hunt, looking for trophy antlers. The Newfoundland government had provided him with a complementary license and had flown him to the remote outfitting camp in one of their forestry helicopters.

The tall, middle-aged man shook my hand as I disembarked from the helicopter. "Hopefully you will confirm my caribou as a record specimen," he said. "I understand you are an official measurer of the Boone and Crocket Club." The gentleman had procured a nice set of antlers but after carefully recording the eighteen different measurements, it came up a bit short of the minimum score for official recognition. I told him the antlers were much above average and he should be proud to have them displayed in a place of honour.

"Well," he said. "I came a long way to collect a world record and this will not do. Please arrange another permit and perhaps you would guide me on my next attempt. With your helicopter it should be quite easy to locate a larger stag."

I stayed at the camp and during lunch I tried to explain that one licence is all that is allowed and that hunting from aircraft is contrary to all regulations. It was difficult for him to accept these backward Canadian rules. The man was no ordinary tourist. He had flown to St. John's by private jetliner from Tehran, a group of Iranian security officials had inspected the camp and its staff prior to his arrival, sealed water jugs had been shipped from Iran, and the cook had strict instructions to use the imported water for all his cooking needs.

Although disappointed with my inability to skirt the rules, he seemed quite down to earth in other ways. During our conversation, it became obvious that he was not an amateur hunter and he showed a keen interest in Canadian wildlife. Apparently, he had acquired 260 varieties of big game around the world, with over 400 record class specimens. The guides said he was an excellent hunter and fun to be with. On my departure, I wished him success in obtaining a nice moose and told him that it would be my pleasure to come back and measure his next trophy.

****

Lee Wulff was held in high esteem throughout Newfoundland. After honing his fly fishing skills in Alaska, he moved to Newfoundland in the early 1950s in pursuit of the Atlantic salmon. With his small floatplane, he established some rustic camps in the back country and encouraged American sportsmen to come to these virgin waters and participate in the best fly-fishing in North America. Lee and his wife were very successful in becoming the first outfitters to attract tourists to this eastern island paradise.

The Newfoundland government contracted Lee to produce promotional movies on salmon fishing, moose hunting and tuna fishing. He and his wife gave exhibitions on fly casting and Lee published a number of informative books on the art of salmon fishing. By 1964, when I met him, he had established himself as the ultimate king of salmon fishing and fly casting. Our introduction was quite unusual.

Sitting in my office on a windy August afternoon, I watched a small Piper Cub floatplane make a landing approach in front of our sea plane base. We had terminated flight operations owing to the three foot waves on Deer Lake. Just as the little Piper touched the cresting waves, the pilot applied full power and climbed away. Our curiosity aroused, some of the staff went outside with me to see where the overshooting plane was headed. The pilot made another circle and then let the plane settle in the nasty water some 600 feet beyond our docks. As the craft bounced off the first big wave, a gust caught the left wing, lifting it high in the air. The momentary loss of control dipped the right wingtip in the frothy water and a slow inverted roll resulted.

Knowing that the pilot was now upside down and under the water, I ran to the shore, grabbing Eddie Oake on the way. We jumped into our 16 foot boat, started the outboard and headed to the overturned craft. By the time we reached the scene, the pilot had managed to evacuate the cabin and was hanging on to the inverted floats. Eddie manoeuvred the boat alongside and I dragged the soggy man over the coaming. He spit water as he shook my hand: "I'm sure glad to meet you, I'm Lee Wulff." We put a line on his lurching machine and slowly towed it to the sandy beach by our dock. Lee came to the office, where we gave him hot coffee and dry clothing. Our maintenance crew, who had experience with overturned floatplanes, soon had his machine flipped over and were examining the minor damage. Lee engaged our crew to repair his machine. The next morning I flew him back to his base in Portland Creek. It was very gratifying to develop a friendly relationship with such a famous outdoorsman, and aviation minded sportsman. Thereafter, we remained good friends.

In 1991, when he was age 86, Lee was obtaining a check ride in the same plane to reinstate his pilot's licence when he slumped over the controls on the landing approach. The instructor landed the plane with great difficulty and discovered that Lee had suffered a fatal heart attack! In 1996, Lee's son flew the plane from Albany, New York to our fishing lodge on the Main River. He came to visit his father's historical old cabin that we had preserved in fond memory of a great outdoorsman.

During lunch at our lodge, we talked of his father's innovative fishing techniques, his great success as a film maker, artist, and author. Lee had continually struggled to protect the salmon, and was vice president of the Atlantic Salmon Federation at the time of his death. His son was intrigued by the story of the watery rescue of his father some thirty years before.

****

Flying introduced me to many corporate officials and managers. For thirty years I was closely associated with the Johns Manville company in supplying their air travel needs throughout Newfoundland. Many of these associations turned into lasting friendships. Tom Stephens was their CEO in the 1980s and 1990s. Aside from his business travels, he was an avid sportsman. We shared many interesting flights.

Tom held the reins of Manville during the difficult times when the asbestos health risks threatened their future. In 1982, the company filed for protection under Chapter 11 of the U.S. Bankruptcy Code. Through innovative leadership, Tom met the challenge head on, shiufting the company focus and selling non-core businesses. Many say that he was instrumental in successfully bringing the company through that difficult period.

Tom projected a calm air of proficiency, always devoid of arrogance. I had the pleasure of hunting and fishing with Tom in Newfoundland, Ontario, Colorado, Louisiana, Arkansas and Wyoming. He was as proficient at these outdoor sports as he was in the boardroom. After leaving Manville, Tom became CEO of McMillan Bloedell, and later head of Boise Cascade. Recent retirement finds him settled in the Colorado foothills with his wife, shotgun, horses, and dogs. He remains active as a board member of five major corporations. Over the years, I gained a very considerable respect for the quiet, effective way that he handled himself both in business and pleasure.

Chapter 19 DeHavilland Heron

The DeHavilland Heron - our four-engine delight

One of our engines had to be shut down! Rick listened to me on the intercom from the copilot seat: "Let's just pull the throttle back to idle. I think we can safely continue the flight without scaring our passengers too much. What are your thoughts?"

The aircraft had four Gypsy Queen engines but the inboard starboard motor had suddenly lost most of its oil pressure. We were nearing the completion of a ten hour ice patrol for senior government officials with the Department of Fisheries and Oceans. They had chartered our Heron aircraft out of Gander to familiarize themselves with the arctic ice forming off the coast of Labrador and the suitability of this particular aircraft for the upcoming job. It was a very important mission for our company in that we were on the brink of landing a formidable contract that would be renewed each spring during the seal hunting season. Losing an engine at this time would no doubt jeopardize the contract.

When the problem occurred we were over 100 kilometers from the coast, over the Labrador Sea. Fortunately the weather was excellent, although we were three hours away from Gander and about the same to Goose Bay. Our load at the time was light since we had only five passengers and had already consumed over half of our fuel.

"We should be OK on three although that one may seize up," Rick responded. "I'll go back and pour them some coffee to distract their attention while you ease the power off."

With most multi-engine aircraft an engine can be shut down and the propeller put into "feather mode," which stops the propeller rotation to reduce the drag. The Gypsy power plants did not have this feature. When the engine was shut down in flight the prop would keep wind milling at a slow RPM.

The DeHavilland Heron had been owned by the Department of Transport in Moncton, New Brunswick. It was used to conduct instrument landing approach calibrations at airports throughout their Atlantic Region. In 1965, DOT upgraded to a more modern aircraft and we purchased CF-EYX from Crown Assets at an attractive price. The aircraft was manufactured in England and therefore parts were difficult and expensive to obtain. As a result, the ministry had a considerable inventory of spare parts which we also acquired as part of the purchase arrangement. Rick and I knew that the faulty engine could be replaced or repaired fairly quickly once we got it back to our hangar in Deer Lake.

Our passengers did not notice the difference in sound as that propeller unwound, nor did they realize that we were now only using three engines. There was a large oil streak emanating from the lower cowling but it could only be seen from the cockpit.

After another hour of manoeuvring over the frothy ice formations, Tom Curran stuck his head in the front office and advised that we could end the survey and head back to Gander: "Everyone seems very satisfied with the flight."

Rick and I breathed a cautious sigh of relief as I slowly turned south to a heading of 195 degrees. The passengers were advised that it would be about two hours and twenty minutes to arrival. Although power for climbing was lacking, I eventually struggled up to 6,000 feet. If we had further trouble we could divert to the strip at St. Anthony, which we would pass by on our direct route to Gander.

The three hour flight was uneventful until approaching the Gander Control Zone south of Twillingate. As Rick called the tower with our estimated time of arrival, out of habit I checked the brakes for landing. There was absolutely no pressure on the left side! This aircraft had a most unusual braking arrangement in that it was fitted with air brakes rather than the conventional hydraulic system. We'd had this hitch before, but on this important trip it was most frustrating.

There would be no problem having a safe landing if the wind was parallel to the active runway. And the Gander runways were ample length for stopping without brakes. My concern was whether I could steer the aircraft to the terminal without the passengers knowing that we had a brake failure. Normally we would have requested a tow truck. Both faulty engine and brake failure on this one "showpiece" trip would certainly imperil our contract.

Rick shut down the other inboard engine on touchdown in order to slow our speed and assist me with turning. With both props stopped on the inner motors, it would be less noticeable to the passengers. We hoped that they would think of this as normal procedure for taxiing.

Luckily the wind was in our favour as the tires kissed the runway. With plenty of room ahead, I carefully walked the rudder pedals to keep on the center line. After decelerating to a walking pace, differential power was used to bring her around in a wide arc in clearing the active runway. I awkwardly manoeuvred across the field to the terminal parking area using alternate power on the two outboard engines. As they disembarked, the officials, including Mr. Smith, the regional director, shook our hands and thanked us for a very enjoyable flight.

"You have a nice machine here and it appears to be well suited for the job: good visibility, comfortable seating, excellent fuel range and quite quiet. Tom and his crew need another overflight tomorrow. takeoff at seven to the same area. You will probably be doing three or four flights each week for the next two months," Smith said, and with that they disappeared into the terminal.

We could have told them that a trip tomorrow would be impossible due to scheduled maintenance, but we certainly didn't want them to revert to chartering EPA's DC-3. It had taken us two years of lobbying and much effort to gain this spring contract. As well, the ten hours for tomorrow's effort would provide much needed revenue.

Rick called Eddie Oake for assistance and he was soon on the three hour drive to Gander with a spare engine, brake assembly, and tools. The boys worked all night in the rented hangar while I ashamedly took ten hours bed time at the hotel. While the repairs were not particularly complex, it was tedious and time consuming for two men. At 6:15 the next morning the two weary mechanics joined me for a successful test flight. We departed on time with the survey officials, making a slight diversion to Deer Lake, where I dropped Rick off and picked up Pierre Meagher as a spare pilot.

The old Heron was a delight to fly. It was a very stable platform. In bad weather you could trim it to the glide path descent on an instrument approach without barely touching the controls until flareout. On the long over ice patrols we had a large, long range fuel tank that was fitted in the cargo compartment. This provided up to eighteen hours of cruise flight. On these lengthy trips we carried a chesterfield in the cabin so that the pilots could alternate with rest periods.

During the 1960s and early 1970s, a large number of foreign and Canadian ships were involved in the spring seal hunt off the Labrador coast. Other groups opposing the hunt were trying to interfere with the program. Using our services, Canadian fishery officers closely scrutinized the movement of both factions. They also monitored the smaller shore boats, the seal population, ice movements and iceberg locations. It was very interesting work and the supervising officer of the contract, Tom Curran, made the forays even more enjoyable.

Tom was a congenial fellow with a formidable stature. His 6'6" frame was as straight and blocky as that of a trim linebacker.

He spent his younger years as a forestry worker. After returning from WW2 with his Scottish bride, he joined the fisheries department in St. John's. After many years of conservation work on fishery patrol vessels he became renowned for his in-depth knowledge of Newfoundland seal herds. Not only was he highly regarded in his department, but the sealing industry had great respect for his remarkable understanding, enthusiasm, and fairness.

In 1964, prior to acquiring the Heron aircraft, we had conducted some ice patrols using an Aero Commander 560E. Tom would squeeze his large frame into the copilot seat in order to direct the surveys. In the beginning we needed his directions since we were totally unfamiliar with the "front" sealing area off the Labrador coast.

"Head for the Square Islands and then go northeast. We should find whelping ice forty or so kilometers from shore," he recommended.

In early March, the female harp seals are choosy in selecting a particular type of ice formation for giving birth to their pups. Since the young whitecoats cannot swim for a few weeks, the nursing mother and her pup remain on the chosen pan for nearly a month, drifting southward in the wind and current. Our first flights involved locating these particular ice fields that soon would be dotted with thousands of whelping seals. Noisy and gregarious, the seal nursery is quite a magnificent sight. These colonies consist of hundreds of thousands of densely crowded animals that blacken the ruptured ice pans in splotches of thirty square kilometers or more. Normally, the band of drift ice extended over 100 hundred kilometers from the Labrador shore. Further to the east, the ice coverage thinned and became more broken, eventually giving way to open ocean and waves of slob. In this Labrador current, icebergs of various sizes are embedded in the drift as they make their way from Greenland and Baffin Bay.

It was not unusual to encounter poor visibility on these surveillance flights. Low cloud and snow showers were prevalent in the moist, cold sea air. Such conditions required flying at low altitudes over the ice in order to plot the seals' and the ships' positions. Using instrument capable wheel-configured aircraft, we were never too concerned with bad weather in that we could always pull up and proceed to an airport under "Instrument Flight Regulations. "We always stayed in radio contact with a shore station to be sure that either Goose Bay or Gander airports were available for a diversion. Of course, there were no navigational aids in that remote region so we kept careful speed and distance plots of our position using a triangulation method. The area was too far north for Loran signal and "ground positioning systems" (GPS) were not yet in use.

With all the turning and circling, it was astounding how Tom Curran's sixth sense made him continually aware of our approximate position. He seemed to use his knowledge of the ice appearance to judge our distance offshore. His mental calculations were seldom in error.

On one occasion we had difficulty locating the herd. The early March storms (Sheila's Brush)* had grounded us for a few days. After forty-five minutes of searching off Grady Island, we could not find the herd.

"See those ravens over the ice? Follow their direction. Go where they're to," Tom insisted. It was out of the ordinary to see these land birds flying toward the open Atlantic some 60 kilometers from shore! "They always know when there's fresh afterbirth and somehow they know where to find it." He was right again. The ravens led us directly to the whelping seals. To me, this was surely an unusual but observable fact of nature.

Other interesting phenomena were often observed on these flights. Occasionally we would fly toward Greenland for 300 kilometers to plot iceberg movement. In April of 1969 we were on such a junket. A gale force wind had been blowing from the northeast for five days. As we approached the extremity of the ice coverage, we observed a large heaving motion in the loosening ice. Further out the waving mass became higher and soon we were over the open sea. The sight was unbelievable. Although the wind had diminished significantly, the huge waves looked like something out of a science fiction movie! The foaming crests were at least 70 feet high and the trough between was a huge dark blue valley, some 300 feet wide. We were left breathless by the awesome sight.

"Let's get a picture of this. No one will believe us," Tom quietly muttered.

I slowly edged the plane down into the trough. It looked frightening but it was not dangerous. The waves were moving so it was necessary to keep a slight bank to stay in the deep valley. There was ample room since our wingspan was only 87 feet. But what a sight! On both sides of the aircraft there was a steep wall of angry, blue water towering above our wingtips and threatening to close the gap. It was a memorable experience, to say the least.

Aside from experiencing the stark, inhospitable beauty of the Labrador winter wilderness, these long flights brought many wonders into view. Often there were polar bears and killer whales searching for a meal along the ice edge. Icebergs, of many beautiful forms, march south in that Labrador Current to their demise in the warmer latitudes of the Continental Shelf, where they eventually melt away. They are treacherous, majestic islands, trudging through the cold northern waters. The sight of these floating pinnacles was of great interest to all on board. In the dazzling sunshine, their scalloped sides are translucent carvings that have been hassled by the unrelenting waves, resplendent in their contrast to the dark blue environment. Some are very expansive, yielding a flat surface that could be likened to a large suspended airfield. On some occasions I felt a fleeting urge to land on the frozen domain. Had we been using a skiplane, no doubt we would have had a stopover.

On the spring patrols, we often operated out of Goose Bay for a few days since it was somewhat closer to the sealing area than was Gander. Being inland 250 kilometers from the coast, this Labrador heartland has a subarctic climate. Blowing snow and minus 30C temperatures are not uncommon. We did not have our own hangar at Goose Bay and sometimes rental space was not available. This meant leaving the aircraft exposed to the elements.

The Heron -iced up in Goose Bay

To get ready for an early morning departure, our crews had to de-ice or remove snow from the wings by hand. On one very cold morning it was impossible to start number two engine and there were no Herman Nelson engine heaters available. Somehow, I had to find a way to get it going before my passengers arrived.

Knowing the aircraft's excellent performance with a light load and cold temperatures, I elected to try a takeoff on three engines prior to refueling. The control tower questioned my request for departure, seeing that one prop was inoperative. The Goose runways are over 10,000 feet long so there was lots of asphalt for a long run. The old bird gained speed sluggishly but finally lifted off. As my speed increased after takeoff, the paralytic propeller began to turn with the increasing air pressure on the blades. After reaching idle RPM, I switched on the magnetos and the dead engine coughed to life. By the time I returned for landing, all the engine temperatures were normal and the aircraft cabin was soothingly warm for my awaiting passengers. They thought I had done the short flight to enhance their comfort. Over the years the Heron was put to various uses. International charters were frequently made to the French Islands of St. Pierre and Miquelon, crews were transported between Deer Lake and St. Anthony during the construction of the new Grenfell Hospital, personnel and cargo flights were required to St. Albans during the construction of the Baie d'Espoir Hydro project, scheduleD services were provided from Stephenville to Sydney and Halifax during the Air Canada strike, freight and tourists were transported to Blanc Sablon, Quebec and a few lengthy trips were made to Montreal.

Shortly after taking delivery of the Heron in the mid-1960s, Air Canada was grounded by a company strike. We did not yet have any pilots with a Class One Instrument Flight License but we were anxious to start a schedule service to Halifax during the work stoppage. In order to maintain a valid instrument flight endorsement, a pilot must endure a proficiency flight check every twelve months, otherwise he must not fly an aircraft without visual reference to the ground. These tests are conducted by a licensing inspector from the Ministry of Transport. The flight consists of takeoff and landing procedures and various other manoeuvres with the pilot's outside view blocked by windscreen coverings. He must show that he can safely handle the aircraft by using only the panel instruments during emergency and approach procedures. Special emphasis is placed on performing abortive landings with one engine inoperative. Passing the rigid test allows him to conduct commercial instrument flight for another year. I had not bothered to renew my endorsement for six years as most of the flying in Newfoundland had been in single engine bush planes. Now an instrument ticket was urgently needed in order to conduct the schedule operations that were at hand.

Our old friend, Ernie Savard, the regional director of Air Services in Moncton, clearly understood our predicament and the need for our services to the mainland. He responded in his usual accommodating manner: "Tomorrow, on your first flight out of Stephenville, you will be doing a station stop at Sydney Airport. I will meet you there and give you a check ride before you proceed to Halifax."

Usually these check rides take about an hour in order to complete all the required procedures. Ernie knew that I had a lot of this type of experience in jet aircraft with the RCAF. He also realized that a group of passengers would be waiting for departure from Sydney in thirty minutes. After conducting a simulated blind takeoff with the Heron, Ernie asked me to do a few steep turns without visual reference through the hooded windscreen.

"OK, shoot me an ILS and cut one engine," he asked. We were required to do a blind approach and overshoot of the runway with unsymmetrical power. This was to demonstrate one's ability to handle the machine with offset thrust in bad weather.

Ten minutes later, after a procedure approach to the runway, we were nearing the threshold lights. "Make it a full stop," he said. "You can handle this stuff as though you've been practicing, and you have passengers waiting to go to Halifax."

So much for an instrument renewal! Pierre Meagher and I continued to make two return flights each day during the strike.

The winter of 1967 brought about unusual ice conditions along the south coast which prevented the supply boat from delivering fresh meats to St. Pierre. Jim Shanahan of Eastern Flying Service at Sydney, Nova Scotia asked if we would provide the Heron to fill the need. The cabin seats were removed to accommodate the large array of frozen meats and milk cartons. The small island of St. Pierre is fifty kilometers south of Newfoundland and would be a 1-1/2 hour flight across the ocean waters from Nova Scotia. Jim had arranged for a Mr. Moraze to be our cargo agent in St. Pierre.

Government House in St. Pierre & Miquelon

St. Pierre and Miquelon are French holdings, heavily subsidized by France. This territory, which was settled by the Basques in 1604, consists of two small 93 square mile islands. After many year of intermarriage with Newfoundlanders, the population of 6,000 is mostly bilingual. Their meager economy is based on fish exports and summer tourism. The French culture and the pompous European political style is still very much alive here. The Governor is appointed by France and he rules his nation with the traditional tendency toward Parisian bureaucracy and the strict application of local power. I learned of these facts upon my first cargo landing at the small airport. Three officious looking immigration officers were at the plane when I opened the cabin door. They were accompanied by two gendarmes. One of them spoke in broken English: "Bonjour Capitaine, may we have your manifest and your entry clearance forms, s'il vous plâit? Also your passport?"

I was taken by surprise since we had been previously operating a few charter flights into this community from Deer Lake without any hassle. The only paperwork I had was a note from Shanahan on which he had scribbled the name of the consignee! Before I could think of a reasonable response, a stout, well dressed elderly man stepped out of the terminal and addressed the officers. He spoke sternly to them in French and then turned to me with his hand outstretched:"You must be Captain Manion," he said. "I'm Henri Moraze. Don't be concerned, I will handle this."

A long discussion took place between Henri and the officials. Henri did most of the talking. The aircraft door was sealed with red tape marked "QUARANTINE." Henri beckoned me to his black Fiat car and soon we were seated in his office, which was located in the back of a large empty store on the waterfront.

"Do not be concerned, my friend. There is some red tape that needs to be carefully handled. The local government has some close connections with other aviation interests and they tend to make roadblocks for would-be intrusive competitors. Bringing in tourists on a charter is acceptable but they don't want your company to threaten their cartel." Henri explained that one must

224

have the right political key to operate freely in St. Pierre. "Since the service that you bring is greatly needed, but of a temporary nature, we will find a quick solution." Henri then checked me in to the Ile de France Hotel.

After an enjoyable lunch in the quite empty auberge, Henri reappeared to advise me of a meeting with the Governor which he had set up for 3 p.m.

"To expedite the necessary documents you must personally meet with "the Préfecteur (Governor)," he said. "He has all the information so it will only be a formality. I have apologized in advance regarding your unsuitable apparel for this high level meeting and those circumstances have been accepted."

Government House was quite modest from the exterior courtyard. Two armed guards escorted me through the secured doors and led me through the foyer and down a marble floored hallway to an elaborate vestibule. The mahogany walls were artfully adorned with large portraits of the French nobility. At precisely 3 p.m. a well dressed lady gave me a generous curtsey and waved me toward the adjoining room. It looked like a wing of the Louvre with all the ornate statues and paintings. The lady bowed and left the room, leaving me standing in front of an elevated, throne-like rosewood chair embellished with a golden coat of arms.

In my smudged flight pants and well-worn bomber jacket, I was completely humbled by the ostentatious surroundings. His Excellency gave a gracious hand gesture as I bowed slightly, and not knowing how to respond, I addressed him as "Your Lordship."

His speech was clear and articulate: "I understand, Captain, that you are a senior director of your company as well as a pilot. Your company is desirous of importing certain products to my country by air on a short term basis. Your services will be of an irregular nature as opposed to being on a schedule. You have contracted a resident agent in Monsieur Moraze to conduct all your business affairs in St. Pierre. Do I have the details correct?"

"Yes Sir, that seems to sum it up," I responded, sizing him up as he rose from his throne. He was probably in his early sixties, dressed in an immaculate grey suit and with a purple stole on his narrow shoulders. His grayish sideburns added to his distinguished air.

"Please come to the desk and provide me with your signature," he said. "I'm sure you understand that we must maintain control of our boundaries and all internal movements therein. This document will satisfy your convention. I am pleased that we've met."

In turn, we both signed the certificate with a regal nibbed pen. Not knowing what else to say and unsure of the proper etiquette for departure, I awkwardly folded the official paper, thanked him, and joyfully left the drawing room. The two official gendarmes were waiting to usher me out of the building to the courtyard. I thought, "Holy shit. What will I get into next?"

During the next two weeks, I had the pleasure of being an overnight guest in Mr. Moraze's home and learned of his colourful history and local prominence. Henri was in his early seventies, with mild blue eyes that flickered a flame of resolution and charm. He was gentle but fierce in action, loved by most, and feared by some. His unpretentious home was graced with opulent antique furnishings staged in a cozy European atmosphere. His wife was quite French, in a modest, motherly way. After dinner Henri and I would retire to his snug den to enjoy more of his vintage red wine. Reclining in the soft leather chairs, we talked of the local event which confirmed my thoughts about EPA being part of the Governor's alliance. As our friendship grew, he gradually opened up about his checkered past. With rascal eyes, he eventually told stories about his exciting earlier life. Henri hesitated between sentences to sip his wine, holding it momentarily beneath his tongue seemed to help his recollections.

From 1920 to 1933, the prohibition law in the United States made it illegal to manufacture, transport or sell alcohol. The result was that risk-taking entrepreneurs found a highly rewarding business in smuggling booze into the States. At St. Pierre, alcohol could be easily and cheaply imported from France or the French islands in the Caribbean. Henri became heavily involved as a middleman in the lucrative trade. Large, windowless warehouses were built on his waterfront land and huge quantities of liquor were stored there. Contacts were made with certain groups in New England and ocean rendezvous exchanges were arranged. High speed boats were used to deliver the liquor to various U.S. ports.

Henri explained: "We were just wholesalers. Businessmen selling a product. Not criminals. The bootleggers were the bad guys who were breaking the laws of entry. Many of them were mob members who controlled the U.S. whiskey distribution. They were the gangsters. It became a big business here and added zest to the local economy. Our boats stayed in international waters where the American law did not apply."

It became a game to have faster boats than the Coast Guard: "Al Capone was one of our biggest customers and he had the best boats available. He negotiated many deals and threw some big parties here at Le Select Hotel."

Capone, at the age of 26, dominated the U.S. whiskey trade. He had 1,000 employees with a payroll in excess of $300,000. I learned that Henri's warehouses had loaded many cargo vessels destined for the States. Apparently the ships' manifests did not always list the entire contents of some containers! "Prohibition ended in1929 but by that time we had become financially secure and had gained some authority in local circles," said Henri.

Yes, I thought, Mr. Moraze does have considerable influence in these French islands, even after 35 years. It would have been a delight to have met him in his younger days. I have no doubt that this vibrant man had quietly dominated the scene in St. Pierre and Miquelon for many years. And had he been such a pioneer in the United States, his dramatic life would probably have been glamorized by a movie or novel.

****

Sable Island is a long, curved strip of exposed sandbar along the western edge of the Gulf Stream. It lies, as a chain of sand dunes, in the open ocean about 280 kilometers southeast of Halifax, Nova Scotia. Over centuries it has been a menace to ship navigation and is the scene of numerous wrecks, the "Graveyard of the Atlantic." A failed attempt was made to establish a French colony there in 1598. It was formerly 65 kilometers long by two kilometers wide, but it is now about 35 kilometers long and 1-1/2 kilometers wide. It is gradually sinking and washing away. The treeless land is comprised of grassy sand dunes which rise to a height of about 80 feet on the northwest side. The grassy hills provide food for the wild ponies that have survived since they were shipwrecked there 300 years ago. The lower south shore is an extensive beach running the entire length of the island and containing an enclosed lagoon.

In 1967, we were asked if there was any way that sand samples could be airlifted to Halifax. A consortium of oil companies was trying to analyze the sand for prospects of oil or gas recovery. Heavy lift helicopters were not available in the region at that time. It sounded like an exciting challenge worthy of further investigation.

Pierre flew our Grumman Widgeon amphibian to the site. After careful scrutiny, he set the machine down successfully on the inland lagoon. We investigated the sandy coastal shore area with a view to using it for wheel equipped aircraft. We also took the knowledgeable advice of the resident lighthouse keepers.

A raised Coast Guard lighthouse and staff house was on the western end of the spit. The seven members of the maintenance crew were thrilled to find that some unusual activity was about to happen on their isolated terrain. Fixed wing, wheel aircraft had never before landed on the island. Their report was encouraging. During north or easterly winds, the sea slackened, draining the wetness from the sand beach to create a hard compact surface. "Don't attempt a landing on the sand while the wind is from the south or southwest, fer she becomes a sloppy mess," they warned.

The next day, accompanied by Pierre in the Widgeon, I flew the larger Heron out for a trial run. After a few touch-and-go landings I found the beach conditions were quite reasonable for the airlift. On some days I believe you could have safely landed a 737 jetliner. We finished lifting the sandbags from Sable during the next two weeks, being careful to forego the operation when southerly winds prevailed. The Widgeon utilized the beach as well, since larger loads could be handled using wheels instead of the lagoon. Only on one occasion did I get the big airplane mired in the soft sand. But with the help of the local men, their tractor, lots of power, and some plywood, we were able to extract the machine without any damage. Our customers were happy and Pierre and I were in high spirits upon completion of this unusual contract. To my knowledge, no other fixed wing aircraft have landed on the Sable sand, either before or after our escapade. Large helicopters are now under contract for transporting the work crews to and from the island.

Thirty years later, the Sable Island area became a major producer of natural gas, which is transported through pipelines over the ocean floor to Nova Scotia. In 1997, a $1 billion pipeline project was announced that would transport 550 McF of gas from Sable Island to Quebec, some 1,125 kilometers away. Apparently the sand samples we carried ashore in 1967 contained optimistic clues that encouraged further exploration, drilling and eventual production.

****

Some 1,300 kilometers north of Pasadena, snowfed streams flow to the ocean through the steep rocky walls of Saglek Fiord. The flow stops for eight months of the year when all exposed water is frozen. On the flat stretch of barren coast, at the base of a 600 meter cliff, an aircraft landing strip slopes towards the ocean. This desolate runway was constructed in 1953 as a resupply strip for a USAF radar station, forming a link in the Distant Early Warning system (DEW Line).

By 1965, the major oil companies were interested in test drilling the sea floor off the coast of northern Labrador. They utilized Saglek as their staging base. Large helicopters, based in Saglek, shuttled the drilling crews to and from the offshore drill ship. Eastcan was an international company that supplied specialized teams from Europe who travelled back and forth to Gander by Air Canada. Our company was contracted to provide transportation between Gander Airport and Saglek.

We began the airlift using our DeHavilland Heron. Saglek was not only desolate, but a very demanding destination. Weather forecasting was unreliable, the mountainous region was not conducive to bad weather approach procedures, the nearest alternate airport was hundreds of kilometers away at Goose Bay, heavy fuel loads were necessary, and the high terrain necessitated taking off downhill on the 4,700 foot runway toward the sea, and with a tail wind component!

The old Heron was not ideal for that job. With a heavy load, the end of the runway came at us quite quickly! Eventually, we replaced the Heron with two Queen Air B-80 aircraft on the contract. They fit the job nicely, having sprightlier takeoff performance, and a brisker climb through the mountainous fiords.

****

Pierre quickly found their frequency: "Wilmington Tower, this is Charlie Fox. Echo. Yankee. X-ray. We are twenty minutes north. Have a small problem and diverting to your field."

"This is Wilmington Tower, we acknowledge your position. Are you declaring an emergency?"

In response, Pierre advised that we had some power loss: "It should not be an emergency, providing you can approve a straight-in approach."

In 1971, I had arranged the sale of our old Heron aircraft. By that time we had used most of our parts inventory and the remaining engines were reaching their overhaul life. The aircraft was in need of interior refurbishing, new exterior paint was overdue and we were acquiring two Beechcraft B-80 planes as an upgrade. The sale to Mr. Desmond Munford was contingent upon us delivering the aircraft to Fort Lauderdale, Florida, in an airworthy state and it included all of our spare parts and the paint that we had purchased. There was very little market for this type aircraft so we were elated to find a buyer who did not quibble about our selling price.

We knew the engines were quite tired, so we should have groundshipped all the crates of miscellaneous parts, three expired engines, propellers, tires, and the two 45-gallon drums of paint and paint remover. That was our first mistake.

"I think we can fit all that stuff in the aircraft," I told Pierre. "We'll keep our fuel load to minimum and save a few thousand dollars in shipping costs."

Pierre shrugged his shoulders in agreement with my suggestion. On June 10, we departed from Deer Lake Airport with a heavily overloaded aircraft. After a fuel stop in Moncton we crossed the Canadian border to land in Houlton, Maine for an overnight stay.

Realizing the cool morning temperatures would provide less strain on the engines during takeoff, we lined up for departure before sunrise on the 5,000 foot runway. There was no wind to help the liftoff. The machine was sluggish, using most of the runway. and then climbing listlessly over the trees. The cool morning air had somewhat awakened the spirit of the Gypsy Queens. Both Pierre and I now realized that we were extremely overloaded and two of our engines were not developing normal power. However, the weather was good so we reduced the throttles for a cruise climb,1,100 kilometers later we landed at Atlantic City for lunch and refueling. The afternoon temperature was 30C. We knew the old bird would strain on takeoff in this high temperature and our assumptions were correct. To avoid another stressful departure enroute, we had taken on extra fuel to proceed directly to Fort Lauderdale. There had been some discussion about ground shipping our cargo from there to Florida but it was only a thought. That was our next mistake.

Fortunately, the runway was long and there were no high obstructions after departure. The heat and humidity, and the big overload were all factors working against us as the machine clawed for each foot of altitude. The engines had been at takeoff power for ten minutes with their temperatures rapidly climbing above the red line. How much more abuse could they take? I reduced the throttles to a climb setting and could almost hear a sigh of relief from the Gypsy Queens. Pierre and I sat silent, listening intently to the beat of the engines and staring at the temperature gauges in hope of reprieve.

Finally we reached cruising altitude and watched as Delaware and Virginia slipped by. Except for our growing concern about overheating, the clear day provided a delightful view of the New England coast.

About midway to our Fort Lauderdale destination the number two engine had to be shut down because of decreasing oil pressure. With the cooperating weather, we considered our options: proceed on to Lauderdale on three engines, as our weight would decrease with the fuel burn, or stop at the nearest airport. Although the plane would maintain altitude, there was little extra power available should it be required. We elected to continue. If we stopped, another takeoff would be out of the question.

Eighty kilometers north of Wilmington, North Carolina, our number four engine began a serious vibration as though some invisible hand had reached out to shake out her life. We both stared with uneasy eyes at the rapid rise in the associated cylinder head temperature.

"Better give Wilmington a call. We're gonna be tourists," I said to Pierre.

As I swung toward the nearest airport we were starting to sink in a gradual descent. With the loss of the second engine, the aircraft could not hold its height and our airspeed dropped dramatically. The only way to keep a safe flying speed was to lower the nose. The power remaining was only sufficient to control the flight on its way to eventual contact with the ground! A sickly, pulsating wobble shook the Heron as the second set of propeller blades slowed their windmilling rotation. There was a drastic finality about the sight of two throttle levers pushed forward against the stops, with the old engines snarling in defiance at the ground with harsh,blaring crackles of their exhausts.We precariously edged closer to the airport, dragging our two dead engines.

Although somewhat demanding, it was not difficult to reach the runway utilizing a straight-in approach. The solid ground felt good to us and no doubt our two good engines exhaled a sigh of liberation as I pulled back the throttles from their strenuous position.

Wilmington offered a wide selection of maintenance facilities, but none of the mechanics were at all familiar with our British engines. At the local motel, a few cold drinks brought us a light hearted giddiness that greatly contrasted with the tension of our recent flight. After discussing the aircraft sale dilemma, it was decided that Pierre should return to Newfoundland and that Eddie Oake be immediately dispatched, with his tool box and know how. Eddie arrived by commercial flight the next day.

For the next two days and nights, he toiled in the heat to remove cylinder assemblies and various other components from our load of time expired parts. I wasn't much help mechanically but I tried to keep his spirits in an optimistic mode.

Finally, the revitalized engines sprang to life with a vibrant display of power. After a number of adjustments and further ground testing, Eddie advised against an air test as it would place undue strain on the old motors. "She should be OK for one more takeoff and your three hour flight to Fort Lauderdale," he said. I could see he was hoping to go home but with the likely prospect of further problems, I suggested he continue with me on the delivery.

Our last leg was uneventful until we joined the busy circuit at the Lauderdale airport. The old bird seemed to taunt us as though rebelling against the change in ownership. We discovered that the air system in both brake assemblies was zero! It was not pleasant to picture the buyer watching us being towed to the parking ramp, since he had insisted on receiving an airworthy aircraft. Having been down a similar road before, I was able to land and slowly taxi the plane to the assigned ramp using differential power on the outboard props for manoeuvring. Sounding calmer than I probably was, I advised the tower that we had cleared the active runway. The heavy airport traffic was more of a hazard than it had been during my brake failure in Gander.

Mr. Munford met us on the ramp: "Shall we do the acceptance flight now or would you prefer to wait til tomorrow?"

Straightforwardly, we advised him that we needed some overdue rest, but he insisted that we join him for dinner. During a great feast of ribs at Pier 66, we learned that Desmond was purchasing two other similar aircraft and that they would all be completely overhauled, painted, and fitted with new turboprop engines. He had arranged a resale to a small airline in Columbia that would use the aircraft on scheduled passenger services.

I was nearing the end of my rope: "Desmond, we are anxious to get home. Surely you don't need another flight to prove this aircraft is flyable? We have just completed a more than 4,000 kilometer flight in an overloaded condition. What more can you ask? Another flight is just bullshit. And you plan for a complete overhaul in any event."

He thought intensely for a moment before responding: "Yes, you are right. Perhaps I've been unreasonable." My smile of relief was difficult to hide as I accepted his certified cheque.

Leaving the aircraft behind was somewhat traumatic. I knew it would be a sad day when I couldn't hear the usual backfires on start up, or enjoy the hypnotic rhythm of the four synchronized Gypsy engines on a dark cloudy night. A pilot often develops a profound relationship with an aeroplane that has seen him through some difficult passages over the years. It was like leaving an old friend who, in spite of some disturbing moments, has been faithful to the end. I'm pleased to have been part of that Heron era.

DeHavilland Heron on Sable Island beach (1967)

Saglek Airport -Northern Labrador

Grumman Widgeon on Sable Island

Chapter 20 A Stolen Camp

Arctic Char at my Tesuiyak fishing camp

In 1967, I decided to expand my fly-in fishing business, hoping to attract American tourists to northern Labrador for arctic char. After a lot of scouting we finally decided on the Tesuiyak River, located about 100 kilometers north of Nain, the most northerly settlement in Labrador. Many northern bands of aboriginals from remote settlements had been relocated there by the government in 1959 so that they could be provided with schools, medical facilities and other services. The Tesuiyak River flowed from a large lake surrounded by mountains and drained into the Labrador Sea. It was a beautiful, pristine site, and after three years of extensive investigation we knew it would produce the best char fishing in Labrador. To haul in nine or ten char every day averaging seven pounds was normal. Many fish over eighteen pounds were released and the largest, almost beating the world record, weighed in at 28 pounds, 2 ounces. This remote site was fabulous for its large fish and spectacular scenery.

The far flung acreage was all Crown land and we were able to get a lease from the Newfoundland and Labrador Ministry of Resources without any trouble. The lumber and building supplies were shipped by coastal boat from Lewisporte to Nain. A Beaver floatplane was used to bring in a workcrew from Pasadena and materials from Nain. When I filled out the papers for the lease I chose the specific site hurriedly, picking a likely looking cove near the inflow of the river. Later, on closer inspection, we realized the site was mostly bog. When it came time to start actual construction, I moved the location of the cabin about two kilometers away to a preferable area near the lake outflow. The new site was beside a white sand beach surrounded by spruce trees with a dramatic view of the lake and the lofty Torngat Mountains. It was not unusual to change locations slightly after signing a Crown lease and there was usually little difficult. But the government did have to be informed by letter of the change. I was busy with other things and forgot this formality. Two years later my mistake came back to haunt me.

My partner, Rick Richard, and I had been having nasty disagreements about the way the business was being run and I was in the process of buying him out. The procedure became quite ugly, and our long friendship dissolved. Rick had never shown much interest in the tourist business, and was not, in my opinion, pulling his weight in the flying operation. After operating the Tesuiyak Camp for the first season, I found out that Roland Reed, an American from Maine who was also interested in the fly-in fishing business, had contrived to upset my plans. I discovered that Rick Richard was in cahoots with Reed. I knew Rick was a good friend of Bill Callahan, Minister of Natural Resources, and since he was also a buddy of Roland Reed, it seemed likely to me there was skullduggery afoot. They filled out lease application forms for the exact acreage where I had constructed my camp. The minister, after collaboration, issued the lease to Reed. Needless to say, I was incensed. As far as I was concerned, he was squatting on my land and stealing my camp.

I contacted the Ministry and explained the situation. But they said nothing could be done because I hadn't followed the regulations, and I couldn't change the lease because the land was now legally in Mr. Reed's possession. It had taken much effort and a large investment to get the camp built in that remote wilderness, and the more I thought about it the angrier I got. When I learned the next spring that Reed had flown in some American tourists and was putting them up at the lodge I had built, I got angrier still.

I had to face the fact that there wasn't much I could do on the Tesuiyak lease and decided to get out of the char fishing business altogether. I had heard that a friend from Goose Bay, Peter Pour, was planning to build a fishing camp further north on the Umiakovik River. I told him I could save him a lot of money in construction costs by disassembling my camp and shipping the whole thing to his site for reassembly. It was a lot cheaper than flying everything in from Newfoundland or Nain. I came up with a price that we both considered fair. All I had to do was get the cabin to his site.

I explained my moving arrangement to Glenn Goobie, a pilot with our company. Glen wasn't easily perturbed by difficult or unusual situations and found my plan quite captivating. We rounded up three of the roughest and toughest scoundrels I could find in Pasadena to serve as the workcrew. I explained the task at hand, telling them there could be some serious trouble so if they weren't up to it they should just let me know now. "This cabin must be taken down and moved no matter what

Captain Glenn Goobie

resistance you encounter from Reed," I told them. They were more amused than concerned and raring to go. Just in case, they packed a rifle onto the Otter floatplane along with some axes in case the relocation didn't go off as smoothly as hoped. We were expecting real trouble since we knew Roland Reed was apparently at the cabin with some fishing customers from Maine.

It was a beautiful day when the Otter landed after a five hour flight north from Pasadena. There was no one at the camp, but it was obvious from the personal gear and food on hand that people were staying there and had only recently left the premises. Reed had taken three American guests out fishing for the day with his Cessna 180. With no one around to object, my men set to work taking the cabin apart piece by piece. The Otter could take quite a load. After a number of trips to Umiakovik (40 kilometers north), there was nothing left but a pile of personal belongings lying on an empty patch of ground. They even dismantled and moved the outhouse. Glenn contacted me by radio as he returned from the last trip and I told him to be sure not to touch any of the guests' personal belongings.

"I'm getting a bit low on fuel," he said. "I've got enough to get back to Nain, but not sufficient to reach Goose Bay. There are three drums of gas sitting here by the shore. Do you think I should use some of that?"

"Use it," I said, without hesitation. "And what's left just dump it. Take out the bungs and roll them around until they're empty. Away from the shore."

I always regretted not being there behind a tree when Roland arrived to find the building gone, cooking utensils missing, personal gear piled in a heap on the shore, and no fuel in the drums.

We found out later that Reed had to hire an EPA plane from Goose Bay to bring in fuel. He and his clients were stranded without shelter for four days while they waited for the aviation gas. Glen wondered aloud how much of a tip Roland got from his tourists."

In the years following, I would sometimes meet Rolly at the post office in Corner Brook but he would try to avoid me. "Hello Rolly," I'd say, full of good will. "How is our fishing camp up in northern Labrador coming along? Will we make a profit this year?" He never did say much. He would just mumble something and turn away.

Coincidentally, the arctic char population in the waters surrounding Nain was drastically reduced by 1974. The Canadian

Government built a modern fish processing plant at Nain in 1970 in order to provide employment for the natives who were taught how to run the plant, net char, and smoke the fillets. All of the estuaries were soon webbed with gill nets. It was a bonanza for a few years. But as the larger fish were depleted, the mesh size was reduced to snare the smaller fish. Since it takes over twenty years for these slow growing fish to reach fifteen pounds, the larger fish can easily be decimated. By 1976, the arctic char tourist camps on the Labrador coast were no longer able to entice guests with promises of big fish. The result was that the camps were either closed or converted to caribou hunting sites.

Chapter 21 Premier Joey Smallwood

Admirers watching departure of Joey Smallwood -Jackson's Arm (1971)

My first encounter with Premier Joey Smallwood was in 1963 at the official opening of the big asbestos mine in Baie Verte. I made three trips to Gander flying in various dignitaries for the ceremony: Mr. Karl Lindell of the Johns Manville Corporation, Mr. M.J. Boylen and his son, and various contractors were among my passengers. For weeks, Ross Sampson had meticulously organized the event, which brought together banking officials, mine managers, local merchants, engineers, and a large number of politicians. The premier and his ensemble had arrived in an Eastern Provincial Airways floatplane from St. John's.

After touring the mining complex, the visitors were directed to the community center where speeches, refreshments and a buffet dinner would be served. Having finished my flying for the day, I was standing near the entrance of the hall as the guests entered. At the doorway, after accepting a token gift to commemorate the occasion, the VIPs shook hands with the mine management, who were in the receiving line. Ross had delegated Jack Kelly to welcome each visitor and hand them a Zippo lighter as they entered.

Jack was a delightful little Irishman whose normal job was as a heavy equipment mechanic. On occasion he was known to indulge quite heavily in the dark rum. Apparently he had visited the open bar on a number of instances while awaiting the arrival of the dignitaries. When I chatted with him earlier, he was swaying in exuberance and his breath was quite lethal.

Joey Smallwood was known throughout the province and was venerated by some. He had brought Newfoundland into Confederation in 1949 as the tenth province of Canada. He was a short, pompous, dynamic little man with a large opinion of his leadership qualities. As he entered the hall, followed by some of his inner caucus ministers, he was cordially greeted by Jack's outstretched hand.

"Good day to you, my lordshp," Jack said while vigorously shaking the premier's hand. "And here is a small gift fer which you may remember this great occasion." Jack handed him a Zippo which had been artfully engraved:

ADVOCATE MINES LTD

Official Opening

Baie Verte - 1963

Joey carefully examined it: "Well, this is very nice but I would like to have half a dozen or so for my colleagues who could not be here."

Jack teetered a bit but was quick to respond: "Sorry, sir, but Ross says I'm only to give out one per person."

Joey shot back: "Do you know who I am? I'm Joe Smallwood, the premier of this province!"

Jack was not won over: "Yes, sir, I knows ya. But do you know who I is? I is Jack Kelly, a senior mechanic at this here mine, and Ross ses only one lighter each!"

It would be another year before I would come face to face with the premier. Our little flying service was thriving after the seal hunt financing. But even though we had upgraded our fleet with some new planes we could not obtain any provincial government work. Their aircraft needs were enormous and all of those requirements were being handed to our competition without a bid or tender call. We knew we could provide many of their services most adequately, and often at a lower price. It became more and more frustrating to see lucrative contracts going to EPA without any requests for our charter service. We had continually written letters to government outlining our services, equipment lists, and references, but never had a response.

I visited the Confederation Building in St. Johns on many occasions to meet with the Director of Transportation Services, the Minister of Transportation,the Minister of Health, and the Minister of Public Services, and various other politicians. These meetings were cordial but yielded no results. The gentlemen that I talked to left me with the impression that they had been directed to use the air services of EPA They would not say where that direction came prom but I concluded that it had to be from the Premier.

Although we were still a very small enterprise, NLAT had become fairly well known by our press releases, search and rescue efforts, tourist promotions, medivac flights, and the blunt opinions that I openly expressed.

Maybe as a result of Newfoundland's small population, it was surprisingly easy, after only one phone call, to arrange a meeting with the premier of the province. I was somewhat unnerved as I waited in the anteroom of Mr. Smallwood's office. I decided I had nothing to lose by being frank and to the point in our upcoming discussions. Finally, Mrs. Bettie Duff ushered me through the heavy oak door and into the large opulent sanctum. She beckoned me to a leather armchair in front of the premier's huge mahogany and then retreated to her secretary side table at the far side of the office. The expansive room, with a wall of windows, overlooked the old city of St. John's and its active harbour.

Mr. Smallwood motioned to me: "Please sit, Mr. Manion, I will be with you shortly." He was having a lengthy chat on one of his three phones. The telephone had a very long cord which allowed him to walk around the desk and briefly shake my hand without interrupting his loquacious conversation: "Look, Jack, I don't care what it costs. We must have that entire causeway completed before September. I will take care of any overruns. Forget about tenders. Just tell Lundrigans to

Premier Joey Smallwood

get on with it Hang on, Jack." The premier dropped that phone and picked up another that was ringing: "Yes, of course I will arrange for them to be at my office tonight at seven and you'd best bring your deputy." He hung that phone back in its cradle and continued with the other call: "I told those people it would be done and it will be done. If you get any more flack just tell them to call me." And with that, he slammed the phone into its rack. He turned to his secretary: "Bettie, call in a press release to the *Telegram*. Describe the unusual difficulty we are having with that land bridge, and tell them that I visited the site this morning and found a solution. But emphasize that it will be finished as I promised."

Another phone rang, and, as he picked it up he turned to me and said: "Please go ahead, Mr. Manion, I will listen as I talk." It was very distracting trying to explain my problems while he was engaged in telephone tag, but he did seem to be hearing both me and the caller. I explained our general services and base locations and suggested that we could save the government considerable dollars if we were not shut out from participating in their air needs. I also mentioned the exemption from provincial sales tax that was given to EPA, the dire need for airstrips on coastal Labrador, and the lack of a winter food supply subsidy to the remote settlements.

When he finally finished the phone call, he paced theatrically back and forth across the office and peered out the window: "Yes, Mr. Manion, I'm quite aware of your rapid expansion with the air service and I am quite impressed with your unyielding style. This province needs more people like you. The outport people, the mining industry, the construction movers, the tourism sector, and the fishing companies are all benefiting from your service. Yes, even EPA is better off having some good competition. I began this career as a little pig farmer and look where I am today. Yes, I understand your position and have some sympathy for your situation." The intercom system on his desk came alive with another tone. He had a direct voice line with his cabinet ministers by way of a keyboard console, he could talk to each of his ministers or listen to their conversations by selecting their number. He quickly dealt with that request, shuffled some folders on his desk, and continued: "Young man, you are correct. Rather than go to lengthy tender procedures, we usually call on EPA for all of our air requirements, it saves a lot of paper work. Now, you might think that is unfair, and perhaps you are not wrong. A long time ago I got in bed with the Crosbie family and as you are well aware, they own Eastern Provincial. That was the only air company in those days and although I have had some doubts about that decision, right or wrong I am still in the same loyal bed. Therefore, Mr. Manion, I suggest that you concentrate your efforts on expanding your services in other areas."

He answered two more calls and asked his secretary to deal with another matter. He then signed a paper she handed him before continuing his discourse with me: "I was unaware that you were not included in the sales tax exemption. You must take this up with my finance minister. Tell John Crosbie that I directed you. Now, regarding the airstrips." He paused, scanning my features. "I will be blunt with you. Yes, we need many improvements in this regard, but to keep this province moving ahead I must always be sure of re-election. There are not many votes on the coast of Labrador so we must satisfy some other places first. Then in due course we can find monies for Labrador." He continued with his trademark repetition: "All these things are in my long term plan. I have a clear agenda, a schedule, a program, a list for the entire province. Not just the island, but for all Newfoundlanders and Labradorians. Now what was the other concern that you mentioned?" He walked over to the open door on the far side of his office and made some inaudible comments to someone in the adjoining caucus chamber. Then he closed the door.

I spoke up: "The people on the Labrador coast are without fresh food from December until the resumption of the coastal boat service in June. Their eggs are spoiled and their meats are moldy, and they have no fresh vegetables or fruit available. They cannot afford to charter aircraft to bring in fresh supplies. They are living in another world. A small air subsidy would correct the problem. The health benefits alone should justify the cost and there would be political benefits as well. Would you consider such a program?"

Rising from his swivel chair, he responded, "Mr. Manion, you have a point. My government is founded on sound economic development. I work diligently day and night to work out programs that will benefit all Newfoundlanders and Labradorians from Cape Chidley to the Grand Banks, from the Port au Port to the Avalon. Leave this matter with me and after some discussion with my federal counterparts you will hear from me in this regard. Is there anything else?"

He reached out to shake my hand: "Do not hesitate to call me should you have further need. You may not have received the response you were looking for today, but I know you have overcome many difficulties already and I have confidence that with your determination. You will be a successful force in this province without my help."

I thought about the meeting as I rode the elevator down from the top floor of the Confederation Building. At least he was up-front about his association with EPA. We would not waste further time in pursuing government work, I thought. Instead we would concentrate all our effort on serving the mining, construction, and tourism sectors.

It did work out quite well. We were able to concentrate and expand our services in other areas and gradually pried customers from the competition. A further meeting was held with John Crosbie, the provincial Minister of Finance. Although his family owned EPA, he seemed interested in my plight and immediately gave us similar exemption from the sales tax. He agreed that we were also vital in assisting with economic development throughout the region. Later, Premier Smallwood requested another meeting to discuss the financial funding for a passenger and food service to Labrador. When you were summoned to his office, you knew you were in for a lengthy lecture, punctuated by a multitude of interrupting phone calls. But the meeting did result in an air subsidy for the Labrador coast. This was extremely helpful to our revenue stream during the winter months. We set up a winter skiplane base in Flowers Cove to move groceries across the strait to Labrador from the wholesale depot. We also inaugurated a scheduled passenger and freight service from Deer Lake to St. Anthony and Blanc Sablon using twin engine wheel planes.

During the 1960s, Joey Smallwood continued in power with a large majority of Liberal seats in government. Gradually he became a one-man government. All of his energy was devoted to staying in power. He tried to run every department, he handpicked all the Liberal candidates, and he ruled like an absolute monarch. Many, including John Crosbie, said he became a ruthless, crooked tyrant. Increasingly, more Newfoundlanders became uneasy with his leadership, including some of his cabinet ministers. In the late 1960s, the Conservatives were gaining some momentum, and that was substantially strengthened by the leadership of Frank Moores.

On one occasion in 1968, before we introduced helicopter service, an early cold snap occurred in October. We were providing air support to twelve large tourist operators who had remote hunting camps. There were six big game hunters and five staff at Wentzell's camp on Angus Lake when the lake froze. They were anxious to go home after their seven day hunt. They had five dressed moose to be flown out and the camp was getting very low on food. We kept in touch each day via high frequency radio while waiting for warm weather to melt the ice and let us land our floatplanes. After the fifth day of delay, the situation became serious. Something had to be done.

The only helicopter in western Newfoundland was on a fulltime contract with the provincial Forestry Department. I called my friend Harry Goodland, the regional director of forestry. After explaining the problem, I asked if he would release the Bell jet ranger for three trips to Angus Lake and we would cover the costs.

"I really don't have clear authority to let you use the machine," he replied. "You will have to call the minister. I'll give you Mr. Callahan's number." Upon reaching the minister, I got a similar reply: "I would like to help but I could have problems if a fire should break out," Callahan said.

"I don't think there's much chance of a forest fire with all the snow around," I said. "This is the only way we can get these people out. Who do I have to reach to get that damn machine released?"

Callahan stammered: "I guess you'll have to call the premier himself. Since this is Sunday I'll give you his home number."

I couldn't believe it! The premier dispatching helicopters! On the third ring, a male voice answered the phone and I asked to speak with Mr. Smallwood.

"This is he! What can I do for you?" Briefly, I explained who I was, my dire need for a helicopter, and the reason I was bothering him at his home. "Yes, Mr. Manion, I understand," said Smallwood. "Tell Mr. Goodland I am authorizing you to use the forestry machine in Pasadena to conduct the rescue operation and let me know if you require further assistance."

It certainly had become a one man show! Joey had clung to power for twenty-one years. But by 1970 the opposition, led by John Crosbie and other former Liberal cabinet ministers, joined with Frank Moores to attack his vulnerability and end his rule. An election was called for October 28, 1971.

Since we had always been opposed to the undemocratic ways of Joey and his favouritism to certain big business groups, it was with great pleasure we learned that Frank Moores had chosen our service to transport him and his squad around the province during their vigorous election campaign. Supporting the Conservatives, our aircraft took to the skies with Moores' team. Two of our floatplanes were embossed with large white and blue Conservative emblems on the fuselage.

Frank Moores had effortless charisma. He was a well spoken revolutionary who showed great enthusiasm as he visited all the coastal communities. The ordinary rural folks identified with him. They accepted him as one of them since he didn't talk down to them and spoke in their colourful colloquialisms. His slogan, "The Time Has Come," was well received and the momentum grew as he gave his views on quality of life issues and rural development. During the crusade, our DeHavilland Otter floatplane transported him to every nook and cranny of the province. We walked through the villages with him, listened to his town hall discussions, and partied with him at night. Our pilots enjoyed the campaign and their association with this man, who had a penchant for fishing, hunting, travel, women and booze.

A few days prior to the election, our dispatch office in Pasadena received an urgent charter request from the Liberal headquarters. Mr. Smallwood was stranded in Jackson's Arm and a plane was critically needed to transport him further north to Roddickton. It was obvious that they had to be quite desperate to ask us for assistance. Apparently, EPA could not supply the aircraft due to maintenance problems. We had one Beaver plane at the dock and no other pilots were readily available except me.

"Tell them we'll have a plane there in an hour," I said to Joan French, who was taking the call.

Hanging up, she looked at me questioningly: "Gene, you can't use that plane for Smallwood! It has a Conservative banner stretching across the entire fuselage and it can't be easily removed!"

As I took off from Deer Lake, I had sinister thoughts of retribution in flying Joey around with the big blue and white placard on the left side of my plane. Landing in the harbour some fifty minutes later, I saw the huge crowd of people swarming the government dock in Jackson's Arm. Carefully. I manoeuvred the plane so that only the starboard side was visible from the shore.

The light breeze was in a favourable direction, allowing me to cut the engine and glide the nose of the pontoons gently into the outer end of the wharf, with the Conservative sign only observable on the ocean side. I crawled out on the starboard float, helped Mr. Smallwood down the ladder, opened the cabin doors, and assisted Joey and his aide into their seats. I untied the plane, gave it a push backwards and crawled under the belly to gain my left seat in the cockpit. Joey looked very at ease in the co-pilot's seat as he shook my hand. The whole community was on the dock waving at the plane as I warmed the engine for takeoff. Impulsively, I taxied to the west and turned for departure. I eased the throttle forward and the big radial engine roared to life. We gained speed, the floats came up on the step, and we raced along on the water very near the shore. As we passed the end of the wharf, Joey reached across in front of me to wave a goodbye to his fold. Looking sideways, I could see the shock on the multitude of faces when the Conservative insignia came into their view! The waving subsided, their arms dropped, and I had a covert feeling of immense delight.

I followed the same procedure at the harbour in Roddickton. Except on my departure, Joey was standing on the dock amongst the crowd when my blue and white sign flashed by on takeoff. I guess it was my modest way of saying, "Thanks, Mr. Smallwood, for the years of unfair Liberal treatment!"

It would not be my last encounter with Joey. On election night the mood had changed. Around 8 p.m. as the voting returns were pouring in, my home phone rang. It was Mr. Smallwood's executive assistant. There was desperation in his voice as he pleaded for an aircraft to take Mr. Smallwood out of Newfoundland as quickly as possible. Joey was rapidly losing the election and they wanted to get him away from the hounding press.

Pierre Meagher and I flew from Deer Lake to St. John's in our twin engine Aero Commander. It was a wicked weather night and the Canadian air traffic controllers were on strike resulting in all aircraft over 12,500 pounds being prevented from operating under "Instrument Flight Conditions." The easterly gale off the ocean at

St. John's created sheets of rain and a murky 200 foot ceiling. The instrument approach and landing went fine. The control tower directed us the service center on the far side of the airport for refueling since we had been instructed to avoid the main passenger terminal.

It was too wet to exit the plane so Pierre and I waited in the cockpit. Eventually, a man darted from the hangar to advise that he was Mr. Smallwood's executive assistant. He shouted through the storm when I opened the cabin door: "The premier's party is slightly delayed. Would it be OK if he sat in your plane while we find his wife? We are trying to hide him away from the harassment of the press."

"Yes, that's OK since we've got to wait for fuel anyway," I replied. A forlorn little figure soon dashed through the pelting rain and entered the cabin. We gave Joey a cordial greeting. After removing his wet topcoat he slumped into the seat behind the open cockpit door. He looked like a sad little mouse that had just lost his best friend.

Jim Collins, a long time friend of mine, was an aircraft operator who offered a refueling service in St. John's. Both he and I had been active for years in supporting the Conservative Party. His bowser headlights glistened on the wet tarmac as the big truck came to a halt beside our left wing. Jim was driving the vehicle himself. He sauntered over to my sliding cockpit window in his yellow rain slicker.

"What in hell are you doing driving that truck on a night like this? Have all your employees finally quit?" I asked.

"I thought you'd be out celebratin tonight instead of screwing around in this weather," he loudly responded. "We should both be tieing one on with the rest of Newfoundland. It's been a long struggle but we finally got rid of that little son of a bitch!" I wasn't sure whether Jim knew that Joey was sitting right behind me and hearing every word he said. He was so elated with the election results that it probably wouldn't have changed his wording. I motioned for him to shut up and pointed at Joey.

"Ya, that little bastard screwed us for years, but the dark

cloud has bin lifted. Tis a proud time fer you and me, we worked ar asses of fer this," Jim finished up.

Although I didn't have much love for Joey, I felt awkwardly embarrassed by these outbursts. "Jim, you're getting soaked and we're in a hurry. Just fill up those tanks and we'll be out of here," I urged, trying to stop his tirade of insults about our passenger.

We were soon refueled and had Mrs. Smallwood comfortably settled in the cabin. The weather had not improved. But departure through lashing rain and fog is always less demanding than the precise flying required for arrival. With the engines humming a synchronized tune, our rate of climb indicator showed a steady rise through the black night scud. Soon a few stars flickered overhead as we began to break through the wispy top of the overcast. At 8,000 feet I eased the throttles back to cruise power as Pierre reported our altitude to Gander Center.

"It looks like a nice smooth ride," I said to Pierre, handing the controls over to him. "I'll go back and play stewardess." We had arranged hot coffee and mini sandwiches in St. John's but our three dejected passengers were not in the eating mood. Mrs. Smallwood was pleasant but subdued, the aide was busy doodling on a notepad, and Joey, slouched in his seat, seemed in a faroff daze.

We made a quick fuel stop at Halifax before setting course for Boston. With the absence of air traffic, due to the controller's strike, the lack of radio chatter was quite eerie. It seemed as though we were the only aircraft in the entire sky. The world was silent as though mourning Joey's departure. Our communication with Boston tower allowed us to arrange a limousine and VIP custom clearance for the dignitaries upon our arrival. We assisted with their luggage and wished them well. Actually, it felt somewhat bizarre for us to be flying Mr. Smallwood on his last official trip. During all the previous years his government would not make use of our services for routine charters. The tide had gone out!

If my memory is correct, I believe that this charter was never paid for. Therefore, it may be construed as the only donation I ever provided to the provincial Liberals during the Smallwood era!

NEWFOUNDLAND AND LABRADOR
LEADER OF THE PROGRESSIVE CONSERVATIVE PARTY

20th December 1971

Mr. Gene Manion
General Manager
Nfld. & Labrador Air Transport Ltd.
Steadybrook
Newfoundland.

Dear Gene:

First of all let me thank you for your assistance during the campaign and secondly to advise you that I have been in touch with Tom Burgess regarding the badly needed air service for the coast of Labrador.

I have received your proposal and intend to follow it through with Tom in this regard. This together with the other brief you presented I would like to sit down and discuss with you when next in Corner Brook and I am sure that we can come to some satisfactory conclusion.

As you are undoubtly aware we still have not formed the government because of the stubborness of Mr. Smallwood but that day is rapidly approaching and at that time, hopefully, we can come up with something realistic and beneficial for all parties concerned.

In the meantime once again many thanks for your co-operation and help, I remain with best personal regards.

Sincerely

Frank D. Moores
Leader of the P.C. Party

Chapter 22 Icing

Aero Commander 560 used for aerial photography and medivac flights

The Gulf of St. Lawrence is a large body of water that extends from the north shore of Nova Scotia to the south coast of Labrador, and from Newfoundland to the Gaspe Peninsula. Really, it is a part of the Atlantic Ocean separated by the island of Newfoundland. During winter, a good portion of the area becomes frozen with moving sheet ice. The lower air mass in the region is moisture laden, which often produces ideal conditions for aircraft icing.

With air temperature at the freezing point, ice forms on the leading edges of aircraft structures as the super cooled water droplets make contact with the cold metal. The ensuing build-up of ice changes the shape of the airfoil, disturbing the smooth flow of air over the wing and tail assemblies and destroying the lift. Some aircraft are fitted with flexible rubber boots or heated leading edges to help dislodge ice accumulation. Some have alcohol dispensers to remove ice from the propellers. Aircraft that attain a speed of over 230 knots are free of this icing problem owing to the heat caused by skin friction.

Pierre Meagher, Jim Bouzanne and I were flying out of Prince

Edward Island for ten days with Dr. Sergeant to employ infrared film over the seal herds. Dr. Sergeant, with the federal Department of Fisheries, had contracted our services to conduct the experimental camera work. The young whitecoats could not be readily distinguished from their icy surroundings using normal photo technology. Jim, who normally worked with the federal Department of Forestry, was very knowledgeable about aerial photography and he was quite certain that infrared film would pick up the body heat of the seal pups and show as red dots when developed. We had not anticipated any severe icing when we departed Charlottetown for the photography mission. Although our twin engine Aero Commander was fitted with wing de-icer boots, this apparatus was very ineffective when severe conditions were encountered.

Wet snowfall was increasing as we completed another photo run over the scattered seals near the coast of Port Aux Choix in northern Newfoundland. I advised Dr. Sergeant that a frontal system had moved into the Gulf and conditions would not be suitable for further photography: "We'll climb up and head back to Charlottetown. It's about 350 kilometers so we'll be about 1-1/2 hours."

Pierre received an instrument clearance for a direct route at 8,000 feet. I was relaxing in the passenger cabin when Jim beckoned to me. "I think Pierre wants you up front," he said.

On entering the cockpit, I heard Pierre asking Moncton Control Center for a higher altitude. He then spoke to me: "We're picking up quite a bunch of ice. Look at the wings. They've given us 10,000 feet but she doesn't want to climb!"

There was a considerable build-up of ice on the leading edge of the wing boots. By the sound of the prop synchronization there had to be ice on the propellers as well. Obviously, the ice was destroying the wing aerodynamics since the aircraft refused to climb, and our airspeed was far less than normal. I was able to throw some ice off the props by bringing the pitch back to a flat position and quickly changing the angle of bite. Pieces of ice rattled against the fuselage, denting the paint as it was flung from the propellers.

We informed Jim and Dr. Sergeant of our trouble: "We're loaded up with ice. The outside air is minus 3C. We must find some warmer air so we're taking her down a bit."

Going down was easy as that's where she wanted to go. The official minimum, safe, instrument altitude was 2,000 feet. Unfortunately, on reaching that altitude, we were still in heavy, damp cloud and the temperature was still minus two. The ice buildup was not lessening. Further action was required.

I spoke to Pierre on the intercom: "We're over flat ice and miles from any land. You're gonna have to keep letting down til we get warmer air. Otherwise she's going down on her own!"

"OK," Pierre said. "Better tell Moncton what we're doing, and get the latest altimeter setting for Grindstone."

We began further descent through the ominous clouds. As we dropped lower, the wet cloud layer became darker. Eventually we broke through the wispy bottoms at 300 feet only to see another white layer below, but that was the carpet of Gulf ice! Slowly the wing ice began to break off in the warmer temperature. Before crossing the Magdalen Islands we were back to normal flight configuration, and able to regain a safe altitude to clear the nearing land mass of Prince Edward Island, and our landing approach to Charlottetown.

Dr. Sergeant said it had been one of his more interesting white knuckle flights: "Jolly good show, old chaps, but not grossly productive from my filming standpoint!"

The infrared photography proved very successful and is now used extensively for wildlife census.

****

A different type of icing occurred late in the year of 1967.

"Lard Jasus skipper, she's bottom up!" Tommy hollered.

It was a wild night on the west coast of Newfoundland. We were always restless on a windy night, fearing damage to the moored seaplanes.With waves washing over the floats, considerable seepage could occur if the pump out caps were not tight fitting.

On December 23, the shudders of the raging gale woke me at three in the morning. Immediately I phoned Tommy Caines, who lived near the seaplane base in Pasadena: "There's quite a storm blowing. Would ya mind meeting me at the base? I'll be there in half an hour. We'd best check on the planes."

With the drifting snow, the entrance road by Bowater Park was barely drivable. Tommy had left his car at the highway and walked in. My four-wheel drive Suburban straddled his tracks as I bucked through the banks. As I peered through the storm I could see Tommy was being drenched with spray as huge waves on the lake broke over the docks. I directed a twelve-volt beam of light at the mooring buoys some 300 feet from shore where the pilots had secured two Otters, three Beavers, and a Beechcraft 18. But where was the Beechcraft?

We soon discovered the big two-engine plane was floating, but it was upside down. The bottom of her floats, still shackled to the buoy, were visible between the breaking rollers. In the raging blizzard, we could do little. The other aircraft, bouncing and swinging, seemed to be riding out the storm without difficulty. We tightened the ropes on the three Cessna planes that had been pulled up on the sandy shore behind the docks. Filled with frustration, we retreated to the dispatch office for coffee.

"We're going to have to get that plane ashore when the wind drops or the floats will eventually fill up with water and she'll go to the bottom," I muttered.

"Not to worry," Tommy said. "We've flipped em over afore in worser places. Best ting, she's near ar shop and not hout in the boondocks. I'll get Eddie and the boys at er come light. An whilst they's gettin de gear, I'll bull a road down through the park wit the dozer."

By noon the next day the wind had abated. Rick and his maintenance staff were well organized for the difficult task of overturning the big plane without causing further damage. It was carefully towed towards the sandy shore at Bowater Park. The front float compartments were drilled to allow filling with water.

As subsequent sections filled, the front of the plane gradually sank to the lake bed. As it reached a near vertical position, with the nose of the pontoons entrenched in the sand, guy ropes were attached to the wingtips to prevent a sideways fall. A strong nylon tether was secured to the inverted tail assembly, and warped ashore to the tracked dozer. Slowly, the tractor moved up the incline, bringing the fuselage past the vertical. In slow motion,the plane gently settled in an upright position with the tail next to the shore. Icicles formed as the water drained from the wings and engine cowlings. In the darkness of Christmas Eve, the craft was inched backwards from the lake on a log ramp. There was no scratch on the plane. The only damage was from the water dunking.

Eddie and Tommy covered the engines with tarps and spent most of the night tending to the propane heaters. This prevented freezing damage to the power plants in the minus 10C temperature. They weren't dreaming of a White Christmas, they were in the thick of one. On Christmas day, Rick and another crew were able to start the 450hp Pratt and Whitney radials. The salvage was complete but considerable hangar work would be required before CF-OII would take to the air in the spring. During the next few cold nights the lake froze, causing another obstacle in getting the aircraft to the hangar ramp about one kilometer up the shore. The Bowater Paper Company cooperated by offering the use of their tugboat. On December 28, we refloated the Beechcraft and I steered her through the icy path behind the log boom tug, captained by Jim Carter. With chain falls and skids, the plane was manoeuvred into the security of the hangar at South Brook, where a complete overhaul and a new paint job would be carried out during the winter.

The Beech 18 performed quite well on floats with a gross weight of 3,970 kg. Some executive customers required a two-engine aircraft to satisfy their company policy. At maximum payload, the float equipped aircraft would barely maintain altitude if one engine became inoperative, but you could extend your flight to reach a suitable lake for safe landing. Although we never encountered an engine failure with the Beech, some pilots said in jest with only one engine the pilot could extend the point of the crash! In the early 1970s, we operated three Beech 18s: one on floats and two on wheels, conducting resupply to the USAF radar sites from Stephenville.

Recovered Beech 18 from Deer Lake. (Dec 24 -1967)

Chapter 23 Helicopters

Bell G-4 helicopters at our Pasadena base (1969)

It was evident in the 1960s that EPA did not have sufficient helicopters to serve the growing demand. We were constantly upgrading our fixed wing fleet and reluctant to borrow further to purchase helicopters. Therefore, we embarked on various joint ventures with different mainland companies who were already in the rotary business. The first such venture was not satisfactory, but in 1969 Larry Campaugh and I made a working agreement.

Larry was the single-minded owner of Viking Helicopters. He was well established at Carp, Ontario, with equipment working across Canada. Viking was just completing a large malaria spray contract for the World Health Organization in Africa, and so they would have a surplus of equipment back in Canada. Viking had a high quality maintenance setup in Carp, experienced pilots, and good connections with the Hughes Helicopter Company. Larry did not have any contacts in Newfoundland but was anxious to get established in the Atlantic region.

A good working relationship evolved. Larry supplied the aircraft, crews, and maintenance and our company did the marketing, dispatching and management of the helicopters in

Newfoundland and Labrador. We started by using the small, piston-engined Bell G-4 machines. But as his fleet returned from Africa, we upgraded to the turbine powered Hughes 500 equipment in the early 1970s. Although the Hughes did not have the VIP passenger appeal, it was far superior to the Bell 206 as a maneuverable workhorse, especially for slinging exterior loads.

Upgrading to the Hughes 500 - working on the Buchans transmission line

After 1967, I had mounting disagreements with Rick Richard, my original partner, regarding helicopters and other business ventures. I negotiated a purchase of his shares, which we finalized in 1968. The name of the business was changed to Newfoundland and Labrador Air Transport Ltd. (NLAT).

A good deal of our work was with mining and exploration companies, moving their drill rigs and core samples. Our experience with seal hunting gave us an edge in supplying helicopters to the Department of Fisheries for annual surveillance and to control the anti-seal protesters. The construction industries were also finding it advantageous to use helicopters in specialized circumstances.

The steel towers for the Marble Mountain ski lift required large volumes of concrete for their base. The steep terrain was no problem for the Hughes. A large sling bucket filled with cement had the vertical lifting completed in five days, saving the contractor thousands of dollars in mountainside road construction.

Electrical power generation and transmission construction was rampant with the development of Churchill Falls, Baie D'Espoir and the Hinds Lake projects. The Power Commission decided to construct a hydro line from Stephenville to Buchans, along South West Brook. The rugged terrain along this 90 kilometer line was not conducive to easy road construction. Larry and I convinced the contractor that we could transport the men and equipment and place the poles by using helicopters. Pole setting by chopper was a first in Newfoundland. We used a Bell 204 for the heavy lifting and two 500s. The job was successfully completed without any major problems. There were more than 200 65-foot wooden poles, each weighing 4,000 pounds. With light fuel the chopper could lift about 4,200 pounds so there was little room for error. During the two month contract, only one load had to be dropped due to excessive swinging with gusty wind pendulum effect.

Bell 204 used for setting hydro poles on the Buchans Line

In 1973, we were contacted by relatives of Mr. Leonidas Hubbard in New York. His friends and families were interested in erecting a bronze plaque at the site where Mr. Hubbard had died of starvation in Labrador.

In 1903, Hubbard, an assistant editor of *Outing* magazine, was interested in adventurous exploration and convinced his friend, Dillon Wallace, to join him in an expedition to the interior of

Labrador. They arrived at Northwest River, Labrador, in mid-July of that year. A Cree guide, George Elson, was hired and they began their trek, which they hoped would take them to Lake Michikamau (via the Naskaupi River), and onward to the George River and down to Ungava Bay. Early in the trip they made a fatal error by turning up the wrong river. The Susan River was a much longer and more arduous route.Inadequate food supplies and the onslaught of winter added to their problems. Facing undernourishment, they turned back in September. On their way out, Hubbard succumbed to starvation. Wallace came near death before Elson managed to locate some native trappers who helped transport him to Northwest River. Hubbard's body was later recovered and taken by dog team to Battle Harbour, where it could be forwarded by ship to New York in the spring.

I was very interested in helping to place the commemorative plaque since I was well acquainted with the Hubbard story and the Labrador wilderness held great intrigue for me. Mac Forgie piloted the Hughes 500. As we inched our way up the shallow, rocky, Susan River I could easily visualize the tragic hardships that those men had endured seventy years ago. It was difficult to believe that northern travel could have changed so much and so quickly. Mac and I comfortably traveled further in a few hours than the early explorers would have gone in six months. We found the site where an inscription had been etched on the flat side of a large boulder, facing Hubbard's last camp.We firmly attached the bronze memorial plate to the rock face and our job was complete. It was a gratifying thought to have played a small, final part in that historic event.

****

Every spring St. Anthony (population 2,600), nestled in a bay on the northern tip of Newfoundland, became the focal point for the seal hunt at the "Front." It was the nearest airport and lodging area to the offshore hunting area, as the seals drifted with the Labrador current. The anti-sealing groups were there to heckle the hunters and their ships, and gain publicity for their cause. The

Department of Fisheries and Oceans also used this community as a vantage point to monitor the protesters, enforce the regulations, conduct photography, and gather scientific data. The RCMP brought in extra manpower in case the feuding became rowdy. The hunt also drew reporters, television crews, and conservationists to cover the proceedings.

International furor broke loose in 1964 when a controversial Quebec film was released. *Les Phoques*, filmed near the Magdalen Islands, showed a hunter tormenting a seal and a seal being skinned while supposedly still alive! Dr. Pimlott, a zoologist from the University of Toronto, said the harassment had been staged by a member of the film crew, and another man, Gustave Poirier, admitted to having been paid to skin a live seal in front of the cameras. But the European papers had already widely published the pictures so the damage was done! Societies throughout Europe launched a salvo of protests against the savage, barbarian hunt in Canada.

The Canadian government brought in strict new sealing regulations in 1965 and 1966, but this did not satisfy Patrick Watson, Peter Lust, Brian Davies, or any of the anti-sealing groups who were now receiving donations to help them with their cause. Brian Davies accelerated his rigorous "Save the Seals" campaign in an effort to stop the hunt and cash from his supporters came pouring in. Davies was funded by a wealthy German, Dr. Grzimek, and a Munich-based humane organization. They brought in veterinarians, news media groups, and photographers to witness the cruelty and arouse public concern. These groups needed helicopters to gain access to the seals. With spring being a slack period for our equipment, we filled some of their requests.

Paris Match, Life magazine, and *The London Daily Mirror* sent representatives to film the "grisly slaughter." We chartered helicopters to these groups. with machines also under contract with the Department of Fisheries and Oceans to monitor the protestors! In one instance, we had two of our pilots subpoenaed to court to give evidence against each other as to how near the photographers had been to the seals. Regulations prohibited anyone from landing within one half mile of the animals. Using our four-engined Heron aircraft, we were also doing surveillance and air-photo work for the government and the Karl Karlsen Shipping Company.

We often lodged at the same motel as the activists and engaged in testy discussions with them. Sometimes they brazenly bragged about the lucrative donations that were coming in. Davies told us he wouldn't need our helicopters next year. He said he would be paying cash for a new Jet Ranger under the name of the International Fund for Animal Welfare (IFAW). Then they started to bring celebrities in to publicize the bloody, barbaric hunt.

In the early 1970s, English model Celia Hammond was photographed on the ice, saying, "I don't know how any woman could watch this and wear a fur coat again unless she was a monster."

Greenpeace began selling protest buttons, t-shirts, and pendants, and Harpy, the harp seal doll, was offered for $20. In 1976, Davies brought seven photogenic stewardesses to witness the hunt, "to deflate the mystique of the ordeal." Franz Weber, from Switzerland, announced plans to spend a million dollars to fly 600 influential reporters from all over the world to witness the violent massacre. He booked all the available rooms in St. Anthony and said he would bring in a hotel ship to house the balance of his entourage. He was ridiculed by the sealers, and the government. Richard Cashin, fishermen's union leader, told him, "Get your rich arse out of the province. Go to hell home."

The ensuing 1977 season brought the likelihood of an explosive situation when Davies showed up in St. Anthony with six helicopters after being chased out of the Magdalen Islands. The RCMP sent in 100 of their force to separate Davies and his group from the militant pro-sealers of the region. The local people formed a human barricade to prevent Davies from accessing his helicopters or acquiring fuel. The police intervened; otherwise the machines would have been damaged by the angry crowd.

Meanwhile, Greenpeace members settled in at Lourdes du Blanc Sablon, across the strait in southern Labrador. Paul Watson pulled one of his usual tricks by handcuffing himself to a ship's winch chain used for hauling pelts on board. He suffered a dislocated shoulder and a good dunking in the cold seawater.

The chaos worsened when Weber, with sixty cohorts, descended on the small coastal town of Blanc Sablon. He had enticed French actress Brigitte Bardot to join him in his fight to save the seals. It was reported that when Bardot deplaned in Gander to clear customs she was dressed in a leopard skin jacket! Weber tried to charter a helicopter from us in St. Anthony to take her to the "ice" but our machines were all booked. We advised them that we could offer a machine in three days. Greenpeace had helicopters, but they didn't want any involvement with the sex symbol. Bardot refused interviews with the press because she said she couldn't express herself in English. Disheartened by the lack of success in Blanc Sablon, her group flew back to St. Anthony, where Davies was waiting to fly her out to the hunting area. Davies grew impatient when she dallied over lunch and left without her. The next day. when she was supposed to go out in our helicopter, she said it looked too stormy. She and her boyfriend, Mirko Brosek, flew back to Labrador in their private jet. On the following morning, they returned to France.

The April I issue of *Paris Match* displayed Bardot on the cover, cuddling a whitecoat. She said her trip to Newfoundland and the flight to the slaughter area over the arctic ice had been a very risky and dangerous mission. As far as anyone knows, she never left the shore and the embraced animal was reportedly a stuffed young seal!

Although the protesters were at odds as they fought for the most coverage, they were quite successful in convincing many non-Newfoundlanders, and the rest of the world, that the seal hunt should be stopped. In retaliation, Federal MP John Crosbie made two suggestions: Canada must ban the import of all French wines because they brutalize the grapes when they stomp them with their feet, and ban the use of pâté de foie gras on the grounds that the French treat their geese with cruelty by force feeding them in order to satisfy the jaded appetites of the wealthy.

To those of us who have been involved in every facet of the sealing operation, it is my opinion that the protest groups are primarily interested in the donations that flow to them through their propaganda. The seals are not becoming extinct. They are increasing in number. The method of killing, while not pretty, is not inhumane, and many Newfoundlanders augment their income during the spring hunt. The growing seal herds are consuming enormous amounts of fish. If the hunt was stopped, a cull would eventually be necessary, as happened with deer in New Zealand. The controversy continues and will no doubt go on until either whitecoats become ugly, or the general public is forced to visit other blood-spattered slaughterhouses. The seal hunt is the only butchery open to public viewing. In any event, the seals were good for our business.

****

"Mayday. Mayday. Mayday. This is chopper TUP. Engine failure 52/04 North by 52/01 West," Dale Caldwell transmitted simultaneously on both his VHF emergency and sideband low frequency radios. The Hughes 500 was about 30 kilometers east of Belle Island when the engine compressor failed on March 28, 1983. The Labrador Sea was 500 feet below, covered with ragged ice floes. As the emergency power failure horn blared and the alarm lights flashed, Dale's front seat passenger, Captain Morrisey Johnson, reached over in a nonchalant manner and offered Dale a cigarette!

"Holy shit," Dale later told us. "There was a good chance that we would all be dead in a few minutes as there weren't many flat places for an autorotation, and this cool old sealing skipper wondered if it was OK to have a smoke! There were sure more important things on my mind about then!"

Dale was on a term charter contract with the Department of Fisheries and Oceans. They were working out of St. Anthony to monitor the distribution of the seal herd and keep an enforcement eye on the sealing ships. Don Clark, the fisheries officer, had been in the helicopter in the morning when they discovered a patch of seals north of Cape Bauld. Two polar bears were molesting the herd and many seals had already been killed but not eaten. This is a common practice of northern bears so they can have a cache of ready meat when they head north, later in the season. The ridged ice throughout the area was heavily packed with few open water leads; Mr. Clark suggested they fly east to where the ships were wedged and advise the captains as to their best route in avoiding the thickest ice.

A number of large sealing vessels were jammed into the pack ice about 40 kilometers east of Belle Isle. Dale landed on the deck of the *Lady Johnson.* After a hearty lunch, Captain Morrisey Johnson asked if he could go with them for a quick look at the ice with a view to finding the best route to the seal herd. Toward Belle Island and the strait, the ocean was 95% ice covered. The fragmented pans had been agitated by three days of easterly wind. The ice was in a crushed state, with hummocks pushed on each other. The small pans had been grinding together and pressed harshly against the Newfoundland coast.

The Hughes was in a descending arc powered only by the air flowing up through the rotor blades and causing them to spin. "I think we can make that small pan to the left," Dale shouted through the intercom. The cockpit had became eerily quiet, with only the sound of rushing air slipping past the fuselage as Dale concentrated on his autorotation.

Brian Nuttall, one of Viking's engineers, happened to be in our Pasadena dispatch office when the Mayday boomed in. Alarmed, Brian tried to contact Dale for more information on his emergency but there was no response for five minutes. Brian, knowing the terrible ice conditions, was very relieved when Dale's voice came through the Spilsbury radio: "We're on a small pan. No damage to the machine. Try to send AHI to pick us up. There's a polar bear nearby and we don't have a rifle." It was unusual for the radio reception to be so clear, especially since the downed helicopter was over 350 kilometers away.

Brian was swift in responding to Dale and his crisis: "Peter Nealy is flying AHI with a biologist on one of the ships. I'll get him to bring you a rifle and his mechanic. We have a complete engine here in the shop and I'll see if we can get a fixed wing charter to take me and the engine to St. Anthony S.A.P."

"OK Pasadena," Dale said. "But things will have to click pretty well… its two o'clock now, and darkness comes early. I now have contact with AHI on the VHF."

Under pressure, Brian was known for his leadership. "Dale, you must have some tools on board," he said. "You should be able to loosen things up and have that dead engine ready for removal when we get there. If all goes well, I'll be at the St. Anthony airport in two hours. Tell Peter to meet me there with his chopper."

While the new engine was enroute, Dale became anxious about the cautious aggression of the bear that was nearing their ice pan. He fired his flare gun at it. The bear lurched, but having scented the men, it continued to threaten their position. He and Don Clark drained some jet fuel and poured it around the perimeter of their ice pan, planning to flame it to discourage the stealthy animal. Within an hour, Peter landed alongside, gave a rifle to Dale, dropped off his apprentice mechanic, and departed with Don Clark and Captain Johnson. Before leaving, Johnson shook Dale's hand and thanked him for the exciting afternoon. "That sure beats being jammed in the friggin ice," he growled.

When NLAT's Piper landed in St. Anthony, Peter was there to take delivery of the new Allison engine. Brian rushed the transfer to Peter's helicopter and they were soon airborne for the 90 kilometer flight to Dale and his marooned machine. Spotting a small apparatus on the vast ocean of upturned ice is quite difficult, but Peter had a good fix punched on his GPS. From Cape Bauld, the most northern tip of Newfoundland, the stranded machine was 57 kilometers on a heading of 073 degrees magnetic. On the forty minute flight, Brian was in the rear compartment, disconnecting various fittings and making sure the new engine was ready for immediate installation.

They worked feverishly in the fading light. The sky had turned to a deep blue and was roiling with clouds that held snow. Dale later remarked that it was probably the fastest engine change ever made: "It would make the record book, and it sure as hell wasn't done in a heated hangar!" After a quick ground run, they loaded the expired engine and Dale and Brian took off for St. Anthony. Peter followed in close formation just in case something was not quite right. Brian was somewhat concerned, having had no time to troubleshoot the installation. Not only was it dark when they sighted land, but moderate snow was falling, hampering their visibility even further.

On that part of the remote coast, there is no habitation and no lights. You have never seen a dark night unless you've been there. With the snowfall and darkness, it was necessary for them to slow down and hover along the crooked coastline from Quirpon Island to the harbour at St. Anthony. A straight flight would have been fifty kilometers but the indents and coves along Griquet, St. Lunaire, Brechat, and Square Bay elongated the route by fifty per cent. They were a tired but elated crew when their two noisy choppers landed by the Vinland Motel.

Viking had some great pilots and engineers who pushed the boundaries in a professional manner. They were always eager and proficient. Scotty Aldie was distinguished by his slinging and longlining skills. He was the lead pilot during the construction of the long Confederation Bridge to Prince Edward Island in 1996. With a Bell 212, he carried the steel crossbeams to the installed uprights and precisely hovered with the load while the bolts were placed to connect the two formations. This required extremely accurate manoeuvring with a heavy swaying load over an area with no relative reference or nearby horizon.

In the late 1970s, Viking was merged with Sealand Helicopters and they eventually became part of the international conglomerate, Canadian Helicopters Ltd. Under the vigilant guidance of Craig Dobbin, Canadian Helicopters became the largest fleet operator in the world.

Chapter 24 The Turnover

Queen Air B-80 aircraft were used to transport oil drilling crews to
Saglek, Labrador, as well as for medivacs, ice reconnaissance
and scheduled flights to St. Anthony and Blanc Sablon.

By the late 1970s, our little company was doing quite well. The
bush planes were busy year around with the mining companies,
tourist charters, construction projects, winter cargo flights to
Labrador, a new floatplane base in Goose Bay, off shore patrols,
oil exploration development and the inauguration of schedule
flights to St Anthony and Labrador. As well, our six helicopters
were in good demand. However, it was becoming obvious that the
recent road construction to the south coast and the other isolated
communities on the island and throughout Labrador would soon
reduce the need for bush plane travel.

Our future seemed to be in developing more feeder services to
connect small remote airports with regional airports at Deer Lake,
Goose Bay, Gander and St. John's. This would require a major
investment in larger and more sophisticated equipment.
Additionally we had a major contract in transporting offshore drill
crews between Gander and Saglek, Labrador. That consortium
asked us to provide a larger 48 passenger plane to cope with their
expanding program. The scope of our operations was rapidly
changing.

During the process of applying for new scheduled licenses, acquiring a large turboprop aircraft, designing a new hangar facility, and upgrading crews, we were approached by Eastern Provincial Airways to consider a merger. The thought of merging with our longstanding, fierce competitor was not too enticing. A merger would place me in a very minority situation. EPA had purchased Maritime Central Airways (MCA) in 1964 and rapidly expanded their scheduled services to mainland Canada. They were now using a fleet of Boeing 737 aircraft.

Eventually, the management of EPA asked for a meeting to discuss an outright purchase of my company. It was a discomfited decision. The future looked bright but a huge debt load would be required to realign our direction. It was also quite troubling to consider the abandonment of this little company that we had started from scratch and taken it through so much difficulty. It seemed as though I was considering the doomed burial of a loved one. Although not too captivated by the idea, I thought that there would be no harm in discussing the matter. Perhaps I would learn more about my competitors.

For the next few months, we held many meetings with Harold Wareham, EPA's vice president of finance, Bert Patey of Labrador Airways and our auditors. Eventually, we agreed to the terms of a sale with a specified date to finalize the closing.

As president of EPA, now the third largest air carrier in Canada, Andrew Crosbie invited me to their secluded lodge for finalizing the sale. He greeted me cordially at the dock as I flew into their chalet on Kekadeck Lake. Andrew was the younger son of Chesley Crosbie and brother of John the politician. Andrew was intricately involved in overseeing the vast Crosbie Empire, and in keeping with family tradition he was also imbedded in Newfoundland politics.

Andrew Crosbie

During our pre-dinner cocktails and the lavish meal that followed, I told him of my first encounter with his father at the Lakeland Motel in 1961: "I will never forget my anger when he smashed his glass on our table and vowed to kick me out of Newfoundland."

"Yes," he said, "Father could be pretty obnoxious when he was drinking."

"You know," I said. "The absurdity in all this is that I was in the process of giving up the flying business that same night your father threatened me. Had that incident not occurred, there wouldn't be any need of you now writing me a cheque!"

Andrew provided pleasant conversation about his family's checkered lifestyle, their many mistakes, and their vast accomplishments. He spoke of their increasing diversification and recent expansion into the offshore oil service industry. I asked why he wanted to purchase my small business.

"Frankly Gene," he said, "you were so successful in competing against us with your small bush planes under tremendous adversity that we don't want to see you get into bigger equipment. It's not your small aircraft that we are interested in as that demand is lessening. But our associate, Bert Patey with Labrador Air, could use those planes in Goose Bay."

While we were savoring our Irish coffee, Andrew handed me the cheque. "Lordy Jasus," he shouted. "Did you feel that vicious tremble?"

"No," I replied. What do you mean?"

He raised his sugar-rimmed glass to clink with mine: "My dear father, Ches, tried desperately to put you out of business, and now here I am buying you out. He detested you as a brazen adversary. As I passed you the cheque he rolled over in his grave, shuddering the whole east coast! I think it measured seven on the Reichter scale. "

I rose from my chair, reached across the table, wished him good luck, and we shook hands with mutual respect. The Crosbies had provided me with an exciting 20-year trip.

First Beaver- purchased from U.S. Wildlife Service

Eddie Oake & Rick Richard loading lumber

Harold Oake - chief pilot (1968)

Gene & Austin Bugden (1969)

Eddie Oake & Rick load deer at Anticosti Island, Quebec

NAT's first Otter

NAT adds 10-passenger aircraft

A new 10-passenger aircraft has been added to Newfoundland Air Transport Limited's fleet and will be used on the Deer Lake-St. Anthony-Southern Labrador scheduled run, says Gene Manion, NAT's general manager.

Mr. Manion Wednesday described the Queen Air B-80 as the most up-to-date commuter airliner for passenger and cargo feeder service.

Purchased in the United States, the twin-engine configuration and airline instrumentation and navigation equipment will permit NAT to operate over its routes at higher speeds and during inclement weather condition, Mr. Manion said.

A new Queen Air costs $280,000. It has a maximum cruising speed of 200 miles an hour but the unusual speed on scheduled runs will be 210 m.p.h., he said.

This aircraft will replace a seven-passenger Aero Commander that has been used on

the run, the aircraft has a 1,000-mile range and is adapted for air ambulance flights throughout the province or to the mainland. It will be permanently based at Deer Lake and will be available for charter when not on scheduled services.

Mr. Manion said the aircraft is fitted for 10 passengers or combination passenger and express loads. A specially designed cargo loading door is installed to accommodate large items being shipped to Labrador.

During 1972 NAT had a 17 per cent increase in schedule traffic over its route to Labrador and a 20 per cent increase is expected in 1973, Mr. Manion said.

St. Anthony was added to NAT's schedule in December 1972 and the company now operates three return flights each week to that point.

The schedule route will be extended to include Port au Choix and Goose Bay if an ap-

plication before the Air Transport Committee of the Canadian Transport Commission in Ottawa is approved, Mr. Manion said.

Future plans of the company are to include service to Burgeo, Mary's Harbour and Cartwright, when adequate landing strips are available there, he said.

The Newfoundland government recently introduced a 25 per cent fare subsidy for residents of Labrador travelling with NAT to and from Labrador.

NAT operates charter bases in South Brook, Furteau and Goose Bay. During 1972 the company transported more than 12,000 passengers and 2.4 million pounds of air cargo on their general services. Mr. Manion said.

The aircraft fleet includes 10 fixed wing aircraft and 14 during peak traffic seasons. Both piston and turbine powered helicopters are also based at Pasadena for use throughout the province.

Gene Manion, general manager of Newfoundland Air Transport Ltd., points to the Air Queen 10-passenger aircraft that the company has added to its Deer Lake St. Anthony-Southern Labrador scheduled run. The twin-engine aircraft is described by Mr. Manion as the most up-to-date commuter aircraft available for passenger and cargo feeder service.

Western Star-Corner Brook

NAT carrying out air surveillance

Newfoundland and Labrador Air Transport Ltd. of Pasadena are now providing air surveillance for the Inspection Branch of the Federal Dept. of Fisheries.

Gene Manion of NAT said the seal herds were presently off the east coast of the province and south as far as Fogo and east of Grey Islands. He said there are a number of Canadian and Norweigan vessels in the area and quite a few long-liners from Notre Dame Bay and Twillingate areas were presenting the seal fishery.

According to one of the NAT pilots, the seal herd is considered to be equal this year to any other season. Mr. Manion said the surveillance will be continued as long as the hunt goes on the quotas are reached. He indicated this would probably take place by mid-May.

NAT are using a twin-engine Beachcraft and a twin engine aero-commander which are good in excess of 10 hours endurance without refueling. The planes are specially equipped with precise navigational aids for obtaining accurate over-ice positions.

Approximately 25,000 patrol land miles are flown during the sealing operation.

Meanwhile, Mr. Manion informed the Humber Log that his company has been engaged by the sealing industry from time to time to assist their ships in locating herds and making air drops of emergency supplies.

He also disclosed that the Fishery Research Branch from Montreal have contracted with NAT in March for use of a turbine helicopter to assist them in their tagging and field studies of seals off the coast of Cartwright, Labrador. This particular operation has been carried out annually since 1965.

The sealing quota this year has been set for 60,000 each for both Norweigan and Canadian ships involved in the hunt while landsmen are allowed to take 30,000.

This picture, as all others, was taken by Gene Manion of Newfoundland and Labrador Air Transport Ltd. of Pasadena. This aerial scene gives readers a rare opportunity to see a herd of seals on the ice off the coast of Newfoundland.

BABY SEAL:— Known as the white-coat, this baby seal gazes directly at our cameraman when he shot this picture on the ice. The white coats are prized for their pelts.

Western Star-Corner Brook

Canada issued a stamp recognizing
the Main River as a heritage site

REFLECTIONS

Tumbling brook that feeds September Lake, a secret site in
western Newfoundland that I named and visited annually
for more than 25 years. September Lake is a place that offered
excellent trout fishing as well as delightful and wild tranquil beauty.
Beteeen the last week of August and mid-September,
the lake was an angler's dream,

Herbert Nadeau's cabin on the St. Paul River, Labrador
Note the ptarmigan hanging by the door. Sandy House, Ace Caines and I
stayed in this cabin during a goose hunting trip.

September Lake Brook Trout

PLEASURE FLYING and WHIRLY BIRDS

Chapter 25 A Wilderness Excursion

Len Chiasson and Ace Caines travelling up Main River before the storm

After the sale of NLAT, an entirely new chapter opened for me.I was now pleasure flying, with no stress from customers or employees. It was a different world, I went where I wanted to go and with whom I wanted. It was not necessary to transport maximum payloads, and pushing bad weather was no longer required.

Every year in late March, I would organize a wilderness holiday with some friends keen to enjoy a winter sport. One of my remote fishing camps was located at the headwaters of the Main River system on the Great Northern Peninsula, a few miles downstream from the Main River Lodge. This site offered a comfortable base camp for our wintry explorations. In 1978, Ace Caines and Len Chiasson accompanied me on a one week safari. We left the highway a few miles east of Deer Lake and used our snow machines to open a twisting path through the forests and river valleys. Extra fuel and all the necessary supplies were lashed on komotiks and towed up the 60 kilometer trail to Eagle Mountain Lake.

Each season it was our practice to investigate a new area and find alternate routes to our favourite sections. We knew the region extremely well since I had been flying over it for 17 years, Ace had hiked and trapped over most of the region, and the three of us had been snowmobiling in northern Newfoundland since1967. We also hunted caribou and moose and fly fished around the Main River each year. We had come to know the region so well that perhaps we were somewhat complacent and even careless in our wanderings.

We spent the first few days hauling firewood for our summer steam bath, ice fishing, and sightseeing along the valley. Although it's common to have   snowfall and high winds nearly every day in that high country, the weather had been unusually good. On the fourth afternoon we returned to camp for a late lunch.

Ace was restless. "We have about three hours of daylight left; let's go for a run up the river to Arluk Tilt," he suggested. "It will be a nice evening and we could come straight back over the mountains."

Arluk Tilt was a small log cabin we had constructed on a remote northern branch of the river for moose hunting and salmon fishing. The trip up the Main River and Keough's Brook would be about thirty kilometers.

Over the years, we had experienced many problems and hazardous conditions on our snowmobile escapades. As a result, we were usually well prepared for whatever might confront us on these excursions. On day trips we carried snowshoes, axe, compass, large scale maps, emergency rations, first-aid equipment, some tools and spare parts, a boiling pot, rope and extra fuel. However, since we thought this would be a short outing, we left our camp with scant supplies. The trip was delightful as we meandered up the river on the bright, smooth snow. Reaching the mouth of Keogh's Brook, we stopped for a chat.

"Let's forget about going to Arluk cabin, and continue up the main branch to Wentzell's camp on Four Ponds," Len suggested. "There's some low cloud over the high range, but it should be a good evening to go back across the mountains from the headwaters."

Ace and I agreed, since a direct course over the hills would be shorter and it was always boring to backtrack. We were aware of the challenging terrain through the mountains, but the snow crust was excellent and the weather looked favourable for a night crossing.

Ace was leading the parade on his Bombardier Olympic as we approached the third of the four lakes near the headwater. We should have been more cautious, since we all knew that the fast current from the lake's outflow often prevented safe ice from forming. Usually, we would divert through the woods to avoid the area, but on this day it looked white and solid. Following in Ace's tracks, Len and I came around the bend to see Ace crawling away from an open hole in the ice where his machine was precariously suspended, but mostly submerged.

Other than having two wet feet and a bruised knee, Ace was uninjured. The two front skis of the Skidoo were sticking up on the ice, the windshield and most of the engine was above the water and the rear section was unsteadily balancing below the gaping hole.

As we pulled the machine out and up onto solid ice, we noticed chimney smoke coming from the old Angus Wentzell hunting cabin at the far end of the lake. Prior to the 1980s, it was extremely unusual to encounter any other winter travelers in this isolated region. The wood harvesting roads were still far to the south and most snowmobilers were hesitant to venture into this far flung district. We decided to investigate.

Reaching the cluster of buildings, we discovered three snowmobiles parked in front of the main cabin. Three young men emerged from the doorway.

"Come on in," one of them said. "We got it nice and warm in here and a wee drop of whiskey might do you no harm."

We recognized Leslie Wentzell as soon as he opened his mouth. As Ace dried his boots and socks, Leslie explained the presence of his coastal group in this remote outpost: "We left home from Daniel's Harbour yesterday morning and came up the mountain trail to Rubbly Plateau. Only planned on a day trip, but we got wandering around the back country up by Leander Lake and got a bit mixed up in our location.We had a compass, but I guess we should've had a map, this being our first trip to these parts."

Leslie grabbed the bottle and took a swig as Ken Perry picked up where he left off: "We were following a bunch of valleys, looking for another way back to the ridge, when we spotted this old camp. Maybe you guys could show us the best route back. We're running a bit short on fuel."

Ace spread his topographical map on the table: "It's too late now to head back, but we'll show you the best route to take in the morning."

"Yeah, and it's starting to snow," Dawson put in. "Could be a bad night in the hills if that black cloud to the west keeps threatening."

Ace continued tracing a pencil line along the chart: "Go down through the four small lakes. After eight kilometers, turn north here up Keough's Brook. You'll pass by Gene's cabin at Arluk Steady, then go right up the brook to Jack Joe's Steady where the river divides. Keep to the left fork and past this old warden's cabin, then on up to Otter Pond. The steep slope will then lead you to the open barrens above the tree line. A compass course of 350 magnetic will bring you to Leander Lake. From there, follow the little brook north past the Spot of Snow Hill. Keep the higher hills to your left and you are back on Rubbly Plateau. The trail down to the coast is on the northwest side of the round hills, on the far side of the ridge. Keep clear of the hole I made at the lower end of the second pond that we marked it with spruce boughs. You could go up Ten Mile Lake, here. It's a shorter distance, but it can be bad reaching the open country cuz the steep shore at the north end."

I asked how they were off for grub.

"We only brought a couple loaves of bread and some tea. Our canned wieners are all gone," Leslie answered.

Before we left we gave them the map, six chocolate bars, and our two gallons of extra fuel and wished them well. They were all in high spirits as they waved goodbye from the doorway.

When we came out of the warmth of the cabin we were surprised to see a radical change in the weather. Large snowflakes were falling and the wind had freshened from the west. I glanced at the outline of the mountain summit where scuddy stratus had already formed around the peak.

Although we seldom headed recklessly into danger, after a short discussion we agreed to challenge the more difficult shorter route. Between us we had an intimate knowledge of perpendicular cliffs and hazardous gullies ahead. In spite of the impending storm and darkness, we felt confident of a successful passage.

The crossing was not the usual sort of hilly pass. The Four Pond Valley was separated from the Eagle Mountain Valley by a high, treeless, bleak plateau. To gain the height of land, we had to traverse several lakes and then locate Tuckamore Brook for a suitable entry up a steep, narrow gulch. There were many other streams, but they were either too steep or filled with impassable underbrush. In good weather it was easy to find the stream, but we had no idea of the storm that was brewing.

Forty minutes after leaving the river valley, we were into the rugged mountain area. The wind hit us with a blast and loose snow whipped round us like wisps of thick smoke. The conditions quickly turned ugly with the increasing ferocity of the wind. Len and Ace were leading the way and I was following close behind. Soon the visibility got so bad that I lost their tracks in the blinding snow. Even our bouncing headlights were useless in the furour of the drift. The pitch black of night and the heavy spindrift conspired to impede our progress. We could no longer make out landmarks, and all the enormous boulders looked alike; we couldn't recognize the small ponds or find the passage. Time and again we ended up in an impassable gorge and would have to stop to try to figure out where we were. Although we were warmly dressed, the fine powdery snow was penetrating every seam in our clothing.

Ace thought we should backtrack to Four Ponds, but we soon found that our tracks had completely disappeared. For hours we circled and searched to pick up a recognizable lead through the tangled scrub spruce. By midnight, over twelve inches of heavy snow had fallen. We began to spin out on the steeper hills and were exhausted from pushing and pulling on the mired machines. The drive belt snapped on Len's Elan, but that was soon replaced from the spare parts duffel bag.

Finally we came upon a large lake that we recognized as East Island Pond. At least we knew we were on the right route and we would find the Tuck Brook access flowing into this lake at the southeast corner. Nearly delirious with exhaustion, we stopped in the swirling snow to discuss our situation.

"This is stupid," I shouted above the howling wind. "We'll never make it across the open country in this storm. We'd be crazy to try! Let's pull into the heavy timber and wait for daylight."

At the southern end of the lake we parked the three machines and huddled under a large fir tree with our backs to the wind. After gathering a pile of dry limbs, we found temporary comfort from a blazing fire, but that was short lived as the rising heat from the fire melted the snow embedded in the branches above us. Still, it was too frigid to move away from the warmth of the fire to be free of the dripping water. Occasionally, we were forced back from the flame with the smell of scorched nylon from our leg coverings. At least sitting on the snow by the fire, only our backs were cold and wet. As the fire pit melted down into the deep snow, we had to stomp around the rim to allow air to feed the flame. Although we were exhausted, it was impossible for us to grab any sleep huddled in our sodden clothes, with the branches dripping and the whirling snow spinning around our heads. While Ace boiled some strong tea, we ate the last of our marble cheese and pondered our gas situation.

With his flashlight, Len checked the fuel quantity in our machines: "Ace has less than one quarter tank, Gene's Scandic is slightly better, and my Elan is about one quarter."

It was a long, wretched night. The heavy snow and gale force wind didn't let up. Anxious to get going, though stiff from sitting all night, at first light we started our machines only to discover that Len had left the cover off my gas tank. The drifting snow had created a slushy mixture of non-flammable liquid.

Highly discouraged by this finding, we headed up the canyon with two of us trying to ride on the small Elan and Ace breaking trail. Within the first hour we had exhausted all the fuel in the small overworked Skidoo. Len and I set out on snowshoes. We compacted a deep path for Ace to follow up the small brook. The forest thinned and grew sparse, and little by little, with altitude, the trees shrank to spiked scrubs. We eventually gained open country above the tree line. This part of the Long Mountains Range is generally avoided by knowledgeable travelers, except in good weather and good daylight visibility and for good reason. Without reasonable visual reference it's easy to become trapped in a deep ravine or unexpectedly stumble over the edge of an icy cliff. We were well aware that two years earlier, a disoriented trekker had driven his machine over the 2,000 foot lip of a fiord near Sally's Cove.

Partway up the slope, the coil on Ace's machine failed. We abandoned our last machine, with survival now dependant on our legs. Upon reaching the barrens, the visibility was almost non-existent in the blowing snow. The encrusted surface was now covered with over two feet of new snow and the relentless wind was moving it from one place to another. Hungry and damp, we trudged southeast by compass with no visible features to guide us.

For hours, with no trees or stumps in our path, we struggled across the high plateau, plodding along the crust covered ground. In the blizzard, it was a long, exhausting trek to the eastern slope that led to the Eagle Lake Valley. At times, the man only ten feet ahead would disappear in the impenetrable gusts. Fortunately we had the wind on our backs. We were thankful for our snowshoes and compass.

By late afternoon, we passed Bean Pond and Jackie's Bone, which were familiar milestones. We could see our destination lake about ten kilometers down the valley. We descended into the forested area. The low drift we had been fighting since daybreak was behind, but the soft snow let our snowshoes sink deep with each weary step. At least it was downhill. Ace and Len were about ten years younger and fit for extended snowshoe travel, but I was exhausted. My knees jarred with each step and it felt like my legs were driving up through my hips.

As daylight faded, I kicked away the snow and pushed open our cabin door. On reaching comfort and safety, all the pain and hardships were quickly forgotten. Soon, the big stove was red with fire and a stew of bottled moose was heating on the open cover. By the time we had consumed the third hot toddy, we were laughing about our foolish exploit, plotting the recovery of our three machines, and even planning our next escapade.

The camp was equipped with a single sideband radio for contact with our aircraft base at Deer Lake Airport. Before noon the next day we had a Beaver skiplane dispatched to carry us back to civilization. Although it was still stormy on the western hills, pilot Pierre Meagher had no difficulty flying us to Deer Lake by routing through the lower country on the eastern slope.

Overconfidence in our knowledge of the country, and complacency about the weather, had led us into a hazardous situation. Hopefully, we thought, our friends from Daniel's Harbour will not be so impulsive on their trip out.

A difficult trek across the barrens in the storm

A snug camp after the storm

Chapter 26 RCAF Search

The fiords of western Newfoundland -magnificent but treacherous

When I arrived home at Steady Brook, my wife Nina greeted me with an urgent message: "The RCMP detachment has been trying to reach you. Apparently some men are missing from Daniel's Harbour. Three days ago they went over the mountains by snowmobile and they haven't returned. The police have organized a big search and they want your help."

After unpacking, I contacted Inspector McGuire at his office in Corner Brook: "Yes, Mr. Manion, our detachment in Port Saunders has set in motion a search plan for the overdue snowmobilers from Daniel's Harbour. They require someone who has an extensive knowledge of the Northern Peninsula and they have suggested your involvement. We will transport you to the area. How soon would you be able to leave?"

Since I'd just arrived home, Nina wasn't really pleased when I boarded Constable Flynn's vehicle the next morning for the four hour drive to Daniel's Harbour. The road had been paved north of Deer Lake through the Gros Morne National Park as far as Rocky Harbour. In the high elevations around Bonne Bay, it was very icy with snow pack. As we slowly drove north along the coast, my driver filled me in on some details.

Surprisingly, the search that was underway was for the same three men that we had encountered at Four Ponds two days before.

"We gave a map and directions to Leslie and Dawson Wentzell and Ken Perry," I told him. "They were confused about the best route home over the mountains."

We pulled into Clifford House's motel on the southern edge of Daniel's Harbour in the early afternoon. There were a number of cars and pickup trucks parked in the driveway and a large Labrador helicopter sat across the road in the adjoining field.

Daniel's Harbour is a coastal town about half way up the northern peninsula. Traditionally a fishing port, it gradually evolved into a mining community with the development of the Newfoundland Zinc Mine in 1967. I was well acquainted with Jim Hogan, the mine manager. Jim was a take charge kind of man who always involved himself in community affairs. As I entered the modest motel, Jim greeted me and invited me to join him and Corporal McIntee for a late lunch.

McIntee was a church-going family man who cared deeply about his community. He couldn't have been more concerned if he was involved in a search for his own son. He and Hogan told me the parents of the missing men couldn't understand why Search and Rescue hadn't moved, They said with my military background and local experience maybe the air force captain would listen to me. After I agreed to talk to him I went down the hallway and knocked on door number 9.

"I'm Captain Trayner," a man said in a deep baritone as he opened the door, apparently about to go out. "Senior pilot with Rescue Squadron #103. You must be that infamous bush pilot that they told us all about. Please come in."

The other man in the room was introduced as Lieutenant Davis. He was slightly younger and wearing an immaculate blue flight suit. I was surprised when Trayner asked Davis to leave the room so we could talk privately. The captain was neat and clean-shaven. He removed his peak cap and dark sunglasses, revealing short-cropped black hair and sharp blue eyes. He had the businesslike air of an energetic and capable man.

"I'll be in charge of the SAR operations here," he said. "When the weather clears, I'll get things underway to find those men. It shouldn't be much of a problem. This crew has been successful in all our last twenty-three missions. Oh, we don't always recover living souls. Sometimes things happen on the ground before we reach the site, but we always make a successful recovery, one way or another."

I gave him a brief overview of our recent encounter with the lost party, described the general terrain in that region and advised him of the growing local discontent. Given his superior air, I hesitated to mention my particular knowledge of the local terrain or my understanding of Air Force bureaucracy.

"Thank you for your guidance, Mr. Manion. I'm sure we'll be able to find you if we have further need." It seemed our conversation was finished and I was dismissed.

Prior to holding a full discussion with McIntee and Hogan, I made a point of bumping into the helicopter maintenance engineer to inquire about any possible mechanical problems and their fuel situation. Although he wasn't anxious to talk at first, I learned that their Labrador Helicopter was due for a major component change after two more start cycles and that the regulations would not permit replenishing their tanks from nonauthorized fuel drums. They had about five flight hours of fuel remaining.

Calling Gander Met Center, I received a comprehensive weather picture. There was a stationary depression over the Gulf, creating a strong southwest flow of moist, unstable air along the west coast of the province. The inland upslope would continue to cause low stratus and wet snow throughout the high country. The lee side of the peninsula would be slightly better. These conditions were likely to persist for two or three more days. But there could be temporary periods of minor improvement as the surface trough waves moved slowly across the province.

Reluctantly, I phoned the Search Command Centre at Halifax to determine their involvement in the operation and to find out if another helicopter would be available. The major was well aware of the situation in Daniel's Harbour, but unfortunately their other machines were either in maintenance or allocated to other important missions.

Later, at our meeting, we studied the maps and terrain data, probable search areas, weather information, the background of the lost persons, their clothing and supplies, and the information that I had obtained about the helicopter situation. We were aware of the dangerous confusion that would inevitably develop if various groups went off in uncoordinated search patterns. We concluded that some decisive steps had to be taken. Corporal McIntee would inform everyone that he was now the "command search controller" and that all rescue attempts and briefings would be coordinated through his office. Meanwhile, the RCMP would immediately charter a Bell Jet Ranger helicopter to assist with the search and I would direct the chartered helicopter in its search activities. Jim Hogan would organize and outfit an experienced ground party to immediately go to the search area from Deer Lake, using my camp at Eagle Mountain as their base.

That night, at McIntee's request, I conducted a town hall meeting organized by Jm Hogan. Friends and family of the missing men filled the schoolroom. The air was thick with cigarette smoke and despair. The pain of constant worry was etched deep into their grim faces. One of the mothers had tears in her eyes as she spoke: "They's been gone tree nights with no food and nare sleeping bags. The weather has been most frightful for dem and that dere helicopter hasn't turned a blade. No one has gone to elp 'em. We can't just sit ere and wait fer 'em to die!"

I chose my words carefully. I wanted to be clear about the weather factors and the futility of flying in the mountains without visual reference. I told of our chance meeting with the lads at Four Ponds and about the map, fuel, and directions we had given them. I told them how we had marked all the hunting cabins on the map and explained the best route for them to take, that we had warned them about staying clear of the fiords and had advised them of the best compass course.

"They are all intelligent young men," I said. "And they know that the best thing to do is to stay in a warm cabin until it's fit to travel. There are usually some canned goods in those camps, and if not, they can stay healthy for many days without food."

There seemed to be some relief when I told them that we were bringing in another chopper and that a ground party was being organized to leave that night for the back country. I was as reassuring as I could be in the circumstances.

Randell Wentzell, an elderly camp outfitter from River of Ponds, walked back to the motel with me. "I knows what they's goin through, cuzz I bin dere," he said. "Tree year hago, we got starmed in back dere wit nuttin.' Fetched up in a snow drifter fer four nights at tirty below."

"Yeah, I heard about your ordeal," I said. "Your hands and feet were badly frozen, as I remember?"

"Yes me son, she was some wunnerful cold . When I gets back ome, dey cuts off me big toe and tree fingers with the gangrene." He laughed as he held up his remaining thumb and forefinger. "T'is nothing ta fear though, fer I's still gots nuff left for two more nights easy!"

I laughed at Randell's dark sense of humor, but he and I both knew that he had got off lucky. The high country is always beautiful and seductive, but it can be treacherous.

Back in the noisy motel bar, I bumped into Trayner's co-pilot, Lieutenant Ernie Davis, as he was returning to his corner table.

He seemed eager to talk, so I didn't interrupt as he opened up about his senior pilot. Apparently Captain Trayner had to cancel some scheduled time off when he was assigned this mission and the squadron was temporarily short of both machines and qualified healthy personnel. Trayner hadn't been to northern Newfoundland before and he was generally unhappy with the entire situation. He had been advised to keep a lid on the fact that the assigned helicopter was due for a major component change after two more flight starts and no replacement equipment was readily available. The squadron command thought it would be bad public relations if the press discovered that the machine was so restricted in its mission Their orders were to be sure not to waste a trip in poor weather or they would be grounded for maintenance. That, at least, explained Captain Trayner's reluctance to get the search off the ground. Ernie went on to praise the outstanding piloting skills of his captain, even if he had a reputation for going strictly by the book. He also told me Trayner was possibly working on a promotion, was known to be somewhat opinionated, and did not take kindly to criticism.

At breakfast the next morning, the dining room windows rattled from the loud vibrations of a landing helicopter. Jack Saunders of Universal Helicopters set his small chopper down by the building. He had followed up the stormy coast from Pasadena. After shutting down, he wasted no time pumping fuel from the sealed drums of Jet A-1 that Jim Hogan had had delivered to the site. A few minutes later, Captain Trayner stormed into the office breathing fire.

"Manion, you had no business calling Halifax Center. Why did you go over my head? And what's with that chopper that just landed?" he spluttered, picking up steam. "What were you doing talking to my mechanic? Who in hell do you think you are? I got a good mind to...."

"Just hold on right there, Captain Trayner!" McIntee said, taking control of the situation. "Now I told you this morning that I was in command of coordinating this search. Let's all be totally clear on that. I won't interfere with you or your crew in the flying of your machine, but everyone will take direction from my office. Is that clear?" It was a rhetorical question, and the corporal continued in his calm but forceful manner: "I've given certain responsibilities to Gene and to date he has been more helpful than some I could name. He has many years of experience with the RCAF, he has an intimate knowledge of the search area, and he has at least shown some real compassion for the relatives. If you have any complaints in the future, please direct them to me!"

Trayner apparently got the message, though he obviously didn't like it much. He did an abrupt about face and left the office muttering, squeezing by Jack Saunders in the doorway.

Jack was a personable, soft-spoken man and an exceptional helicopter pilot. He had accumulated many hours of flying time in Newfoundland, but the mountainous region to be searched was not well known to him. We filled Jack in on the situation. He said he was ready to go when we were and it would be great if I would ride with him as he wasn't familiar with the area.

In the meantime, conditions had worsened considerably, with very little visibility in the heavy, wet snow. Everything was on hold except for Jim Hogan's ground party. On my suggestion, Jim had appointed Ace Caines and Sandy House to lead the ground party. The Newfoundland Zinc Mine provided vehicles, food, gasoline, extra clothing, medical supplies, sleeping bags, block and tackle and an array of other equipment. He had briefed the four-man search party and got them underway the night before. They would pick up Tommy and Edward Caines at Portland Creek while enroute to the Sop's Arm starting point. From there, they would proceed by snowmobile to the Eagle Mountain camp, arriving around midnight if things went well.

Sandy House was one of the best bush men in the country. He was famed for his resourcefulness and knew the area as well as Ace. Tommy Caines, Ace's older brother, had guided, hunted and fished all his life. He was an invaluable companion in the woods. If I was ever lost or in serious trouble in the wilderness, I certainly would want Tommy involved in any rescue effort. He was always optimistic and as a situation worsened, the more ingenious he became. Edward was an experienced guide, mechanic and carpenter. The four men made a great team; they were all in outstanding physical condition and it was certain they would scan every nook and cranny of the backcountry they knew so well.

We received a message through our Deer Lake dispatcher that the search party had arrived at Eagle Camp early that morning and would soon be heading north to the Four Ponds and Keough's Brook area. They reported difficult trail conditions and continuing bad weather.

At Daniel's Harbour, the wet snow turned to heavy rain in the afternoon. We were still grounded. Even the local people realized that it would be impossible to fly in such conditions. Still, there was some comfort in knowing that a ground search was underway.

Corporal McIntee informed me that Captain Trayner would not be interested in my accompanying him when the air search finally got started:"He told me it wasn't normal procedure to have a civilian onboard during such a sortie and if the mission was aborted after four hours, they would be proceeding to Gander or St. John's directly from the search area."

"That's fine with me," I replied. "Jack and I will do our own scouting with his Bell."

I had a restless night listening to the rain pelting the roof and bouncing off the window. The friction with Captain Trayner bothered me. I did realize that he was in a tight spot, with the dicey fuel and maintenance requirements, and I was also aware that many Air Force pilots would question the idea of putting their trust in the uncertain talents of some bush pilot they didn't know. After the all night rain there was reason to be even more concerned about the fate of the lost men. And to aggravate our fears, the temperature dropped rapidly in the morning, covering everything with sheets of solid ice. McIntee was solemn in giving his report.

"I spoke with our medical adviser and he's not optimistic about our finding those men alive," he said. "If they're not in a cabin, there's a good likelihood of hypothermia from the soaking rain and the freezing temperatures. This could well be fatal and, as you know, dead people are much harder to locate."

"Don't share that assessment with the locals," Jim piped in, still worried about the deteriorating state of mind of the villagers. "They're already pessimistic enough."

The freezing rain stopped by late morning. Jack and I worked for two hours removing the ice envelope from his fuselage and rotor blades. Across the street, the big Labrador presented a greater task for the air force team. As we were completing the de-icing the wind picked up, but the visibility along the coast was improving. I phoned Pierre Meagher at the Deer Lake dispatch office for a weather update since he was in radio contact with various stations, as well as the Eagle camp. He said he'd talked to Ace and there was no sign of the missing men.

I asked him about the current weather and about whether Ace had said anything about the conditions at the higher elevation.

"It has started a lifting trend here at the airport with a 1,200 foot ceiling and very light snow," he said. "Winds are 350 degrees at 25 mph and gusting. Ace says there's light snow and the cloud is on the high hills to the north and west of camp. He says there's better visibility to the east and it's a bit brighter overhead. The Gander forecast office gave the last hourly for Daniel's Harbour at 400 feet obscure with six miles in light snow. They said a temporary clearing trend should take place on the eastern slope for the next few hours. They also said it will become 'shitters' again toward sunset."

"Thanks Pierre," I said. "Keep a close handle on it. Jack and I may go for a look with CG-NLB. We'll contact you on channel six."

I discussed the matter with McIntee, Jim, and Jack Saunders. They agreed that our only window would be during the next few hours. We had to go and we had to go now. Jack said he would start his machine while I grabbed the emergency pack, some extra clothing and the sleeping bags. I said I'd be with him by the time the chopper warmed up.

As I slipped and slid across the icy street to the Jet Ranger, the five-man Air Force crew was just finishing their de-icing of the big SAR chopper. Corporal McIntee followed me to the aircraft with a large duffle bag. "Here," he said ominously. "Take these body bags and tell Jack if you recover any bodies, go directly to Corner Brook. Don't bring dead people back here."

I threw the packsack in the rear cabin and climbed into the left seat beside Jack. As Jack was applying flight RPM, Captain Trayner ran toward us. Crouching under the rotor blades, he opened my cockpit door. In the pulsating downwash, Jack had to reduce power to hear him.

"Where in hell do you guys think you're going in this weather?" Trayner boomed, at the top of his voice.

"We're going to have a look behind the mountains," I shouted back. "This may be our only chance."

Trayner's face was contorted with frustration, his eyes wide and glaring: "If you fly in that little machine and we don't, how do you think that will make us look?

Closing the door in his face, I shrugged: "That's your problem, Captain!"

Jack was rolling the power on again, but Trayner wouldn't let up, and banged his fist on my window. I opened the door again.

"You are forcing me to fly against my better judgment," he roared. "Will you please ask your pilot to shut down and will you think about coming with me?"

Jack gave me a victory smile and thumbs up as he began shut-down procedures. I wasted no time gathering my gear from the back seat and ran across the road to board the air force chopper. Trayner beckoned me to sit up front in the co-pilot's position. Lieutenant Davis gave me a conspiratorial grin and a friendly pat on the shoulder as he relinquished his seat to take up a location in the rear cabin.

Trayner was on the intercom as soon as I donned my headset.

"You know the country and the weather, so I am totally relying on you for navigational direction," he said. "Just tell me where to go, but keep us visual with the ground. Here's a local chart."

"I don't need it," I replied, placing it back in the flight bag. We lifted off in a torrent of swirling snow. Behind the classic sun-glasses, Trayner was as calm and free of emotion as a statue carved in stone. He went through his checklist thoroughly, every inch the professional.

"Mr. Manion," he said. "If you screw up, or it gets too hairy, I'm pulling this baby up and we will be proceeding IFR directly to St. John's. We are only going back to Daniel's Harbour if we're successful in retrieving live souls. Have you got it?"

In reply, I calmly suggested he follow the coast south to Sally's Cove. The machine was huge, with a morass of dual instrumentation, radio equipment and state of the art navigational tools. As we flew down the coastline, I was very uneasy, torn between feelings of responsibility for dragging this crew into a dangerous, perhaps unwise rescue mission, and the commitment I had made to the villagers. The two paramedics and the engineer were securely buckled in and kept watch through the rear windows. I reached down and tightened my seatbelt as the gusting wind buffeted the giant bird we were all depending on.

I kept an eye inland as we passed a string of fiords, some eight kilometers to our left. The largest of these huge canyons was Western Brook Gorge, cutting a narrow gully eastward through the high coastal mountains. I was hoping that the weather to the east had sufficiently improved to allow a visual passage from the far end of that fiord to the interior plateau. I had used this passage previously in similar weather conditions. As we approached Sally's Cove, I directed the captain to turn east into the mouth of the fiord. Entering the dark, eerie canyon, the passage at first looked impossible. The vertical rock walls loomed over 2,000 feet from the lakebed to the top edge on both sides of the helicopter. The rims were enveloped in swirling gray snow cloud and the far end was obscured with a canopy of dark stratus. For a brief moment, Trayner's eyes met mine; seeming to ask why in the world we were flying up this dead end gorge.

"We may find an opening at the far end which will allow access to the eastern slope," I said. "Otherwise we'll have to go all the way around these mountains to the Humber River. This could save us one hour of flight time if it works." I warned him to watch out for some serious turbulence in the gorge. With high winds, the airflow funnels up the chasm and bounces violently off the cliffs. Pilots generally avoid these areas during high winds.

The intercom crackled with the captain's message: "You'd best batten down the hatches. We expect some rough air."

It would be tight, but there would be sufficient room to turn around at the far end if the fiord was found to be impassable. I stared ahead as the big machine pitched and yawed through the tunnel. Rounding the last bend, we saw a small ray of light sky between the rocks and the ragged cloud.

"Beyond that opening things should improve," I said. "If you can squeeze her through."

Even for a seasoned flyer, it was a breathtaking few moments as the captain threaded the machine over the boulders, with the bouncing rotors cutting through the wispy cloud base. In front of us, the sky brightened considerably as we safely passed the high divide. Pointing to the right, I directed Trayner toward Eastern Brook Lake which flowed down in a series of ponds to the headwaters of the Humber River at Upper Lake.

The ground party had scanned the country as far north as Otter Pond, so I planned to concentrate our aerial effort north of that area. Carefully picking our way to avoid the higher elevations, we flew up the winding Humber past Beaver Pond and September Lake. After we crossed Ruhr's Ridge, the route to St. Paul's Lake was relatively easy. Turning east we flew down the Main Valley passing below Bean Hill, still topped with stratus. We were now in the region north of my Eagle Mountain camp, a region with which I was intimately familiar. Now very comfortable with my navigation, I directed the machine across No Moose Valley to gain access to Keogh's Brook on the north side of the Main River. My small cabin at Arluk Tilt passed beneath us before we reached the headwaters at Otter Pond. From here it became more difficult. The terrain sloped up to the high, treeless tableland that extended to the interior chasm behind Portland Creek Gulch.

The high plateau was obscured in an icy crystal haze. There was no horizon or visible reference as the sky blended into the snow-carpeted surface creating a leaden void.

"That's the region where they probably went astray," I said, pointing ahead. Trayner rolled back both engines to hover RPM.

"It looks impossible to stay visual in these conditions, but I'll do one swing up that slope," he said. The intercom clicked: "Keep your eyes open, gentlemen, we are in the zone."

We were going uphill now, climbing slowly toward the height of land that separates the watershed of the Main River and the divide above Portland Gulch. The big chopper crawled noisily along the bleak gradient. We skimmed along above the endless white canvas, a vast, vague, colourless tract stretching to an uncertain horizon. Visibility deteriorated rapidly as we circled around the higher hills searching for ground reference. The only option was to turn back down to Otter Pond.

"Let's do one more swing up the hill," I suggested.

"OK, but that will be it," the captain said, and then called Search Control Center on the high-frequency radio.

"Halifax Control. This is Trident Rescue One Zero Four, aborting search due weather. Returning to Torbay momentarily. Stand by for IFR flight plan. Over."

I was heartbroken by our failure, but I knew it was the correct decision under the circumstances. It was an extremely dangerous flight environment and the poor visibility simply ruled out any hope of a successful search. There really wasn't any choice. Still, desperately, my mind searched for another option.

"Let's set her down at my cabin and wait for conditions to improve," I pleaded.

"No way," Trayner replied.

On the last turn over the gradient, I caught a fleeting glimpse of what might have been a partially obliterated caribou track.

"There was a track up there, probably caribou. Can we have another look?" I asked, clinging to a slender hope. On the next swing, one of the observers shouted through the intercom.

"It could be a snowshoe track and it's heading straight up the hill!" he said.

The twin rotors banked again. Now the light was sufficiently penetrating the crystalline haze to show dim shadows on the surface. Straining our eyes, we caught the faint silhouette of raised imprints angling in a straight line up the incline. The captain concentrated on holding the directional gyro on course as he manoeuvred low over the deceptively featureless slope. As we inched up the difficult grade, we picked up diffuse trail patches every hundred meters or so. The blotches we were seeing were not depressions. The wind had blown the loose snow away from the compacted snowshoe tracks, transforming them to raised imprints that were casting dim shadows on the lower surface. Visibility was negligible until we began a slow descent on the other side of the gradient. We lost the indicators, then found them again as we continued to head in a straight line down the slanting highland.

The hillside was speckled with boulders and stunted juniper brush and arctic willow scrub thrust their spines above the snow, becoming more numerous on the terrace below the ridge. The intercom was quiet as we squinted and strained our eyes at the empty terrain. Our ship lurched and swayed in the buffeting wind fanning up the ravine. The sparse brush thickened into groves of alder and tuckbrush as we slowly rumbled again down the fractured bluff. We lost the trail, but it was obviously leading down to the head of the gorge. The vegetation changed dramatically in the lower reaches of the valley. The sparse juniper gradually thickened into a dense forest of larch and black spruce.

We descended into the bottom of the canyon, where the steep walls engulfed Portland Inner Pond. Rocky chasm walls decked with snow and scrub brush gave way far below to a winding furrow of lake ice. Tall fir and the corrugated trunks of spruce flanked the shore at the head of the ravine. The topmost boughs swayed violently in the wind. The chopper shuddered with each gust lashing against the fuselage as Trayner carefully circled the inside terminus of the fiord. Feathery snow was still falling. The intercom crackled to life.

"Hold course. Smoke at two o'clock! Someone's waving a red shirt!"

It was an awkward spot; the trees beneath us were eighty feet tall, the terrain was vertical and there was no opening in the forest to permit a landing. The end of the lake was about a mile away, and the water there was not frozen enough to land safely.

Without hesitation, the captain sized up the nasty situation. Before committing to a hover, many assessments have to be made: Is there sufficient power to maintain a stationary position over the towering trees? Where is the best opening to lower the hoist? Are the downdrafts and turbulence too severe? What is the average wind direction? Is there sufficient visual reference, and what is the escape route if something goes wrong? But there was not a moment of indecision.

"I'll enter a hover inside that dead spruce," Trayner said. "Kim, deploy the hoist. Paramedics, prepare for descent. Ernie, call me the numbers. Please acknowledge."

"Hoist being deployed."

"Ready for descent."

"Looks OK, Captain. Maybe port ten feet. OK, steady now."

I was impressed with the speed and efficiency of the entire crew. They all knew exactly what was required. In no time, the chopper was stationary over a small opening and a paramedic was being lowered through a small clearing on a body harness, and transmitting directions to the winch operator. The co-pilot was peering down through an observation window and relaying positional data to the pilot so he could remain directly over the recovery hole.

Only another pilot could appreciate the tremendous skill and concentration that Trayner was demonstrating. The slightest miscalculation would have tangled the dangling umbilical cable in the swaying trees. His greatest difficulty was maintaining our static location in the unpredictable gusts of wind conspiring to shift us from that critical position.While monitoring the instruments, Trayner's right hand gently milked the control column and his left hand adjusted the collective lever up and down while delicately rolling the throttle quadrant. His feet worked the tail rotor pedals to keep the nose directed toward the changing wind. He made small reflex adjustments in response to his visual reference and to the audible directions being transmitted by Ernie. All the while, his composure was as cool and calm as if he was watching a mildly interesting video. Had I not known better, I might have thought Trayner was just carrying out a simple, routine manoeuvre.

The voice in the earphones came from the ground: "All three are status eight. Basket not required. First one secured. Take him up."

I left my seat in the cockpit to see if I could be of help by the open evacuation door. Leaning out, I grabbed Leslie Wentzell as he came up to the gate and pulled him into the cabin. He stared at me through a mask of frosted whiskers.

"For the love of God, Manion, don't you ever go home?"

We hugged each other like long-lost brothers. Soon all three men were safely on board, the hoist was swung in, and the door was closed and latched.

"Recovery complete. All secure. Good to go," the crew chief advised.

Trayner motioned me to return to the cockpit as he began turning the helicopter back toward the mountainous route we had just taken.

I quickly turned on my intercom. "There's no need to retrace that route through the high country," I said. "You can turn west and go out the fiord. It will take you directly to the coast at Portland Creek. That's only a few miles south of Daniel's Harbour."

"OK, navigator," he answered, reducing power and easing the big machine around toward the coast. "Halifax Control, this is Trident One Zero Four. Mission complete. Three souls on board, status eight. Landing Daniel's in fifteen. Will then proceed St. Johns, IFR."

The search route had taken us in a semicircle behind the Long Range hills. In a direct line, we were now only 30 kilometers from our departure point. Proceeding out the fiord, I savoured the play of clouds against the curtained walls and the black craggy ledges that we were leaving behind. The winding canyon led us to the flat coastal plain where visibility had improved under the lingering stratus cloud.

We learned that the lost trio had abandoned their snow machines the same day they left Four Ponds. The heavy, loose snow, together with steep elevations, had created impossible barriers for their spinning snowmobile tracks. They had proceeded on snowshoes through the worst of the blizzard, heading blindly across the windswept tundra by compass. The storm, sweeping across the open tableland, carried snow for miles without obstruction, dropping some in every coulee. Eventually, confused, battered and forlorn, they descended into a valley where some relief was found in the shelter of the forest. There were times when they walked in circles only to come back to their recent tracks. In places, they broke through the crust to sink armpit deep into the snow. Their bootlaces were caked and frozen, and their tattered pants flapped around their legs, encrusted with ice. The dark of night was upon them when they reached the bottom of the ravine.

Recognizing the seriousness of their predicament, they scooped out a cavern from the ten meter snowdrift that had formed on the south side of the chasm. The snow cave kept them dry and sheltered from the blizzard as they huddled together for warmth. The next morning they built a roaring fire to dry boots and mitts outside their den, but the exertion of gathering the wood cost them more energy than the fire provided warmth. Although tired and famished, they had survived their ordeal unscathed because they didn't panic and used common sense. They were convinced by their surroundings that they had stumbled into the eastern end of the Portland Creek Gulch. Had they not been rescued, they had hoped to walk out to the coast when the weather cleared.

We later calculated that their directional error may have occurred because they failed to apply the thirty degrees of westerly variation for the region.

We circled the town and made a low victory pass over the gathering crowd at Daniel's Harbour. Landing by the motel, the chopper would have been mobbed by a swarm of relieved and jubilant townfolk had Jim Hogan not secured the area surrounding the landing pad. The big rotors slowed to an idle and the cabin crew helped the bedraggled threesome disembark. Trayner completed his checklist and reached for my hand.

Captain Trayner and I had taken an instant dislike to one another. We both had an idea of how things should be done, and our ideas had bumped up against each other. But as often happens when lives are on the line, we had learned a lot about each other on that short flight together. I took his hand gladly and shook it firmly. We clearly now both regretted that we had got off on the wrong foot. I had seen Trayner in action under the most difficult conditions and could only admire his incredible skill as a pilot and his coolness under pressure. He was a real professional and I told him so.

"I hope one day I'll have half your skill handling a chopper," I told him.

For his part, the captain made it clear he now appreciated the crucial importance of my knowledge of the backcountry. He knew that my "interference" had ultimately played a key role in the successful conclusion of the rescue.

"I'm truly sorry we didn't get off to a better start," he shouted over the din of the engines. "If I'm ever involved in searching this high country again, I want you with me right up front."

There were warm handshakes and hugs of mutual respect with the crew of the Labrador as I disembarked. Avoiding another start cycle, the big helicopter engines roared with increasing rpm and lifted from the field, climbed into the cloud layer, and disappeared from view before the whine of the rotors faded into the grey overcast.

A few weeks later, I received a letter of commendation from Inspector McGuire of the RCMP for my participation in the search and rescue.

CH-113 Labrador helicopter

GENE MANION

ROYAL CANADIAN MOUNTED POLICE   "B"   DIVISION   GENDARMERIE ROYALE DU CANADA

YOUR NO.
VOTRE Nº

OUR NO.
NOTRE Nº

Corner Brook Sub-Division
April 13th, 1978

Mr. M.G. Manion,
Forest Drive,
Steady Brook,
Newfoundland.

Dear Sir:

     I have received a report from Cpl. McIntee of
Port Saunders Detachment regarding the recent search for
Leslie and Dawson Wentzell and Kenneth Perry.

     I have noted with particular interest the part
you played in the search and I wish to thank you for giving
us the benefit of your time and knowledge which obviously
were so important in bringing the search to a successful
conclusion. Cpl. McIntee has also commented very highly on
the manner in which you spoke to the relatives of the
missing men and offered reassurance.

     While I do not wish to detract from the role
that many government agencies can, and do, play in rescue
matters, I feel we would be vain to think that they are all
that is required. Certainly, this case illustrates again
that in the final analysis no combination of these efforts
will ever replace fully persons like yourself whose traditions
and knowledge of local conditions will continue to be of such
vital importance in these endeavours.

     Thank you.

Yours truly,

J.B. McGuire, Insp. for
O.C.Corner Brook S/Divn.AOD

Chapter 27 The Wheelbarrow

Pierre Meagher inspects new high-grade tire
at airstrip in Charlottetown, Labrador

Ralph House and his wife Rachel spent their early years in a small, isolated, hand-hewn house on the upper reaches of the Charlottetown River in Labrador. It is now called Campbell's Cove. Being a seasoned trapper, fisherman and woodsman, Ralph eked out a bare existence, fishing on the coast near Triangle in the summer and trapping on the barrens during the long winter. The nearest settlement was the small village of Charlottetown (previously called Old Cove), some 25 kilometers downstream where the estuary merged with the Atlantic. By 1941, before moving his family to Daniel's Harbour on the island of Newfoundland, they had a child named Ivy. Later, after moving to the island, they increased their family.

I met Ralph in 1965. During the 1960s and 1970s, he worked as our head guide at the Main River Lodge. Even in his older years, he was still wiry, energetic and a very capable outdoorsman. It was always a pleasure to hear him tell of his early life and of the hardships in Labrador.

His son, Sandy, inherited his father's talent for fishing, trapping, hunting, and back-country competence. He had a yearning to see the remnants of his father's old home, visit the graveyard where his grandparents were buried, and test the trout fishing on those legendary waters. Always anxious for a new venture, I arranged a fishing trip to Labrador that would include Sandy.

Pierre piloted the twin engined Cessna 402 that transported Ace Caines, Sandy House and myself from Deer Lake to the northern landing strip at Charlottetown. The 300 kilometer flight took less than two hours. We were met at the airport by Sandy's uncle, who offered us transportation to Campbell's Cove in his nine meter fishing boat. Sandy's uncle had constructed a small cottage near the remnants of Ralph's old home and it would be our abode for the next five days.

Leaving Charlottetown for upriver journey

Although the weather offered frost at night, we had an enjoyable stay. The trout fishing was very productive and our inland treks were always stimulating; we constantly wondered what was beyond the next barren ridge. The nearest soil for community burial was located across the river from our camp site. Five days later, returning to Charlottetown, we met a funeral flotilla of eight boats coming up the river on their solemn journey to the graveyard. The homemade spruce casket and the minister

Ace, Pierre & Gene with sea trout in Labrador

were on the lead boat with the relatives and mourners following in a stately file.

On returning to the airport we had another surprise in finding that the right tire on our airplane was flat. Upon jacking and removing the assembly, we saw the tire was beyond repair. Sadly, we soon discovered that our base in Deer Lake did not have a spare, and that it could take four or five days (owing to the weekend) to acquire one from Montreal and then transport it to our location. Pierre and Sandy needed to get back to work and I knew I would go up the wall sitting around the motel in Charlottetown.

Gloomily, Sandy and I played cribbage, not really wondering where Ace had gone. But then, Ace burst through the door with optimism in his eyes. "I may have found a way out of this," he said. "I been all over town checking trailers, ATVs, and everything with wheels. None of those tires were right, but I just took a tire from a wheelbarrow. She's not new and she's not very thick but tis the right size!"

At first thought, it sounded ridiculous, but after further discussion we agreed to a test trial. Although only one-twentieth the strength of a normal aircraft tire, it did fit. Cautiously we lowered the jack to see if it would stand the weight. Sandy pumped in more air with Ace monitoring the expanding rubber. Pierre said the gravel runway would soon tear up the flimsy casing, and therefore a trial taxi would not be advisable.

We agreed to go for it. All of our gear was placed on the left side of the cabin and the three of us sat in the portside seats. Gingerly, we taxied to the east end of the strip for takeoff. Putting as much weight as possible on the good wheel, Pierre applied full power with partial flaps and locked the brakes for a quick departure. We clenched our teeth and said a silent prayer as he released the brakes. The cold air and slight headwind helped us gain flying speed very quickly. Pierre held full left aileron to provide more lift on the right wing. The starboard wheel came off the ground without the anticipated blowout and we climbed peacefully away on our southbound heading.

Deer Lake had a paved runway, which we convinced ourselves would be easier on our fragile tire during the landing. As we held the right wing high, our other wheel kissed the surface. We slowed, the right wing came down, and then both main wheels were firmly rolling. The nose gear gently relaxed onto the asphalt and just as we all breathed a sigh of relief, she blew! The plane lurched sideways but had slowed sufficiently for Pierre to keep us on the runway using the opposite brake.

Eddy brought the mule to the runway and towed us back to the hangar. The maintenance staff laughed in disbelief when they saw what Ace had contrived. "Well, at least we learned something. A non-reinforced, two-ply tire will stand one takeoff and half a landing. Had it been a new wheelbarrow you would'a had a successful arrival!"

"Yes, Eddy," I said. "Perhaps you should add this discovery to the company maintenance manual. The engineers in Moncton would love it."

Once again, Ace and the mechanics from the coast had been able to devise an unorthodox means to get us out of a jam.

Chapter 28 The Magic Carpet

My backyard, where I replaced the birch tree with a helicopter

In 1982, my wife Nina came barging out the patio door at our home in Steady Brook, yelling, "For the love of God, what are you doing cutting down that beautiful birch tree?"

I sheepishly explained I was going to purchase a helicopter, learn to fly it, and keep it here in our backyard: "The removal of this tree is the first step. It has to go, it's interfering with my rotor blades!"

The die was cast. It was now absolutely necessary to proceed with my plan. I had great respect for Bob Brough, who had been an adversary when he flew with Universal Helicopters in Newfoundland. With his help, I purchased an elderly Hughes 500-C machine in Calgary. Bob and Gloria-Jean adopted me into their home in Kingston, Ontario while I learned the art of piloting my new machine.

Fixed wing pilots have a humorous concept of the helicopter and those who fly them. Helicopter flight is a bunch of spare parts flying in close formation. Don't ever sneak up behind an old, high-time chopper pilot and clap your hands as he will instantly try to lower the collective and dive for cover. Then he'll get up and beat the hell out of you. Chopper pilots always fly in a mode of intensity, like being spring-loaded. while waiting for pieces to fall off their ship. Flying a chopper at any altitude or condition that precludes a landing in less than ten seconds is considered very foolhardy. With an engine failure, during a proper auto rotation the machine flies as well as a twenty case coke machine. Your glide ratio is slightly better than that of a square brick. While hovering, if you start to sink a bit, you pull up on the collective while twisting the throttle, push with your left foot and move the stick left to hold your spot. If you now need to stop rising, you do the opposite in that order. If there is a wind blowing, you do these procedures many times each second. Do you still want to fly helicopters?

A chopper does not want to fly; it is maintained in the air by a variety of forces and controls that are working against each other, and if there is any disturbance in this delicate balance, the machine stops normal flight. There is no such thing as a nice glide in a helicopter. We fighter pilots in the RCAF had a prayer: "Lord, I pray for the eyes of an eagle, the heart of a lion and the balls of a combat helicopter pilot!"

Having said all this, I must admit that flying a chopper is one of the most satisfying experiences I have ever encountered: skimming through a mountainous river valley with the trees going by the rotor blades at 170 kilometers per hour is something we should all be able to do at least once.

As manager of Viking Helicopters in Newfoundland and Labrador for many years, I had done a lot of flying in helicopters but had never taken the time to become licenced. Bob Brough, with his patience and skill, soon had me hooked on the new type of vertical piloting. It was different but not terribly difficult.

"If I push the one rudder pedal, the machine rotates in that direction. If I hold it, the chopper goes round in a circle. If I want to go forward, I ease the cyclic stick ahead and I can go backward by bringing the stick aft. Now we will hover, which is merely moving low and slow over the ground in the ground effect of our downwash. The lift on the blades is changed by raising or lowering the collective control with your other hand and of course, the throttle is a twist grip on the outer end of the collective. Have you got all that so far?" Bob asked.

"Holy shit!" I said, as he turned the dual controls over to my command. Determined to gain the new rating on my licence, I worked diligently, following Bob's instructions every day, and in the evenings I studied the intricacies of their unique aerodynamics. I was thrilled by the complex manoeuvres that could be accomplished, particularly the exacting transport of swaying exterior sling loads carried on the belly hook. Each day things became easier, and within a month Bob said he thought I was ready for the final check ride with an MOT inspector. Having previously flown over 11,000 hours in fixed wing aircraft, I thought the transition to helicopters would have been more difficult. My biggest problem was in defragmenting my brain regarding the glide distance during engine failure procedures. When Bob cut the engine on the helicopter, my mind was automatically programmed to choose a landing site some distance away. But during autorotation the chopper dropped and we would fetch up far short of my predicted ground contact. It took an extra few hours of simulated malfunctions and serious concentration before I was comfortable in judging the steep glide range.

After completing the helicopter training, Bob Brough informed me that he had just sold a Hughes 500D model to a doctor in Fort McMurray, Alberta. He had to deliver the machine from Kingston and return with a small piston model 300. He asked me to accompany him and share in the flying. Eagerly, I accepted. The low level 4,000 kilometer flight across Canada was most enjoyable in the fast, well-equipped Hughes. When we got hungry we landed by a roadside diner, and when it was time for rest, we slid down to a good motel.

The spring weather was very cooperative until we reached Manitoba. After refueling in Winnipeg, our next planned stop was Saskatoon. However, low ceilings and heavy wet snow made a direct route impossible. The forecast office informed us that better weather prevailed to the north, so Bob diverted toward The Pas. This route took us across the desolate scrub terrain between Lake Manitoba and Lake Winnipeg. The visibility was minimal as we sped low over the wilderness.

I tried to keep track of our position but map reading was difficult in that featureless region. Our ground speed became noticeably slower, which I thought was due to Bob reducing power for better visibility. "No," he said. "We're picking up some icing on the blades." Looking outside, I saw that the radio antennae and the landing skids were enveloped in a cocoon of clear ice!

"Our speed is down 60 knots and the ice is building quickly. I think we best land and wait this out," Bob cautioned. He lowered the collective and we gently settled to a stop on the slushy tundra. As the rotors slowed to a halt, it was amazing to see the two inches of ice that had encircled the inner hubs, and all the forward facing parts of the airframe were shrouded with inches of frozen water. That was my first experience with helicopter icing. It had accumulated in less than twenty minutes, and would have soon totally destroyed the lifting capacity of the rotor blades. For the next two hours we sat in the cockpit watching the outside temperature gauge gradually increase; warmer air was moving in and the ice formations were beginning to melt from the machine.

We removed as much ice as we could reach. Bob said the outward portion of the blades should clear off with fast rotation. Soon we were westward bound again, through the diminishing super cooled water droplets. Our diversion had consumed additional fuel, and after making calculations we scribed a direct route to Yorkton Airport. The icing problem was over with, but nearing our new destination, heavily falling snow made our progress quite difficult.

Upon contacting Yorkton Tower for entry clearance to their control zone, we were advised by the traffic regulator that the airport was closed since the weather was below safe operating limits. With only fifteen minutes of fuel remaining, it was necessary to land the machine without delay. Bob circled the area, looking through the blinding storm for a reasonable place to put down.

"There's a big ranch house and barn on our left. Surely they'll put us up for the night," he said, as he quickly spun around and reduced power. After we explained why we had landed in his yard, the burly farmer greeted us with typical prairie hospitality.

"Well." he said. "If ya can burn diesel there's a big tank full over there, just help yerself." Soon we were pumping tractor diesel into our tank and checking with the airport for their advisory. Before nightfall, the weather cleared sufficiently for us to make the short flight, although it might have been more interesting to have stayed at the ranch.

Fort McMurray was an astonishing site, with bustling activity in the tar sand excavation pits: huge drag lines were swinging buckets the size of small houses, and the gigantic dumpster trucks shuttled back and forth like play toys in a sand box. From five hundred feet, it looked like a science fiction movie.

The next day Bob and I settled into the small piston chopper to chug back east at ninety kph. On most days, the cars below were passing us. It was a long but enjoyable flight back to Kingston. And Bob thought I was now ready to pass a commercial flight test.

In Toronto, the written exams and the check ride went smoothly and I was soon enroute through the Eastern provinces, anxious to get back to Newfoundland. The flight was most enjoyable until departing Moncton. The direct route to Halifax involved crossing ten kilometers of water over the Bay of Fundy but I was soon to find out that the whole area was completely socked with fog. This necessitated an overnight stop so I circled the small village of Parsborough, seeking a suitable place to land. I chose a large open yard behind a private residence, settled the machine on the grass, shut down the engine, and proceeded to secure the rotor blades.

I was suddenly interrupted by a young high-spirited boy who came running toward me waving his arms. "Hey mister, do you own a truck?" he asked with bulging eyes.

"Yes, I do, but why do you ask such a question?"

Breathless with excitement, he asked, "What colour is your truck?"

"My truck is dark green." I was becoming curious as to where this conversation was going.

"When I saw you landing I thought it must be Magnum P.I. but his truck is the same colour as his chopper!" The young lad seemed quite disappointed with the discovery. Coincidentally, my helicopter was the same model, and had been painted in a very similar colour scheme as that of the Hawaiian television detective.

The following day, after refueling in Sydney, I crossed the 140 kilometers of water in the Cabot Strait with the commercial whirly bird endorsement in my pocket. On June 6, I circled Steady Brook and gently settled the Hughes 500 in my backyard, beside the stump of the recently choppped birch tree.

The little Hughes was a dream to fly. For the next twenty years I used it at every opportunity: to fish virgin waters that were inaccessible by other means, to photograph wildlife, to access the back country in pursuit of moose, caribou and ptarmigan, and to assist the environmental protection groups in their ongoing battle with hydro developers and clear cutters. I made many trips to Labrador and used the machine extensively in managing the Main River hunting and fishing lodge from 1985 until 2002. It really proved to be a magic carpet.

Gene with Bob Brough and new helicopter at Kingston Airport (1982)

Chapter 29 Beautiful Labrador

Northern Labrador -The land God gave Cain

In August of 1987, Willy Wilson, Tom (my Chocolate Lab) and I waved goodbye to our friends at Deer Lake Airport with Northern Labrador as our destination. The heavily loaded Hughes 500 helicopter lifted off the ramp and turned to a northerly heading. Deer Lake Flight Service cleared us from the local frequency and added, "Have a good trip." Yes, I thought, you're damn right we will.

Tom, the big retriever, was soon asleep, stretched out between Willy's legs with his tail curled around the rudder pedals. He thought it was just another fishing trip. There was little conversation between Willy and me. Either he recognized my deep thoughts and didn't wish to intrude, or he was carefully probing his own mind for an affirmative response to the suggestion that this would be a good trip. Willy had had a long and varied aviation career: flying bombers in WW2, spending time in a German POW. camp, instructing with the RCAF, conducting excursions worldwide in Transport Command and piloting Hercules freighters with Pacific Western Airways in the Canadian Arctic. We were friends of long standing and great fishing buddies. We had shared many exciting adventures over the past 35 years. His trust had always been unfaltering but I was certain that many foreboding questions were now lurking on the periphery of his mind. "What have I got myself into? What kind of a wild adventure are we on now?"

The mystical desolation of Labrador has impressed many travelers since Leif Erickson came ashore in the tenth century. And ever since my first glimpse of Labrador from a jet interceptor in 1956, I'd had a tremendous yearning to explore that intriguing area up close.

This formidable land mass stretches 1,200 kilometers from the Strait of Belle Isle to Cape Chidley, covering about 400,000 square kilometers. It has a hostile, breathtaking splendour with very little human habitation. There are fewer than 300 miles of road and only 32,000 inhabitants within its boundaries. Only specific regions have been developed, such as Schefferville with its iron ore mines, Churchill Falls with its hydro project, Goose Bay with its airport, and recently the Inco mining complex at Voisey Bay. There are a number of small fishing communities along the Atlantic coast from Forteau to Nain, but the rest of the country has changed very little since Jacques Cartier called it "the land God gave Cain." It will undoubtedly be one of North America's last frontiers owing to its remoteness, unnavigable rivers, cost of transportation and the shortness of the summer season. The swarms of mosquitoes and black flies also tend to interfere with an objective assessment of its beauty and charm.

During my commercial bush flying days in the 1960s and 1970s, I became well acquainted with the spectacular scenery, the unforgiving harshness of the climate, and the wonderful hospitality of the coastal livyers. However, my business wanderings through Labrador prevented me from reaching destinations of my choice and biding there a while.

We were heading to northern Labrador for a two week escapade, with fishing as an excuse. The rear compartment was crammed full of camping gear, food, sleeping bags, and emergency supplies. Our intention was to fly north to the Okak

Bay area and then fish and camp our way south in some of the virgin rivers.

After an hour of scenic flight, we found that the Strait of Belle Isle, which separates the northern tip of Newfoundland from the South Coast of Labrador, was covered by a disturbing tongue of fog. The historic Viking settlement at L'Anse aux Meadows and the St. Anthony Airport were obliterated from view. Visual flight below the murky layer was not feasible. The higher Labrador hills were   visible to the west. Although it would be a longer route, I elected to go on top and turned toward Bradore Bay, Quebec. A 30 kilometer transit over hostile ocean and fog bank seems like a long voyage in a single engine chopper. There would be little forgiveness should the engine malfunction.

The southern shore of Labrador is not a friendly looking landscape, with its rocky, treeless hills sloping sharply toward the turbulent sea. We were relieved to be across the menacing strait, so frequently a barrier to small plane travel. A strong easterly breeze was whipping the whitecaps on the lake near Lanse Au Claire. Landing by the seaplane dock, we scrambled to locate warmer clothing in the 10C degree chill.

Prior to landing, we had passed east of Greenly Island, a few miles off the coast near the Quebec border at Blanc Sablon. This island is significant in the aviation world. In April 1928, two Germans and an Irishman left Dublin in a Junkers aircraft (named Bremen) with New York as their destination. For 37 hours they battled unexpected winds and fog. Without navigational equipment or sun sights they had no idea where they were when they crash landed on a rocky island just before they ran out of fuel. To their astonishment, they learned from the lighthouse keeper that they were on Greenly Island, some 900 kilometers off course, and that they were the first aircraft to cross the Atlantic from east to west! The "Bremen" holds an honoured place today at the Henry Ford museum in Dearborn, Michigan.

Soon we were climbing over the barren hills for the 260 kilometer flight to Cartwright. Inland, the undulating terrain became wooded. From the headwaters of the Forteau River to

Hamilton Inlet, the boreal forest clothed the rolling landscape. As we droned over the seemingly limitless expanse of wilderness, we watched the different habitats merge with each other: swampy alpine meadows, and dense coniferous forested valleys, their lower slopes interlaced with bogs and lakes. From 3,000 feet we had a great view of the changing topography. Near Port Hope Simpson, on the Alexis River, the green fir carpet suddenly changed to an extensive charred ruin that had been transformed a few years earlier by a devastating forest fire.

We landed at Art Lundrigan's summer home in Cartwright to say hello, only to find that he had gone in his chopper to the Eagle River for fishing. Without delay, we replenished our fuel before heading across the wide gulf at Hamilton Sound.

Thirty minutes later it became evident that we wouldn't be crossing Groswater Bay that evening. The moist easterly flow had engulfed the entire region with massive fog banks. I eased the machine down to skirt the shoreline of the Backwater Peninsula as I recalled using that route years ago while flying a floatplane in bad weather. Soon that route became impassible as the land merged with the low clinging fog. Darkness was settling in and our options were quickly running out. I tried a valley by Gnat Ridge that would lead to Rigolet, but that was also a dead end.

Turning back to the coast, I asked Willy on the intercom, "Where would you like to sleep tonight?"

We couldn't have found a more inhospitable spot to be weatherbound. The entire peninsula was a mass of swamp and muskeg, only slightly higher than the upper tide levels. The higher ground was completely covered with spindly black spruce and larch sticks, sufficient in density to prevent an open landing area with our forty foot rotor blades. We made a few large circles in the dimming light searching desperately for a small clearing, not knowing how uncomfortable we soon would be in that woeful marsh!

At last, we landed in a small wet clearing but found that knee boots were needed to step out into the squishy bog. Misty darkness overtook us as we unloaded our tent and Coleman stove. Swarms of mosquitoes waited to launch their inevitable attack until they were sure that it was too dark for us to leave.

I had encountered mosquitoes previously but never like that! I lit the stove, but before I could assemble the cooking gear clouds of thirsty insects descended on me. My hands were covered with crawling masses fighting for a taste of blood, and my boots and pants held a frenzied collection of swarming vipers, desperately trying to probe through my garments. Upwind of the kitchen I kindled a damp, mossy fire that threw up huge clouds of black smoke but it had little effect. I held my arms in the smolder but few of the mosquitoes seemed to mind its acrid pungency; the majority stayed put and dug into my flesh. Besieged with their frenzy, I gave up the cooking to help Willy with the little tent, only to find him similarly overcome with the distressing bugs.

Finally we crawled into our insectproof abode, which had already been invaded by the enemy. We swatted and bashed them until there were only a few hundred inside. We then zippered up the awnings and settled for cheese chunks and whiskey for supper. The surfaces of our drinks were dotted with paddling mosquitoes racing to reach the far side of the mugs.

"Are we having fun yet?" Willy asked, as he fished out a few Olympic swimmers from his cup of Crown Royal. "Why in hell didn't Noah swat those two mosquitoes on his ark?"

Upon almost completely ridding our nylon enclosure of the noisy bugs, I heard Tom whimpering outside. In our plight, we had forgotten about the dog. We opened the front enclosure and my poor wretched pet crawled inside, bringing hundreds more buzzers with him. From nose to tail, from paws to shoulders, his unfortunate body was covered by a seething mass of insect life. His belly and nose were bleeding from the voracious bites that he had encountered. It took us another half hour to rid his body of the tiny vultures. The humming sounds outside were frightful, even after we slid into our sleeping bags. There were thousands of tiny feet and wings beating against the nylon wall. As they hit the rigid pavilion, it sounded as if someone were throwing sand at our tent. The little black flies were more considerate in our enclosure as they settled on the fabric wall, showing little interest in our flesh.

Willy spoke wearily. "The experts say that only female mosquitoes bite. If that's the case, then I've never seen a male!"

The next morning we woke early, but a quick glimpse outside sent me back inside. The murkiness and rain continued, with visibility further reduced by mosquitoes and fierce little black flies. Hunger eventually forced us to face the elements but we didn't linger long over our morning coffee. We were determined to leave this hellish swamp we'd christened "Camp Misery."

As the rotor blades gained momentum, I nastily wondered how many bugs were being slaughtered by the impact of each revolution. In a slow hover toward Rigolet, we were finally able to cross Hamilton Sound and make our way inland, hoping to reach Bob Skinner's salmon lodge on Big River.

A formidable rocky bluff, veiled in stratus, prevented our entry into the Big River Valley. Knowing that MicMac Brook flowed into the river, I banked to the left, following the stream, but there was no daylight ahead to separate the rocks from the cloud base. Suddenly a small, bright opening appeared between the boulder structures on the ridge. I slowed the machine and inched through the cleft in the granite wall. The somber entrance gave way to a deep, wide canyon. Its steep slopes were masked by large stands of spruce and fir. The broad, glaciated floor was matted with a lush carpet of willow and alder that bordered the swift flow of Big River. We were relieved to be within fifty kilometers of the estuary and happily headed down the tunnel, which was still capped with ugly weather. Bob's camp was soon spotted beyond the gravel bars, where it was snugly tucked away at the base of the cliff next to a wide, riffled salmon pool. The cozy cabin and Bob's generous hospitality made a welcome change from the torment we had experienced the night before.

After a good rest and leisurely breakfast, we left Big River for the next fuel stop at Hopedale, some 80 kilometers away. Our fuel consumption had been quite high since leaving Cartwright owing to the many diversions and the low altitude at which we had been forced to fly.

I was uneasy with the slight headwind which was eating into our diminishing fuel. I was constantly reevaluating my decisions: should I climb higher to reduce the fuel usage or would the wind be more obstructive at an increased altitude? The townsite and airport swept by underneath just as the fuel low warning light began flashing. Ahead, on the upper ridge, stood a large radar antenna, an obsolete reminder of the defence system used during the Cold War. The rotor blades brushed by the lofty installation and I slid her down the steep slope to a clearing that was littered with forty-five gallon drums of mixed vintage.

Willy remarked," The only time you have too much fuel is when the plane is on fire!"

Tom romped around the strange setting, eagerly marking out his territory and taking ownership of the entire storage area. The Coast Guard had told me they had fuel here but, on examination, all the drums were empty, including the two they had reserved for our use. Fortunately, it was only a short hop back to the airstrip and our remaining fuel served us well. Delighted, we filled the empty tank with Jet A-1 from the RCMP storage and hastily departed for Nain.

It being late in the afternoon, I suggested an overnight stop on the Kogaluck River. Within an hour, we were circling the new mining development at Voisey Bay. We passed over the elaborate government-funded fishing camp at the mouth of the Kogaluck (also called Assiwaban River) and followed the winding course upstream. Around the second bend, the placid water became a swirling froth as it vigorously escaped the base of a massive two-stage waterfall. Volumes of cascading water danced and tumbled down the rocky staircase, throwing up a misty jet of cold steam. I eased the chopper up and over the 130 foot ledge to clear the breathtaking scene below.

We skimmed low over the quiet river above the falls. It was a still, clear evening with brilliant sunset colours reflecting off the water. Westward, the Labrador plateau rose rapidly to mask the sinking sun and a gentle stillness hung over the valley.

The winding ravine curved its way toward Cabot Lake. At each

Camping in Labrador

turn the flow had created flat, sandy islands that were dappled with caribou tracks. We chose one of the sandbars for our campsite, trusting that its openness would deter the flying natives. After supper, we tidied the kitchen and sat by a crackling fire on our folding stools. All was still; the far shore was dark and indistinct. Flecks of foam drifted silently in the current. The crisp black sky began to sparkle with stars. There was barely a sound, except for the steady lapping of the faster water as it rounded the sandbar. Wonderful, peaceful, Labrador isolation at last.

We stayed up late, in front of the smoldering embers, and discussed the trying circumstances that William Brooks Cabot must have encountered during his exploration of this area at the turn of the century. By strange coincidence, we discovered by reading from his diaries that our choice of campsite coincided with his. Cabot was a wealthy Bostonian with a curious longing for the unexplored north country. Around 1900, he wandered through this same region for a number of years, either alone or with a coastal native, establishing friendly contact with the Montagnais Indians, who inhabited the area further west. He established his reputation as a competent outdoorsman.

Excerpt from Cabot diary, August 26, 1906: *"Except for the wind it has been two good days traveling since we left the portage at the big falls. We were eager to camp under the canoe on the edge of a long sandbar. Fourteen hours of continuous paddling and poling is a long shift. Here the stream is five or six hundred yards wide, swinging through a timbered sand plain with high hills of sliding eskers on both sides. These bars are usually free of mosquitoes and there are some fine trout in the eddies below the gravel points, but they are not always abundant in this lower section."*

It was a very moving experience to be reading from Cabot's diary while camped in the same timeless wilderness setting some 80 years later. It seemed as though our spheres of existence had merged, allowing us to share the site with those early travelers.

Nain is a small, bleak settlement huddled below a rocky hillside on the craggy coast. It is now the most northerly community in Labrador inhabited year around. The population consists of about 800 people of mixed race, mostly Inuit. North of Nain there remain only ghost colonies which were abandoned and resettled over the years as the missionary influence waned and the Newfoundland government relocated the natives for centralized education and improved medical attention. These old village sites bear the biblical names of Ramah, Zoar, Hebron, and Okak and were founded in 1752 by the Moravian missionaries. Those settlements are now merely names, with remnants of dilapidated buildings.

After years of lobbying the government for airstrips that were vitally required in this isolated region, they are now a reality. As of 1987, Cartwright, Hopedale, and Nain have excellent gravel strips suitable for small twin engine commuter planes that shuttle passengers to and from Goose Bay and the big hospital at St. Anthony. The airstrips are equipped with radio beacons, passenger facilities, snow clearing, and runway lighting. Modern wheelplanes are now able to provide regular schedules to these remote areas in bad weather and at night. There is no disruption of service while waiting for the bays to freeze or thaw. In contrast, I vividly recalled the days when we served these settlements with old Beavers, Norsemen and single engine Otters equipped with skis or floats. We didn't have any protective hangars, weather advisory, or fuel storage tanks. How miserable it had been, digging out the snow covered fuel drums, rolling them down to the bay ice and hand-pumping precious fuel through old felt strainers at minus 30C.

Willy and I take a strolling tour of the town to purchase groceries at the government store, which a few years ago was a Hudson Bay Trading Post. A couple of children race past us on makeshift minibikes in a drag match. The narrow, muddy street is lined with makeshift homes and jumbled shacks. Most of the buildings are forlorn and grimy in appearance, the yards cluttered with rusty snowmobiles, broken komatiks, empty cans, piles of twisted wood, old packing crates, and scattered garbage. The weeds and wild flowers have grown up through the debris, adding a touch of contradictory beauty. Dogs and dirty children are abundant.

Many of the doors and windows are open on this hot day, so the loud Inuit scolding can be heard from the street. The occupants seem to be in harmony with their surroundings. Showing their shy friendliness, the street stragglers cheerfully respond to our greeting. Near the town water outlet, we talk with an elderly man while the children load water buckets to drag home in their crude wagons. The weatherbeaten lines on the old man's face reflect the struggle he has had with the tough coastal environment: "We still got the regrets fer when we was forced ta move down from Chidley, but now me son manages de fishin plant ear in Nain so tis not all fer nuthin." He also informs us that the general store is closed for lunch: "You shan't find no bread there anyhow cuzz ar women all makes he at home. No need fer hit ta be up fer sale, fer he would go green on de shelf." We thank him for the information, complete our brief tour and head back to the airport past the old Moravian Church, which was reconstructed in 1900 after a fire destroyed the original place of worship. Although somewhat forlorn, Nain had an intriguing charm.

Soon we were speeding northward again over the rugged terrain, reflecting on the fact that in less than one hour we'd fly over country which would take months to traverse by foot or canoe. Our path crossed the mouth of Fraser Canyon, where in 1910, Hesketh Prichard made his epic traverse up the canyon and westward to the George River. We looked down on the wide expanse of Webb Bay, and soon we were amidst the Kiglapait Mountains. These jagged formations rise rapidly from the sea to more than 3,000 feet. There is swift repetition of lofty peaks, followed abruptly by vertical valleys which create a breathtaking panorama.

Out to sea, two large sails loomed up out of the dark water. They were the trailing edge of the annual procession of icebergs that migrate down the coast, having originated on Baffin Island or from the Greenland glaciers. They may take as long as two years to complete their southward voyage to eventual dissolution. During the long winter season the icebergs are locked in the frozen pack ice. With spring breakup, the entire mass is moved southward by the Labrador current. Like stately ships in an armada, they pass in review along the cruel coastline, often reaching the Grand Banks, some 1,400 kilometers further south, before disintegrating in the warmer waters. Some years it is mid-July before ice conditions permit coastal freighters to reach Nain.

The windswept terrain unfolded beneath us. As far as one could see there was a myriad of lakes. Many lakes had islands, and those islands had their own little lakes and islands. The large river systems twisted tortuously between mountains, fighting their way to the coast. There is no neat line separating the treed taiga from the barren tundra; the two areas run well into each other. There are pockets of tundra deep inside the forested area and an oasis of trees far out in the sweep of the barrens. Nor is the tundra of one type: there is alpine tundra high on the slopes, shrubby tundra close to the boreal forest region, and mossy, lichen-covered areas where the vegetation disappears. North of the timberline, the sheltered valleys still harbour a green profusion of trees. They are delicately placed in a lush carpet of lichen, like a parkland designed by man.

Reluctantly, I made a wide turn over the structural remnants at Okak Bay (57-33 degrees north). Obtaining fuel further north was a major problem, otherwise we would have journeyed onward to Saglek or Cape Chidley. Now, we would slowly retrace the 1,300 kilometer passage back toward Corner Brook, fishing along the way.

At the turn of the century there were several Eskimo settlements north of Nain with small populations: Zoar, with 92 inhabitants; Hebron, 256; Ramah, 92; and Okak, 362. Once or twice each year a Moravian supply ship would arrive with provisions and pick up furs and dried fish for the return journey to Europe or St. John's. Unfortunately, the foreign crews brought contagious diseases to which the native population was highly vulnerable. Influenza, rickets, tuberculosis, smallpox and typhoid took their toll, despite the humane attention of the capable missionaries.

In the fall of 1919, a tragic epidemic of Spanish Flu struck the isolated outposts. The outbreak occurred while many of the men were away on hunting or trapping journeys. It spread rampantly. When the men returned home (some themselves dying of the illness) they found nearly all their women and children either dead or dying. Those who had not already succumbed to the disease were too weak to dispose of the dead except to stack the bodies in abandoned buildings. Since their dogs were not being cared for, this resulted in ravenous hunger. The wild dogs molested people and broke into buildings to feast on the corpses. It was a gruesome ordeal for the sickly survivors. It being too difficult to dig grave sites, many bodies were taken on sleds and dropped through holes in the offshore ice.

One third of the Labrador Inuit population died during the 1918-19 pandemic. Settlements were abandoned and survivors moved to Nain, Hopedale and Makovik.

To the north, the landscape is even more striking as the Torngat Mountains proudly display their 4,500 foot peaks. Sadly, the fiords of Nachvak and Mugford would not be viewed on this trip. The splendour of this wild, uninhabited land is absolutely breathtaking! In 1891, Alpheus Packard wrote: "This area of the Labrador Peninsula is less known than the interior of Africa or the wastelands of Siberia."

Enroute to Frank Lake, I showed Willy my old Tesuyiak fishing camp, which I had sold to Peter Pour and moved to Lake Umiakovik in the land dispute with Roland Reed seventeen years before. The adjoining large body of water called Frank Lake is held back by a narrow but massive rock formation at the eastern outflow. On the side of the escarpment, the trapped water suddenly tumbles over the ledge and falls more than 20 feet to a swirling, deep pool before continuing its hasty one kilometer journey to the ocean. I settled the chopper on the smooth boulders so that the granite cliff would provide some shelter in the event of strong westerly winds.

Our chosen campsite was on the rock ledge, near the lip of the falls. It was a breezy location but provided a commanding view. We used an assortment of stones to secure the tent, and quickly assembled our lodgings. That evening vista is etched in memory. Perched high on the flat dam-like surface, our campfire reflected an eerie light on the dark cliffs across the falls. The ten kilometer lake was calm and black, but the outline of the lofty peaks beyond was silhouetted through the golden band of brightness in the northern sky. Overhead, the star pulsations seemed in tune with the surging sound of cascading water. After roasting char fillets over the hot coals, we huddled closer to the fire, sharing a deep feeling of contentment in that frontier environment.

At 5:30, I awaken to a mystical glow inside the tent. Outside, I am amazed at the striking scene that engulfs us. The stunted spruce and tamarack trees on the valley slope are bristling with a white frost, and below the ravine is completely filled with fog. The upper surface of the stratus is reflecting the fading moon while the reddish glow of the rising sun shines up through from below. The lake is also covered in a blanket of fog and we seem suspended on our ledge, as though floating through this rare spectacle of nature. I urge Willy to come out and share the experience. Slowly the imagery dissipates with the heat from the rising sun, and by coffee time things are back to reality.

Many enjoyable days were spent fishing, camping and

"Willy, a big salmon just swirled down there!"

exploring on our southward journey. We flew from river to river, selecting likely looking salmon pools on the upper reaches of the splendid rivers. North of Hopedale, we encountered mostly arctic char and sea trout. Salmon became more plentiful as we dabbled in the streams south of Hopedale. Caribou or their tracks were numerous along the sandy shores. We encountered black bears on many occasions, but they paid little attention to us as they walked the riverbeds looking for fish. A large wolf scampered beneath us as we circled to land on the Hunt River shore. Black Ducks, Mergansers, Goldeneyes, Buffleheads, and Harlequin ducks were common sights on most streams.

One evening, while camped on a sandbar below the falls on the Adlatok River, we gazed in awe at a weird display of Northern Lights. They cast a spell over both sense and sight. They began with pale, teasing yellowish streaks and then quickly intensified. The shifting light broadened with twisting colours, and soon the entire northern sky was a glowing mass of swirling fire. It faded, and then reappeared as a bright luminous belt. Scattered rays shot up in all quadrants, and then weakened to soothing wavelets, like a fluorescent gateway to the arctic's mysteries. "They are God's searchlights," Willy proclaimed.

On August 21, the morning dawned cool and sunny at our

sandbar on the Kanairiktok River. Willy had been up early to catch a trout breakfast, but the salmon did not respond. Soon after breaking camp the industrious turbine responded quickly as we ascended the stunning river. Most waterfalls have a majestic beauty but the overflow on the Kanairiktok is a sight to behold. For over 180 kilometers this major river carves its way seaward through tortured rocks as it drains the tableland toward the Quebec border. Near the coast, it suddenly disappears over a steep escarpment with three spectacular spumes of spray. I circled to allow Willy to video the scene. On the last swing, we glided down into the canyon, where the confused waters rushed along in a swirling frenzy, throwing an enormous horsetail skyward. We marveled at the grandeur.

Further south, we stopped in several fishy-looking pools but were unable to unravel the mysterious whereabouts of the elusive salmon. By late afternoon we accepted defeat, left the confines of the great valleys, crossed over the barren tableland, and slid down the picturesque headwaters of Luscombe Brook. Needing bread and refreshments, I located Premier Frank Moore's "Tree Top Cabin," which was tucked away in the fir trees about 18 kilometers from the ocean. It was a cozy, well-appointed retreat overlooking the stream. No one was home, but true to Labrador hospitality, the doors were unlocked. We borrowed some groceries and a bottle of Crown Royal, leaving a note to suggest that Frank restock his liquor cabinet for future guests.

After a few splendid days on the White Bear and Paradise Rivers, we made our way toward Cartwright airport through a threatening weather system. Hampered by strong winds and low ceilings, I chose to overnight on the upper section of the North River. After finding a suitable location, we set up camp in a sheltered cove at the junction of a rattling stream that entered from the south. The water level appeared low on the expansive pool near the confluence of the two rivers. The slow moving water did not impress us as a salmon pool but we agreed that it offered serenity and comfort.

The peacefulness was quickly shattered when the bulging cumulus clouds, rolling from the Mealy Mountains, released their wet fury amidst squally winds. The sound of shaking canvas and disturbed water, however, did not keep us awake.

The following morning we discovered that the pool next to us was full of salmon. We surmised the fish were waiting for higher water to continue their migration up the shallow shoals and we congratulated each other for having so cunningly chosen this location!

During the next four days, the pool provided us with the best salmon fishing of the entire trip. They were fiercely interested in only two fly patterns: the Blue Emsen and a black dry fly, tied on a number eight hook. When the flies went into the water, there would often be two or three fish racing to grab them. Since we were releasing our salmon, we tried not to overstress them before easing them to the beach to dislodge the tiny hook without hurting their gills or removing them from the water. At the lower end of the sandbar we found some brightly coloured brook trout, two to three pounds each, in shiny red and black spawning colours, far too pretty to eat!

We emerged from the tent on August 24, yearning for the heavy sweaters we failed to bring. Unfortunately, it was time to leave the honey hole. We dismantled the camp and loaded the helicopter for departure as threatening thunder clouds were building in the west. While we were stowing the gear, a violent gust of wind picked up our little tent, rolled it across the sand, and set it in the middle of the river. We laughed at the incredible sight of the red bundle being whisked down river in the current. I raced along the shore in chest waders to intercept it at the next point. Tom thought it was great fun and swam out, only to get tangled in the dangling ropes. A pair of Greater Yellowlegs screamed and fluttered at us, as though delighted with our pending departure from their home.

A vague, let down feeling prevailed over us on our flight south. We thought of Robert Service's comments:

"Now there is a land ... have you seen it?
It's the damndest land that I know,
From the big dizzy mountains that screen it,
To the deep fiords and valleys below.
Some say God was mad when he made it;
Some say it's a land to shun;
Maybe but there's some wouldn't trade it
For no land on earth - and I'm one."

We hoped that Labrador would never change, and would remain a place still only marginally touched by time, where the climate dictates the way you live, and where a visitor cannot forget that he is merely a visitor, a privileged one at that. Two weeks before, the controller at Deer Lake Airport had wished us a good trip. Well, he certainly had that right!

Tom, my Labrador, logged many hours in the helicopter

Camp at Frank Lake Falls

Chapter 30 Lost Liberator

B-24 Liberator

On the last leg of our 2,500 kilometer excursion through the beautiful Labrador wilderness, Willy and I were heading to the airport at Blanc Sablon, the most easterly Quebec settlement, for one more fuel stop. We would fly on to Deer Lake that evening. But first there was a mystery to solve.

Fourteen days earlier, on our way north we had chatted with Ron Letto, a veteran bush pilot in south Labrador. During our stopover in Blanc Sablon, he told us he thought he'd spotted a downed aircraft on one of his floatplane trips. He said it looked like a large military aircraft of some kind.

As we passed Port Hope Simpson, I suggested we make a slight diversion to the west to see if we could find the spot where Ron had given us the coordinates. With our helicopter we might be able to get a better look. After fifteen minutes of circling in the area Ron had noted, we were about to give up the search when Willy saw a bright reflection from what might have been a piece of metal to the east. On closer examination, we discovered what appeared to be a large four engine aircraft, barely visible on the side of a barren slope. It was difficult to ascertain the type of plane since it was almost completely covered by brush and surrounded by evergreen trees. There was no clearing of sufficient size to set the helicopter down without entangling the rotor blades, so with dusk approaching, I noted the exact position on the GPS and proceeded to Blanc Sablon for fuel and then back to Corner Brook.

Unable to let the matter rest, I called Ron Letto, who was living in L'Anse au Claire, on the south coast of Labrador, and asked him to join me on another flight to the downed bomber. He was eager to go. The next day, I picked up Ron at Blanc Sablon Airport for the 112 kilometer flight into the wilderness.

We located the site of the crash easily enough, but couldn't find any safe place to land the helicopter. The nearest clearing was two-kilometers from the wreck. After setting the Hughes 500 down, we grabbed our lunch sacks and headed through the scraggy tundra on a compass course. It was a hot and frustrating trek. The mosquitoes and deer flies plagued us. For thirty minutes, we wended our way through the thick tangle of spindly trees and scrub. Then suddenly we stumbled into a partial opening and an almost surreal apparition peeked out of the undergrowth.

What an awesome sight! The huge B-24 bomber was completely intact, as though it had been carefully lifted and dropped in the midst of this virgin tundra that became its final resting place. Coniferous brush and stunted spruce had grown up around it and obscured much of the 70 foot aluminum fuselage, a sight at once eerie and breathtaking. Machine guns pointed skyward from their turrets. We stopped and stared in stunned silence. Four massive engines were still in place on the 110 foot wingspan, and the propeller tips were slightly bent. There was some fire damage evident behind the cockpit, but otherwise the aircraft looked ready for another mission.

Eighteen thousand Liberators were built by the Consolidated Aircraft Company during the war. The plane had an operational weight of 32 tons, a cruising speed of 345 kilometers per hour, a ceiling of 28,000 feet and a range of 6,000 kilometers, with 3,615 gallons of fuel. It was powered by four Pratt and Whitney 14 cylinder radial engines that each developed 1,200 horsepower. The armament consisted of six .50 caliber Browning guns, two each in the nose, upper, lower ball, dorsal turrets and in waist position, and four .303 guns in a tail turret with 5,200 rounds of ammunition. The internal bomb load was 3,632 kilograms, with optional external bomb racks. It was a formidable war machine. We knew it was probably still fully armed.

Walking around the enormous hulk, we found a rocky, elongated trench that still faintly described the landing path, suggesting the plane had gone down in a level, controlled emergency landing. The US Air Force markings were clearly visible on the vertical stabilizer: 42-50506. There could be no doubt that this was a Second World War vintage aircraft and we were anxious, if somewhat leery, to have a look inside. As we constructed a spruce ladder to climb into the overhead cabin, it played on our minds that there was a good chance we would find the remains of the crew, unless they had parachuted out or somehow survived the crash and walked away.

The door opened easily and swung to the side. With growing apprehension, we warily stepped inside the waist of the bomber. It was a huge tube of sheet metal riveted to ribs and cross members, about seven feet high and eight feet wide. The crew seats, with harnesses unbuckled, appeared to have been vacated before the crash; there were a few bundles of unused parachutes lying in the aisle. It had the uncanny feel of a killing machine with its guns still in place in the turrets, and full belts of live ammunition hanging from the magazines. Toward the cockpit, we saw signs that there had been a small fire over the inboard fuel tanks. There were charred remnants on the cabin floor. From the rubble, I picked up some military medals, USAF hat badges, a few French and English coins, a bombardier's headset, and an assortment of uniform buttons. The cockpit was intact and unmarked except for the cracked glass of the instrument panel, the only sign of a crash. We found the fire extinguishers fully charged and operational, and the machine guns still swung easily on their mounts. Ron sat in the tail gunner's bucket seat, examining the oxygen tanks, while I took pictures of the cabin from several vantage points.

While eating our lunch, we tried to imagine what must have happened and what had been the fate of the crew. There was no sign of human remains and from the condition of the plane it didn't appear the impact would have been sufficiently severe to cause their death. Perhaps they had abandoned the aircraft after the crash and died of exposure or starvation. But I wondered why they hadn't bothered to secure the fuselage door. Had they remained with the plane for a few days, one would think that the cabin would have been far less tidy. It also seemed strange that the portable "Gibson Girl" emergency radio was still neatly stored in its case. There seemed to be a lot of unanswered questions, but the silent hulk wasn't offering any explanations. The mystery tugged at my mind all the way back to Blanc Sablon.

Back home, I reported the finding to the Coast Guard and the RCMP. A few days later they confirmed our suspicion that the wreck had never been recorded. Further enquiries with the United States embassy in Ottawa led me finally to Sergeant Barry Spinks in Washington. Barry was a dedicated historian who worked with the USAF Military Archive Library in Baton Rouge, Louisiana. After a few days of intensive research, he was able to provide a full account of the events surrounding the remarkable history of the lost Liberator.

B-24 J, number 42-50506, was deployed in July, 1944 to the 8th Air Force in the United Kingdom and assigned to the 491 Bomb Group of the 855 Bomber Squadron. The aircraft participated in various bombing raids over Germany, targeting storage depots, communication centers and shipyards in Berlin, Hanover, Cologne, Hamburg and Gelsen-kirchen. The Liberator also took part in raids to destroy supply lines in 1944 during the Battle of the Bulge. It was the lead aircraft in an attack on the Wehrmact General Staff Headquarters bunker in Zossen, south of Berlin. Records revealed that the Liberator was engaged in five bombing missions in February 1945, another twelve in March, and two in April.

In May of 1945, as the war in the European theater was

drawing to a close, the aircraft was redeployed to the United States for possible use in the still raging Pacific conflict. Enroute to North America, the bomber developed electrical problems over Iceland. The fuel gauges and radio communication systems were inoperative. After fifteen days, repairs were completed and the five-man crew departed for New England via Goose Bay on June 16. On board were Captain Robert Eckert, co-pilot Captain Warren Carter, navigator Lt. Francis Bujalski, flight engineer Sgt. Paul Clift, and radio operator Staff Sgt. Charles Dillard. But the flight was far from routine. Ice built up on the wings, causing greater fuel consumption and necessitating reduced speed. The fuel gauges became erratic and radio contact was intermittent. When they reached Goose Bay, the airstrip was socked in by a raging spring snowstorm. Three landing approaches were attempted, but even at minimum altitude the runway was not visible. The pilot, worried about the remaining fuel with the faulty gauges, elected to take the craft to 4,500 feet and have his crew bail out over the airfield. On the last pass, Eckert engaged the rudimentary autopilot and hit the silk. The abandoned plane was tracked on the tower radar for over one hour before contact was lost.

In a follow-up conversation, Sgt. Spink informed me that the pilot and co-pilot had since passed away, but he was able to provide phone numbers for the other three crew members. When I contacted Lt. Bujalski he was elated. "Well, I'll be damned!" he exclaimed. "Did you bring back my duffle bag?" He went on to explain that they had left all their uniforms and belongings in the aircraft when they bailed out. With the sudden stop when his chute opened, Bujalski's mukluks were lost and he landed on the edge of a large river in his socks. He laughed, recalling he had heard stories about Indians living in Labrador and he didn't know if they would be hostile to foreigners. He therefore had mixed emotions when he saw smoke coming from a log cabin in the woods nearby. Soon two men came down the shore. They warmly greeted him and took him to their cozy cabin where they gave him hot soup and a pair of boots. He was very surprised to find that these bushmen spoke good English.

"The natives put me aboard their boat and took me to the airfield just across the Churchill River. When I reached the base, my four buddies were at the bar, already half-snapped. They had landed at the airport and thought they would never see me again."

I told him about signs of the cabin fire. Had the men stored their personal belongings in the rear of the aircraft, there is no doubt their belongings would have survived the ordeal.

I was also able to reach Scott Carter in Montana. His father Warren had been the co-pilot on the final flight. The younger Carter was compiling the history of his dad's Air Force career and was extremely pleased to learn of my discovery in Labrador. He gave me additional information that allowed me to return the various "Military Achievement Medals" and hat badges to their rightful owners.

The following spring, I flew a group of men from a Louisiana military aircraft museum to the site. They were assessing the feasibility of removing and restoring the aircraft, but the cost of retrieval proved to be prohibitive.

The old Liberator still lies in its final resting place in the wilds of Labrador, its work done, its crew safely delivered, and the mystery of its disappearance finally solved after 42 years.

Each trip to Labrador usually involved some new adventure, either for me or my passengers. Mel Yull and his son Duncan, from Sarasota, Florida, accompanied me on a salmon fishing expedition to the Sandhill River in 1988. On our return to Deer Lake, foggy weather forced us to land in the small fishing village of Bear Cove on Newfoundland's Northern Peninsula. As soon as we landed, a robust young man, dressed in torn coveralls and floppy hip boots, emerged from the dock shack, waving and smiling. "Come on in boys outa de wet. Me woman will boil up the kettle. Where in Satan do ye come from on this marly day? Tis not fit fer flyin. Even de damn gulls are walkin."

Our new friend, Victor, said he would fetch a drum of fuel while we enjoyed our tea and biscuits. In less than an hour his old truck backed in by the helicopter with a sealed drum of Jet-A-1.

He even provided a hand pump and hose which he insisted on operating himself. We soon had a full tank, and the weather was looking brighter. But before we could leave, Victor asked us to follow him to his fishing shed on the wharf. Inside, he pried up a wide floorboard and pulled out three mickey bottles. "Here," he said. "I want ye each to have one. When ya drinks her down, you'll mind the time ye was stuck at Bear Cove. We makes she on the bad days, tis over hundred proofs. Try spiken her wit de horange juice. It'l repair yer nerves."

After many years in similar situations, I was accustomed to such coastal resourcefulness and hospitality. But the incident left Mel and Duncan speechless. They were astonished that such sincere generosity was shown to complete strangers.Weather delays are not always annoying, I'd learned over the years. Sometimes they create a window for further education.

Chapter 31 Arluk Ordeal

Helicopter landing pad at my Arluk Tilt retreat

In late June of 1980, a helicopter dropped off Ace Caines, his son Faron, Sandy House and me on the headwaters of Keough's Brook, a small tributary of the Main River. We were about 100 kilometers north of Corner Brook and a good distance from the logging roads and clearcut machinery scarring the land further south. We had brought along a tent, food, chainsaws, windows, felt roofing, and various tools. The pilot was instructed to pick us up in five days.

I had long dreamed of building another rustic log cabin in a remote, unspoiled setting, far from the increasingly beaten path of the growing hunting activity; as more and more hunters were discovering Newfoundland's pristine northern wilderness. By the late 1970s, the privacy of Eagle Mountain and the Main River camps was steadily being encroached upon by float planes, thoughtless snowmobilers, all-terrain vehicles, hunters, and loggers. The time had come to get serious about carving a piece of paradise. The tranquil headwaters of Keough's Brook, with its abundant salmon population, nesting waterfowl, and substantial moose and caribou herds, seemed the perfect choice.

The site we chose was about sixty kilometers from the ocean within sight of the Long Range Mountain headwater. There on the * "steady," the river was squeezed by a rock outcropping, creating a damming effect which formed a wide pool of relatively slack water above. Our battered tent was pitched by the outflow of the steady. As we ate a quick meal of moose stew, an invigoraing evening chill moved in when the sun descended behind the mountains. It seemed too early for sleep, so we continued our work until long after dark, felling trees, peeling logs, and laying a foundation by lantern light.

By the third day, we had the walls erected and chinked with moss. It looked like a stockade from another century. The asphalt covering went on the roof, the stove was installed and the window and door frames slowly took shape. The weather turned cold and misty, but we barely noticed as we began the inside work: erecting bed frames, making shelves and hewing out a rough set of chairs and a table. There was a peaceful view across the flat water where we expected to watch countless future sunsets. The sturdy, steeply pitched roof was ready to support the tons of snow that would inevitably test its strength. As I stood in the salmon pool, the glistening resin on the fresh-hewed logs of the cabin was barely visible through the stand of spruce trees, a mere two casts away.

When the helicopter finally arrived to take us out of the bush, we watched, perplexed, as it circled twice, then headed off to the east without attempting to land. Thirty minutes later it returned. The pilot told us that when he first saw the cabin he was certain he had somehow followed the wrong tributary. He knew there had not been any buildings there when he dropped us off a few days ago. On our way in, we had neglected to tell him the purpose of our trip.

Over the years, the little cabin never disappointed me as the ideal retreat. It provided many restful, idyllic escapes to the back country. We had built the perfect place of escape in the most ideal spot. Or so I thought.

Flash forward 20 years. Sitting on the cabin porch, I watched the afternoon light fade gradually until the tall fir trees cast no shadows and the green landscape paled to gray. Whistling faintly, the rising wind swayed the forest branches back and forth above my barbeque pit. As I lifted the crisp golden sea trout from the barbeque grate, light sprinkles of rain hissed on the coals and danced on the shallow steady nearby. The sky was now leaden and lowering over the higher mountains to the west. Above the din of the bubbling stream,I heard distant cries from the hungry *Whisky Jacks that huddled beneath the thick coniferous foliage.

"Looks like some heavy rain on the way," I muttered to myself, carrying my dinner into the little cabin. A bright fire crackled in the stove, its open draft casting a flickering sheen on the log ceiling. I took down the old black kettle from a nail behind the stovepipe and filled it with water and loose Red Rose tea. I left it simmering on the stove while I enjoyed my fresh trout and baked potato. The helicopter was firmly secured on the log pad that we had erected over the edge of the stream. The rotor blades were tied down for the night, but still they waved at me gently in the mild breeze. I thought again what a great place this was to iron out the wrinkles of the soul without anyone or anything getting in the way. I thought everyone should have a place like this to spend quiet times alone.

We had called the cabin Arluk Tilt. Arluk is an Inuit word meaning trapper or woodsman and tilt is a Newfoundland name for a lean-to or makeshift shelter. Thoreau advised us to "drive life into a corner and reduce it to its simplest terms." Solitude somehow refocuses a perspective warped by the other world, the world out there.

Lightly dozing in my sleeping bag, I was repeatedly awakened by flashes of lightning and the rumbling and boom of distant thunder. The thunder grew closer and the lightning more dazzling. The patter of rain went from intermittent to a steady pour. Then the sky opened up, with sheets of blowing water batteing the cabin. I hunkered down in my bed, safe in the warmth of the covers until the thunder grew distant again and I dozed off. Occasionally during the night, I awoke briefly to the sound of torrential water spilling off the roof onto the plank porch and loudly beating the sodden ground. Just as daylight was emerging, I was startled from sleep by a loud cracking and thumping noise outside. Thinking it was probably a moose bumping on the wooden walkway, I opened the door to have a look. The terrain I knew so well was now unrecognizable.

It was an awesome sight. The small brook had been transformed into a raging river, and the flat steady above the camp was now an expansive lake. The water had risen about six feet since the evening before and was still creeping up the bank. The once placid stream was tumbling over the boulders, through the trees, and swirling around ledges. There was frothy white water in the narrows by the camp and it boiled down stream as far as I could see. A number of tiny islands in the steady had disappeared, with only the tops of a few spruce trees sticking up above the surface. My stone barbeque and bench were just visible in the fast-deepening water of the shifting shoreline. The helicopter pad had become a floating raft.

Chopper pad in midstream -after water level had dropped about three feet

I understood the hydrology of this river and was aware of its quick rise and fast fall during wet and dry periods, but in twenty years I had never witnessed such a huge rise in such a short time. The noise that had startled me had been the more than 40 foot wooden walkway breaking apart and washing away. The bridge extended from the fire pit to the helicopter pad. Luckily, I had secured two steel cables from the upper corners of the main log platform to attachments around large boulders; otherwise the pad and the chopperwould have been swept down the raging river. The two large sling loads of lumber I had dropped alongside the pad were gone. There was now about 60 feet of angry water between the shore and the landing pad. The pad had become an island in the middle of the torrent. I knew I had to act quickly to save the helicopter. I didn't know how long the cables would hold.

Heedless of the cold, with no time to get dressed, and wearing only a pair of undershorts, I ran to the shed for a life jacket and rope. Not able to find any long rope, I grabbed an electrical extension cord from the generator and tied it to a tree some twenty meters upstream. Sloshing around with bare feet, I grabbed my small 12 foot aluminum canoe and attached the end of the cord to the bow. I pushed away from the shore, and tried to swing the canoe in a pendulum motion toward the pad, side-paddling for all I was worth. Battling the speed of the water and turbulence of the waves, I could only get to within a few feet of the raft. Desperate, I stretched out my hand, and then lunged to grab the nearest piece of the log ramp. The canoe swung broadside and was quickly overturned, flinging me into the angry flow of churning water.

I went under until my knees struck the bottom, and then was propelled back to the surface long enough to gasp for a breath before being pulled under again. There is no doubt, the life jacket saved me from drowning, but I was being carried downstream at a torrid pace along with the bouncing debris of broken limbs and floating branches. There was a point jutting out from the left shore ahead and I frantically tried to swim toward it, but the current was too strong and carried me past. The outcrop created a back eddy behind the rocks where the current was less treacherous. I swam as hard as I could, and then to my great relief, I felt my feet touch bottom. Half swimming and half walking, nearly breathless, I reached the riverbank and grabbed an overhanging limb. I finally pulled myself, gasping, onto the shore. It was only while stumbling barefoot along the rocky shore to the cabin, as the adrenalin flow subsided, that I began to shiver. Momentarily, I had time to think about how close I had come to going under for good. But there was no time to worry about that.

The overturned canoe was thrashing about like a cork, but still held fast to its tether. With no time to waste, I hauled it in, emptied most of the water, and then increased the length of the cord by a few feet to create a wider arc. I hoped the longer swing would now allow me to reach the helicopter pad. Without much trepidation, I plunged back in. This time, with the swing of the arc increased by the extra length of cord, and with some more frantic paddling, I quickly came alongside the submerged ramp. Guiding the canoe to the side of the float, I grabbed the underwater logs and pulled myself out of the bucking canoe. The raft was pitching dangerously, so I quickly removed the rotor blade straps, climbed into the cockpit, buckled the safety harness, and started the engine.

With time running out, I was unwilling to wait for the normal three minute warmup. I lifted the machine a few feet off the sunken pad in a low stationary hover to check the instrumentation. I hadn't taken the time for a pre-takeoff check, and my blunder caused the entire glass enclosure to fog up with condensation! I couldn't see anything outside the cockpit. Holding the machine just above the water was very tricky since I was completely blind to my outside surroundings.

Quickly, I unlatched the door to permit some visual height perception of my hover height above the water. Given the inherent instability of a light helicopter, both hands are continually required to maintain a static position in a low hover. One false move and the machine could drop suddenly to the surface or move sideways towards obstacles I couldn't see. There were high trees on both sides, so I knew I had to clear the windscreen for at least some visual perception before daring to rise out of the hover. It was a serious predicament. The defogging control was located above my right shoulder and should have been activated prior to liftoff. I wasn't sure I could reach it with my left arm, but there was no choice since I couldn't take my right hand from the cyclic control. Reluctantly, but swiftly, I released the collective control and reached overhead with my left hand and pulled out on the hot air control. Luckily the machine stayed in position and the windscreen began to clear. The pounding of my heart diminished and I began to breathe normally again as the outer world slowly came into view.

It was still raining heavily, with wispy clouds hanging low over the trees. After lifting from the hover, it was only a short flight to secure a landing site on an open bog behind the camp. Walking back to the cabin, through the brush, without shoes was painful going and my whole body began to tremble. For most of the ordeal, I hadn't noticed the cold, but now, with the worst over, I felt wet and exhausted. I knew I had been exposed to the elements for too long, and I knew enough about hypothermia to be concerned. Fortunately, there was still some dry kindling by the stove. I soon had a fire going and wrapped myself in a sleeping bag, and summoned up enough energy to make myself a good stiff drink. Despite the warmth of the fire, my body continued to shake in a frightening manner for over an hour.

I had escaped with a few minor scratches and bruises. As I sat shivering, I reflected on how suddenly things could change. To me, Arluk Tilt was as close to paradise on earth as anyone could hope to get, but on this day it had very nearly sent me to my reward somewhat earlier than anticipated. When the storm passed and the river subsided, Arluk Tilt returned to its former blissful state.

Chapter 32 Main River Fly-Outs

Manville Guests arrive at Deer Lake enroute to Main River Fishing Lodge

After selling my business, I still had my helicopter and spent the summers ferrying executive customers to the Main River Lodge for fly-fishing. Once there, I would take them to spots along the river (now recognized as heritage site) where the salmon were plentiful but where the water was too shallow or fast for a float plane to land. The lodge, which we had built in 1962, was expanded and upgraded in 1984 and evolved into a summer retreat for the major customers of Johns-Manville. By 1987 Intertape Polymer Inc. of Bradenton, Florida had also become a partner in the operation. The two companies booked the seven-week fishing season each year to entertain their guests, sending groups of eight for a stay of four days. With a staff of nine, I managed the operation for both the fishing and fall hunting.

Main River Lodge was located in one of the most beautiful areas of Newfoundland, and it was always a pleasure to introduce strangers to this pristine paradise. If fishing conditions weren't quite up to scratch at the camp pools, or just for a little variety, there was always the option of taking guests further along the river by helicopter. I would normally drop off three groups comprising two fishermen with a guide in each party, and then return at the end of the day to take them back to the lodge.

On one occasion, I had taken two parties from Intertape Polymer to different pools on the river, dropping them off as usual and telling them I would pick them up at 6 p.m. that evening. We were short a guide that day, so I agreed to take a customer from Drummondville, Quebec and double as his guide to make up a third party. Michel, a heavyset man well over six feet tall, was very enthusiastic about the fishing adventure and he had all kinds of questions. We flew to the bluff pool, and since the water was low, we landed on a small grassy spot by the river bank. It was a beautiful afternoon, and when Michel caught a four pound salmon he was elated. As five o'clock rolled around I decided it was time to pick up the other fishing parties, but when we got in the helicopter, the engine wouldn't start.

I finally had to tell Michel that we were stranded until morning.

"But what does that mean?" he asked, clearly shaken.

"Nothing to worry about," I said. "I just have to get another helicopter in to take us out. If I can't reach them on the radio, we'll just stay here the night and get out tomorrow."

"Here for the night!" he said. "Tabernac! What the hell are we going to do?"

"Well, we'll do some more fishing. We've already got one good fish for supper. We've got two sleeping bags so we can just enjoy a pleasant night in the outdoors. There's even a couple of beers left for you as cocktails."

"But what about tomorrow? How will they find us? How many days do you think we'll be out here?" The questions came fast and furious. You'd have thought we were a thousand miles from nowhere. We were only twenty-kilometers from the camp and there really was nothing to worry about. I sent a mesage to Ace, our camp manager, told Michel I thouht he'd got it, and we'd likely be picked up about 9 a.m. the next day.

"You THINK they got the message!" he said, wide-eyed. Then he let loose with another burst of colourful expressions in his native tongue. "What in hell happens to us if they didn't get your damned S.O.S.?"

I've never seen anyone go so fast from being a good-natured, at peace with the world guy to being on the edge of panic. I tried to calm him down and finally suggested we might as well get some fishing in, since we were stuck here anyway. He wasn't interested in fishing but I did talk him into relaxing with our two beer while he watched me fish. Later, I cooked the salmon he'd caught for our supper and he seemed to calm down with something in his stomach. It was soon dark and I suggested we turn in for the night. The mosquitoes were making a meal of us on the shore, but I could sleep anywhere, so I suggested Michel sleep sitting up in the chopper. He insisted he was too big for the chopper and couldn't sleep sitting up. It was then he caught sight of the ELT on the side of the helicopter. The Emergency Locator Transmitter is activated automati-cally after a crash, or it can be activated manually in a real emergency. Michel asked if I had activated it.

Hell, no," I said. "You only do that in a real emergency."

"A real emergency!" he shouted. "What the hell do you call this?

By now I was growing weary of explaining to Michel that there really was nothing to worry about, so I suggested again that we turn in, and everything would all work out in the morning. Since I had no trouble sleeping sitting up, I wrapped myself up in my sleeping bag in the front seat of the helicopter, while Michel bedded down by the fire. I had just dozed off when I was awakened by a banging on the door and there was Michel, wide-eyed and breathing heavily. He told me the fire had gone out. With panic creeping back into his boice, he said he'd heard wild animals all around and we needed the fire to keep them away.

I tried to tell him there were no wild animals around to worry about, but he looked at me like I was crazy. I got out the flashlight, hunted around for some dry wood and soon got the fire restarted. He bedded down again by the fire. It must have been three in the morning when a pounding on the door awoke me again from a deep dream. I could hear Michel's heavy breathing punctuating his complaints before I got the cockpit door open.

"Gene, Gene, are you in there? I'm telling you there are animals out here. I heard them in the woods behind me. I'm sure I saw a bear."

The chances of seeing a bear in that part of the country at night were slim to none, and I told him so. "If it was anything, it was probably a moose," I said to reassure him, but he still seemed to be on the verge of hyperventilating.

"Well I'm not going back out there with those moose around unless you go with me," he said. When i said I wasn't moving, he climbed into the back seat and wrapped himself up in his sleeping bag. Before long, he was sound asleep. With his thunderous snoring and the shaking of the chopper every time he shifted his great bulk, I soon gave up on sleeping there myself and left the chopper to bed down by the dying embers.

Morning daylight revealed a heavy mist in the air and dark clouds shrouding the hills on both sides of the river. I suggested we go fishing while we waited for the helicopter. I was now as anxious for it to arrive as he was. I worried that the low, gathering clouds would hamper visibility; we'd be stuck there for ages if the weather turned nastier. I was sure I didn't want to spend another night out there with him.

We had been fishing for quite a while, but I could see Michel's heart wasn't in it. He kept glancing at his watch. Finally he waded over to me and said, "Well, it's five to nine and they still aren't here." I looked at him in disbelief, but answered as calmly as I could manage, "Be patient, they'll be here eventually." However, to be honest, with the discomforting weather, I wasn't too sure.

Exactly three minutes later we heard the whump-whump of the approaching helicopter, and Michel's face lit up. "Pretty good," he said. "You were only out by two minutes." And I think he meant it!

That night over dinner, all the guests were in high spirits. The other two fishing parties had also spent the night in the wilderness and couldn't stop talking about their terrific experience. Michel, his composure fully restored, regaled the group with his adventures, the terrific shore lunch he and I had cooked up, and the wild animals he kept at bay by a roaring fire. "Really," he said modestly, "there was nothing to worry about, but there were a few moments when I wondered if we would ever be rescued. But no matter, as long as we had our fishing poles, we could have stayed out there until the snow flew. What a wonderful experience. I wouldn't have missed it for the world."

Main Rier Lodge – chopper pad and lakeside sauna

On another memorable fly-out trip, I had dropped off one group at Sunshine Falls and another at Island Pool. By mid afternoon a frontal system brought low ceilings and drizzle to the region. Not wanting to have the guests caught out overnight, I wiggled my way down river and managed to retrieve the fishermen at the falls. Back at the lodge, with the weather worsening, it seemed foolhardy to attempt reacing the roup at Island Pond.

Irv Memelstein was there with his guide, Edward Caines. I knew Ed was a very competent bushman and although wet and uncomfortable, he would get them through the night without harm. During the afternoon, I paced back and forth watching the cool mist that shrouded the forest. Feeling somewhat guilty about being in the warm cabin while Mr. Memelstein was stranded without a sleeping bag, I decided to attempt another flight. It was a general practice to fly in much worse conditions when there were no passengers on board. I threw a tarpaulin, a food pack and some extra sleeping bags into the rear compartment, thinking that if I could possibly reach their fishing pool, I would spend the night with them and bring them some comfort. After a tricky flight, I finally landed on the Island Pond sandbar and saw Irv huddled over a blazing fire with Edward, trying to dry some clothing. I was in the process of shutting down the engine for the night when Edward and Irv came sloshing over and opened the rear door. They stuffed in their fishing gear along with two salmon. Big Irv, who'd fallen in the river and got his clothes wet, was wearing Ed's too small yellow rain slicker. He had his right foot on the entry step but couldn't swing his body weight any further. I told him to grab the strap and I would put my shoulder under him to boost him up to the seat while Edward pushed. As we heaved I heard a ripping noise and felt a mass of wet, bare flesh flop onto my neck. The crotch in his pants had parted, dropping his slimy testicles on my shoulder! Jerking backward, all three of us fell in a heap to the ground amidst hysterical laughter. The weather had not worsened so we were able to return to the warmth of the lodge. That evening, some grand stories were told around the dining table. Embellishment was not required! Irv later wrote a poem to capture the vivid incident. It was titled "Wet Flesh On The Main."

Conclusion

Gene grudgingly departs with his chopper as
it is loaded for shipping to Oregon. (2004)

In 2002, after relocating to the Thousand Islands in Ontario, I found the helicopter somewhat impractical in that this well developed province had a myriad of roads and ease of ground access to most regions. Reluctantly, I sold the little magic carpet to an outdoor enthusiast in Oregon during the year of 2004. It was as though my best friend had left me.

For the past 53 years, my involvement with aircraft has been a continuous love affair. Operating along the edge was often turbulent, conveying both heady life experiences and the possibility of a tragic mishap. Aviation has introduced me to many wonderful people, taken me to amazing places, and taught me a sense of humbleness and a clear respect for nature and all the creatures of the air. What a fascinating trip this has been!

THE END

End Notes

1   The team at NLAT: Rick Richard, Frank LeDrew, Eric Watson, Pierre Meagher, Hugh Atkinson, Eddie Oake, Nina Manion, Holland Smith, Bob Baker, Ross Sampson, Bob Hutcheson, Ace Caines, Ed Enns, Clayton Pilgrim, Stirling Lush, Earle Johnson, Otto Fuhrer, Don Bonia, John Manuel, Dave Mahoney, Duke Perkins, Hollie Cadman, John Booth, Ralph Collier, Joan French, Glen Goobie, Harold Oake, Austin Bugden, Al MacDonald, Jean LaTiece, Bob Moss, Alaine Guidon, Mike Ross, Alain Gavel, Tommy Caines, Graham Hancock, Garland Patey, Lorne Bradley, Peter Knox, Howard Mercer, Murdock Mayo, Eddie Coates, Ches Walker, Gerry Pumphries, Palmer Tibbo, Loretta O'Neil, Ricky Carter, Art Wildish, Jud Bursey, Denis Bursey, Bob Thurston, Don Ward, Paddy Doyle, Gordie Rezac, Roger Penny, Denis Mullins, Seaward Curry, Jim Bouzanne, Bob Brough, Larry Campaugh, Henri Moraze.

2. Even today, some fifty years later, not much has changed on coastal Labrador except for a few improvements in their roads, airports, education, health care, and a new mining development at Voisey Bay.

3. The hood, a larger migratory seal, also called a bladdernose or blueback, congregates on the pack ice off Labrador and in the Gulf of St. Lawrence during the spring whelping season. They usually choose heavier ice to the seaward of the harp seal. The male is much larger than the female, weighing up to 320 kg. Hood seals are thought to be monogamous, remaining with the young pup and its mother during the nursing period, mating with the female shortly thereafter. A large proboscis that overhangs the upper lip is its most striking characteristic. They

are aggressive, and when angered the nose bladder is rapidly inflated and the red nostrils are flared. The young pup is about thirty-six inches in length at birth. The fetal coat is light grayish in colour and is shed before birth. The young seals are slate blue, shading abruptly to light silver gray on the sides and belly. The black muzzle extends behind the eyes. Young "blueback" skins bring a premium market price. Females mature at five years and produce one pup every year in March. They leave the pack ice, migrating to the area around Greenland and the Denmark Strait, and arriving by early May. The hoods are not nearly as plentiful as the harps, with only about 6,000 taken annually.

4. FBA-1 (Found Brothers Aircraft): It is interesting to note that an EPA Found Brothers floatplane crashed in Williamsport, Newfoundland, killing the pilot, Neil Bridger, and the three passengers in 1967. Apparently, the wings stalled in a tight turn after takeoff in a gusty wind situation. Twenty-seven of these planes were built before the company stopped production in 1967. Later, Bob Beamish purchased the company, and with Tony Hamblin and their quest for perfection, their specialized engineers vastly improved the design with modern techniques: they installed a larger engine, improved the payload, enhanced the appearance, increased the wing lift, and improved the seating and instrument panel, and so on. The new model, Expedition E 350, was certified by the FAA and the Dept. of Transport in 2007. A great, new, modern Canadian bush plane has emerged.

5. Three years later we learned that the Heron, while on a routine scheduled flight, had crashed into a high mountain range in Columbia, killing all twenty persons on the aircraft.

6. In the early 1980s, Andrew Crosbie, an adventurous St. John's businessman, struggled with a large debt during recession, high interest rates, and his battle with alcohol. Eventually the Crosbie

Business Empire came tumbling down in bankruptcy. Andrew died in 1991 at the age of 56.

7. The Main River Lodge became one of the most superb wilderness fishing and hunting lodges in the province. Each year it was expanded and improved. For years, it was a favorite destination for many international guests. Our company was contracted to operate the facility, providing staff, maintenance, supplies and transportation. The managers of Advocate Mine after Bob Baker were Bob Hutcheson, Ross Sampson, Jack Cole, and Eddie McKenna. They, and a long line of CEO's at the Manville Headquarters, devotedly supported the lodge operation with the necessary budget approvals.The mine closed in 1983 when Johns Manville filed for Chapter 11. That year, I took over the camp and was general manager until 2002. It remained a great wilderness retreat for various corporations until 2004.

Many of the productive and well-defined holding pools on our river section were named in honour of the Manville executives who returned each year to flail the waters. Karl's Korner was named for Karl Lindell, vice president of International Mining. Hutch's Hideout for Bob Hutcheson, president of Canadian Johns Manville; Colton's Cache for Dudley Colton, vice president international Division; Orth's Hole for Bob Orth, vice president international sales); Chet's Run for Chet Sweeny, Specialty Products; The Sampson Trail for Ross Sampson, manager of Advocate Mines Ltd.). Two other pools are called Gene's Jump and Nina's Nook. These salmon pools were marked with appropriate signs and the original names remain entrenched to this day.

We retained and maintained one of Lee Wulff's old log shacks as a historic monument to that great author and sportsman.

With great difficulty, we kept the paper companies from clear-cutting and road building in the area. It remains one of the few salmon lodges on the entire island that is not road accessible. Dedicated to preserving the pristine wilderness of the region, we were partly responsible for having the Main River declared a Canadian "Heritage River." With great difficulty, another ecobattle was successful by stopping Kruger Paper Company from building a huge hydro dam on the Humber River.

8. Frank Pye. He continued to amaze everyone with his uncanny ability to complete difficult projects ahead of schedule and under budget. In 1969, Frank was accidentally killed by a rifle shot while he and a friend were poaching moose out of season. He left us, his wonderful wife Anny, and a large family to grieve his loss. He was a good friend and an amazing contractor.

9. Big Game & Fishing Outfitters that we serviced in western Newfoundland during the 1960s and 1970s. Bill Newell, Ben Alexander, Joe Peddle, Bob Skinner, Frank Hann, Clifford House, Sted Wentzell, Angus Wentzell, Randell Wentzell, Shanadithit Camps (owned by us), Sam Caines, Jim Carey, Gerald Byrne, Sandy Parsons, Sted Brophy, Eric Patey, Len Payne, The Keoughs, Cow Head Outfitters, Max Butt, Gid House, Harvey Sheppard, Reg Coombs, Gerry Pumphrey, Sandy Parsons, and Peter Paor. (These outfitters each had from one to six remote camp sites located from 30 to 150 kilometers from our bases at Pasadena and Goose Bay).

10. Prince Abdorreza Pahlavi of Iran is widely recognized as the greatest worldwide hunter and wildlife conservationist to have lived. As a hunter, his peers could only include those like Jay Melon, Herb Klein, Elgin Gates and C.J. McElroy. He was very dedicated to hunting, more at home in the mountains than in his palace. The prince passed away in 2004 at the age of 80. He set up game reserves across the globe, implemented strict game laws in Iran, donated huge sums in funding and used his political pull for the preservation of wildlife.

Glossary

Sealing Statistics:

Average annual catches (ships and landsmen):

Year	Pups	Beaters & Adults	Total
1830			315,000
1831			683,000
1853			
1895-1911	253000	46000	299,000
1912-1940	160000	49000	209,000
1941-1950	74000	46000	120,000
	(Low catch due war time)		
1951-1960	226000	116000	342,000
1972-1975			150,000
1978			180,000

Sealing, aviation and other Newfoundland jargon

Beater: a young harp in its first year after molting to a soft spotted gray coat at 4 weeks

Bedlamer: a juvenile harp from one to five years with a spotted coat harp shape markings appear as it reaches sexual maturity

Blue Back: a new born hood seal, which has darkish blue fast-fur, having shed its first coat prior to birth

Boil-Up: A strong tea enjoyed during a break from work (on land or sea)

Capelin: a small herring- like fish that migrates in large, gregarious swarms

Copying: running across small, floating ice pans

IFR: Instrument flight rules; piloting the aircraft with no visual reference outside the cockpit

Livyer (livier): Permanent settlers as opposed to migratory fishermen

Mauzy: damp, dark, and cloudy weather

Outport: An isolated coastal settlement

Ragged jacket: a young harp, undergoing its first molt from a Whitecoat to a beater (about 2 weeks of age)

Rifter: A pan of ice that has been pushed up on its edge

Scrammed: numb with cold

Scoff: A big, unexpected meal, usually made in one pan

Sculping: Killing and skinning seals

Sheila's brush: A fierce March blizzard

Slob ice: mushy sea ice

Stall turn: Rotating the aircraft 180 degrees, by partially stalling the airflow over one wing

Steady: A slow, pool in a stream

Swatch: a dense gathering of seals

Swilers: seal hunters and skinners

Tilt: A lean-to or rough overnight cabin for shelter

Tuckamore: A small stunted evergreen scrub with gnarled roots and twisted branches

VFR: Visual flight rule; maintaining visual reference to ground and horizon

Whelping: the act of giving birth

Whiskey Jack: A gray jay, a bold wilderness bird

Whitecoat: Newborn harp seal prior to loss of soft white fur which it has at birth

Willy-wa: Extreme gusts of winds that blow down at the surface and then disperse in all directions

References

Gratefully, references from the following publications were helpful in verifying details regarding people, dates, places, statistics, and technical information.

Smallwood, Joseph. The Book of Newfoundland (Vol. 3 & 4). St. John's: Newfoundland Book Publishers (1967) Ltd., 1967.

Wells, Janice. Frank Moores: The Time Of His Life. Toronto: Key Porter Books Limited, 2008.

Crosbie, John. No Holds Barred: My Life In Politics. Toronto: McClel-land and Stewart Limited, 1997.

Chantraine, Pol. The Living Ice. Toronto: McClelland and Stewart Limited, 1980.

Coish, Calvin. Season of the Seal. St. John's: Robinson Blackmore, 1979.

Mowat, Farley. A Whale for the Killing.Toronto: McClelland and Stewart Limited, 1972.

Walls, Martha. Book of Everything.Lunenburg: MacIntyre Purcell Publishing Inc., 2006.

Ingstad, Helge. Land Under The Pole Star. New York: St. Martin Press, 1966.

Brown, Cassie. A Winter's Tale. Toronto: DoubleDay and Com-pany Inc., 1976.

Service, Robert. The Best Of Robert Service. Toronto: McGraw-Hill Ryerson, 1953.

Hotson, Fred. The Bremen. Toronto: CANAV Books, 1988

England, George Allan. The Greatest Hunt in the World. Toronto: Tundra Books, 1969.

Government of Canada. Information Pamphlet-The Canadian Sealing Industry. Ottawa: Department of Fisheries and Oceans, 1979.

Government of Canada, Sealing-A Canadian Perspective. Ottawa: Dept. of Fisheries and Oceans, 1989.

Grenfell, Wilfred and Others. Labrador. New York: The Macmillan Company, 1909.

Mitchum, Allison. Island Keepers. Hantsport: Lancelot Press Limited, 1990.

Forbes, Alexander. Northernmost Labrador. New York: George Grady Press, 1938.

Cabot, William Brooks. In Northern Labrador. Boston: The Gorham Press, 1912.

McGrath,P.T. The Outing Magazine. New York: 1904.

Prichard, Hesketh. Through Trackless Labrador. London: William Heinmann, 2004.

The Western Star - re clippings and finding Liberator, Corner Brook.

The Evening Telegram - re election and political events. St.John's, 1971/&1978

The Financial Post - re Gulf seal hunt, Toronto, 1976.

Globe and Mail - re Watson accident, Toronto , March 1963

About the Author

Gene was raised on a small dairy farm on Wolfe Island, Ontario. At seventeen, he graduated from high school and joined the RCAF. During a seven-year stint as a pilot, he instructed NATO air-students, and flew jet fighters during the Cold War. Thereafter, he spent 43 years in Newfoundland, flying bush planes, commuter craft and helicopters. Although this is his first book, he has written a number of short articles for various local, outdoor magazines and aircraft publications.

He served as vice president of the following organizations: Third Level Air Carriers of Canada; Newfoundland Outfitters Association;Tuckamore Wilderness Club; and Salmon Preservation Association of Newfoundland. He also played a lead role with the environmental group that prevented dam construction on the Humber River and stopped clearcut logging of old growth forest on the Main River watershed.

His interests include: sailboat racing, skiing, gardening, photography, fishing, and hunting. Gene now lives on the shore of Howe Island, Ontario, where he enjoys a mellow retirement with his wife, Nina, along with his dog and his boat.